An Element of Love

JULIA FOSTER PORTER
Founder of Children's Memorial Hospital

An Element of Love

A History of The Children's Memorial Hospital of Chicago, Illinois

by Clare McCausland

THE CHILDREN'S MEMORIAL HOSPITAL   CHICAGO, ILLINOIS

Dedicated to the Children

Contents

Foreword

AN ELEMENT OF LOVE is a history of the first one hundred years of The Children's Memorial Hospital. Founded by Julia Foster Porter in 1882 as a memorial to her son, it was called The Maurice Porter Hospital until 1904 when circumstances led to reorganization, a new name, and the placing of the management of the Hospital in the hands of a Board of Lady Managers and a Board of Directors.

The title of this history comes from a 1931 speech of Dr. Joseph Brennemann, Children's first full-time Chief-of-Staff. He was defining "The essence of a good hospital" for the Children's Hospital Association:

> The children may be well cared for; the medical staff may be made up of able clinicians and investigators; the superintendent may be as wise as Solomon and as just as Aristides, and may see that the whole machinery of administration is well oiled and the physical equipment faultless; the boards of trustees and the women's board may be actively interested and may do all that could be desired in other ways; the nurses may be intelligent, faithful and well trained; the interns and residents may be well schooled and prepared for their duties . . . and yet the vital spark will be lacking if there is not back of it all an all-pervading spirit of cooperation and of kindliness or, as Emerson has so beautifully expressed it, "an element of love that penetrates it like a fine ether."

This book is a story of people—the lay men and women who, with the medical staff, have guided the Hospital through one hundred years of growth. The medical, social, economic, and political forces which have shaped Children's are part of the story. So, too, is the growth of Chicago from a town rebuilding itself after the great fire of 1871 to the vast urban complex of today.

Most of the story comes from the Hospital's archives: handwritten minutes and a few pamphlets in the earlier days; annual reports and minutes in unbroken succession from 1904 to 1981; and a few partial histories written in 1915, 1941, 1961, 1967, and 1970. To this core, significant material has been added from the infinite resources of some of Chicago's libraries: The Joseph Brennemann Library (C.M.H.), the Chicago Historical Society, the Library of the American Academy of Pediatrics, the Newberry Library, the Chicago Public Library, and the University of Chicago's Regenstein Library.

It would be difficult to list all the persons who have helped bring this history to fruition. The generosity of several members of the Board of Directors and the Woman's Board made the project possible in the first place. Many others—board members and members of the administrative and professional staffs—have patiently answered my questions and have shed light on obscure moments in the Hospital's story. Not only have they been generous of their time in talking to me, but they have also looked in their attics for records and in their memories for anecdotes.

I am particularly indebted to Lucille Crawford who, over a period of several years, collected hundreds of documents in one small office, thus saving me months of leg work. The insight into the Hospital which Mrs. Crawford gained through her search for material, as well as from her vantage point as director of volunteers for over ten years, she has shared with me freely.

Suzanne Edwards, Children's Director of Public Relations, has given me unfailing support throughout the work on the history. She has lightened my task in many ways: she has turned up pertinent material; she has helped to select the illustrations; and her thoughtful comments have strengthened the text.

Finally, I wish to thank the History Advisory Committee for its help: Dr. Joseph D. Boggs; Mrs. W. Newton Burdick, Jr.; Ms. Suzanne Edwards; Mr. Earl Frederick; Mrs. Paul W. Guenzel; Mrs. Howell B. Hardy; Mrs. A. Loring Rowe; Dr. Matthew M. Steiner; Mr. William Swartchild, Jr.; and Mrs. Henry P. Wheeler. They have read the manuscript section by section, corrected errors, and commented on its approach and emphasis.

Kathleen Ineman, my editor, has smoothed rough edges of the text; Raymond Machura has designed the book with great sensitivity.

CLARE MCCAUSLAND

Chicago, 1981

An Element of Love

PART ONE   *1882–1904*

---

*"A child had died
and there was no hospital
in Chicago devoted to the
care of children."*

CHAPTER I

Chicago in 1882

A CHILD born in Chicago in 1882 was not, medically speaking, a fortunate human being. His chance of dying before his first birthday was overwhelming, for children under five accounted for over 50 percent of all deaths in Chicago in the eighties. The possibility of early death went up if he were born to poverty. If he lived beyond his first birthday, he would certainly be exposed to a host of contagious diseases: measles, typhoid fever, diphtheria, whooping cough, scarlet fever, and the ever present diarrhea in all its forms. He could, perhaps, escape smallpox, since, after a long fight, vaccination against it was mandatory in Chicago's schools after 1867.

If he became ill, moreover, there was no pediatrician down the street to cope with his problems. He was more likely to be treated with a home remedy. Every housewife had a dozen "tried and true" ones at her finger tips. There was sulphur and molasses to thin the blood in the spring, a mustard poultice to relieve a "tight" chest, a spoonful of camphor and goose grease for whooping cough, a bag of asefetida hung around the neck to ward off colds, a small quantity of "spirits of juniper" (gin) for scarlet fever—to name a few. Daily newspapers advertised patent medicines guaranteed to cure everything from scrofula to dropsy. *Home Remedies* and *What to Do Till the Doctor Comes* were within easy reach on many a household's book shelves.

Although individual doctors were interested in children's diseases, there was not a single pediatrician in Chicago in 1882; nor, in fact, was pediatrics recognized as a special branch of medicine. In that period the most powerful voice raised in behalf of special medicinal treatment for children was that of Dr. Abraham Jacobi of New York. Out of his study of children's diseases came several recommendations ahead of his time. Among the first to link bad water and bad milk to the high death rate among babies fed artificially, he advocated boiling all water used in an infant's diet. On another front he advocated using intubation to treat diphtheria in children when that method was still highly experimental. His book on the diseases of women and children (1860) was largely ignored—most of the first, and only, edition was sold as waste paper for $68.00. But by 1870 his growing fame led Columbia University's College of Physicians and Surgeons to appoint him Clinical Professor of Diseases of Children—without, however, granting him a seat on the medical faculty. Although his own practice was never limited to children, Dr. Jacobi is usually called the Father of Pediatrics.

Chicago boasted no such physician. In 1882 the city was only eleven years away from the Great Fire. The foundations of a vibrant new city had been laid in those years. Leading citizens were proud of its astonishing commercial and industrial expansion. Downtown, solid business blocks of stone, brick, and iron dramatized the building boom. Freighters plied up and down Lake Michigan carrying materials needed by the growing city. Eight hundred and fifty passenger and freight trains arrived daily on twenty different lines. Railroad yards were equipped with block signals and other new railway devices; in another year every train would have Westinghouse air brakes. Thousands of cattle, hogs, and sheep were driven into the stockyard every month for processing in the great packing houses. Chicago was rapidly becoming the chief meat provisioner of the country. Hundreds of small mills and foundries vied for space in the center of the city near the Chicago River. Every day saw the installation of more telephones—the city boasted 5,000 by 1886. And electric lights were fast replacing gas lamps in commercial establishments. The first cable car carried a number of distinguished Chicagoans on its maiden journey from Madison to 20th Street in thirty-two minutes in January 1882.

This rapid expansion carried its own toll. Black smoke belched from thousands of industrial chimneys—only momentarily checked by an anti-smoke ordinance passed in May 1882. Lacking public transportation, laborers in mills, foundries, and stockyards had to live near their jobs. Consequently, hundreds of jerrybuilt shacks mushroomed around work centers, always with an outdoor privy at the rear. Rarely did these cottages house one family alone. A head count in 1881 in the 14th Ward, one of the most congested, placed 18,976 persons in 1,107 buildings. The laboring force of Chicago, housed in crowded, filthy homes, turned for comfort to saloons, gambling "parlors," and houses of prostitution for entertainment. These establishments flourished in Mayor Carter Harrison's city, where personal liberty was an important part of his political philosophy. The whole added up to proliferation of diseases and encouraged the great epidemics of cholera and typhoid fever, which periodically swept through the city.

Not every Chicagoan lived in this way of course. As the city grew from half a million in 1880 to almost a million and a half by 1890, many of the more affluent moved away from the crowded center of the city. A few clung to a mile or so of the area south of Lincoln Park, but others sought space near Grant Boulevard on the far south, Prairie Avenue a little further in, Fullerton Avenue north of Lincoln Park, and Washington Boulevard on the west. From these peaceful, tree-lined enclaves, Chicago's elite swept into the city to dine in elegance at the new, entirely fireproof Palmer House, or the Tremont, the Sherman, or the Grand Pacific Hotel. Each had a magnificent view of Lake Michigan, an orchestra, and flowers on the table—a post-fire innovation. The nights when Johnny Hand played for the great Assembly Balls, downtown Chicago was filled with shining landaus and buggies. Shabby crowds lined the streets, watching the gentlemen in their stiff collars and tall hats and the elegantly dressed ladies with their jewels and elaborate coiffures. It was a city of contrasts.

Although their homes were removed from the crowded, unsanitary inner city, these fortunate Chicagoans did not escape the consequences of such conditions. Nor were they indifferent to them. They could not ignore the health hazards which resulted from unsanitary housing, the epidemics of typhoid and cholera which knew no boundaries. In fact, the health of the city received almost as much of their attention as building churches, promoting cultural institutions, and strengthening financial ones—both before and after the Great Fire which devastated the city of Chicago in 1871.

An obvious starting point to improve conditions was the Board of Health. It had been established when Chicago was granted its charter in 1837, but its record of achievement was uneven. For a short time, indeed, its duties had been turned over to the Police Department, but public indignation following a severe cholera epidemic had forced its reinstatement in 1867. At that time it had made smallpox vaccination mandatory in the schools and had built quarantine facilities near the city hospital. Both actions were useful in curbing epidemics, but the quarantine house was often over-crowded and always badly run.

By 1869 the annual budget to improve public health had risen to $80,745.00—from $2,000.00 in the fifties. But even that was not enough to finance its tasks, particularly inspection of food—meat, fish, flour, bread, and milk. A study at the time revealed that 7 per-cent of the meat sold in Chicago was unfit to eat, 3 percent was ac-tually tainted. Dirty milk was a scandal both then and after the Great Fire of 1871. It was a special target of physicians in the seven-ties and eighties. They were all too aware that milk dealers often diluted their milk with polluted water; the results were increased disease and more deaths among children. Thomas Nast highlighted the situation in a famous cartoon in *Harper's Weekly* in 1878. Called "Swill Milk," it pictured death as a milkman ladling out milk from a huge canister into a pitcher held by a shawled mother. In her arms was a baby, clinging to her skirts were four other emaciated children. Swill milk was a name given to milk from cows fed on distillery wastes—not an uncommon practice then.

The Board of Health was also negligent in policing the disposal of waste from the packing houses, breweries, glue, hide, and tallow factories. Much of it was dumped into the Chicago River which emptied into Lake Michigan, the source of the city's drinking water. Although by ordinance each district in the city was supposed to have two public scavengers, at times there were only two in the whole city, and they often merely hauled away refuse from one section and dumped it in a less congested one. In 1882 improper waste disposal in a burgeoning city was still a prime source of polluted drinking water.

So, also, many citizens suspected, were Chicago's overcrowded cemeteries. Water was never far from the surface in the low lying city; it too might well have been polluted by the mass burials of victims of smallpox and other epidemic diseases. Prominent citizens— many of them doctors—began appearing before the Board of Health urging them to move bodies to more remote areas and stop new burials in the center of the city.

After the Fire, civic leaders pressed so vigorously for reform that the City Council changed the Board of Health to a Department of Health with wider authority. In the eighties this Department was attempting to inspect and regulate sanitary conditions in small factories, boarding houses, lodgings, and tenements. Their suggestions, although supported by a Municipal Code in 1881, were too easily ignored and difficult to enforce. In 1882 more than one-third of Chicago's residents still had outdoor privies. But the Department was moving in the right direction, and it was a highly visible authority upon which civic leaders could put pressure.

Strengthening Chicago's hospitals was a second road to improving the city's health. Without exception, leading citizens had served on the governing boards of these institutions from their founding. There were just over a dozen in Chicago in 1882, serving approximately six thousand to eight thousand patients a year (statistics differ and, at best, are vague). Many had been established by churches. The Roman Catholics had opened Mercy, Alexian Brothers, St. Joseph, and St. Mary; the Episcopals, St. Luke's; the Lutherans, Protestant Deaconess' Hospital. Germans supported the German Hospital to serve its people; the Jews built Michael Reese. Homeopathic doctors treated their patients at Hahneman. Some hospitals had specialties: The Smallpox Hospital, Illinois Charitable Eye and Ear Infirmary, The Chicago Floating Hospital, and Woman's Hospital. After the Civil War, Cook County Hospital belonged to Chicago and was the chief medical center for the poor.

But not one hospital at the beginning of 1882 was focussed solely on the treatment of children's diseases. The Mary H. Thompson came the closest to that specialty. Started in 1865 after the Civil War, it had defined its role as the "care of women and children of the respectable poor," particularly Civil War widows and orphans. Destroyed by the Fire of 1871, it started again under new auspices; but under Dr. Sarah Hackett Stevenson's supervision, it still had limited beds for children. It was the only hospital to do so before the Maurice Porter Memorial Hospital opened its doors.

CHAPTER II

Mrs. Porter's Hospital

1882–1891

I T WAS in this setting that a young widow, Julia Foster Porter, decided in 1882 to open a small hospital for children. She was thirty-six years old, and had been a widow for six years. Her husband, the Reverend Edward Clark Porter, had died in Racine, Wisconsin in 1876. He had been rector of St. Luke's Episcopal Church there for nine years—all but one of their brief married life. There her two sons had been born: Maurice in 1868, James in 1871. After her husband's death, Julia wound up her affairs in Racine and returned to Chicago to live with her mother, Nancy Smith Foster (Mrs. John Herbert Foster) at 1012 N. Clark Street, on the corner of Clark and Belden. Although she had lived on that corner from the time she was thirteen until she was married at twenty, the house to which she brought her two small sons was new to her. The old home had been destroyed in the Great Fire of 1871—it was the last house to burn in the north district. Dr. Foster had immediately built another on the spot. Adjusting to a new house was not difficult; it was more painful to accept her father's absence, for he had died in an accident in 1874.

Julia settled in with her mother, glad of her companionship and that of her sister Adele (Mrs. George E. Adams) who lived around the corner at 350 Belden Avenue. The Adams household was a lively one; in time there were four little cousins for Maurice and James to play with. Their father was active in the social and political life of Chicago and the Adamses entertained lavishly. Most of the city's distinguished citizens came to dine with them and to talk of the rising Newberry Library, the Field Museum, the Art Institute, and the

Orchestral Association. George Adams was a patron, trustee, or member of all of them. And from 350 Belden Avenue he went to Springfield as a senator in 1881.

To the more quiet establishment next door in 1878 came James W. Porter, a bachelor cousin of Julia's husband. He was close to the family, not only as a Porter relative, but as a former colleague of Julia's father when he had turned from medicine to the real estate business.

Although the household was quiet, to take part in civic affairs was its way of life. Julia had grown up hearing her father talk about Chicago's problems. His training in medicine made him a valuable member of the governing board of the Chicago City Hospital (renamed Cook County Hospital in 1866). And it added authority to his plea before the Department of Health to stop burial in one of the city's main cemeteries. Located on open land north of the city's center, the cemetery had once been on the fringes of Chicago, but by the time the area was named Lincoln Park after President Lincoln's assassination, the city was growing all around it.

His concern for people was expressed as a Director of the Chicago Nursery and Half Orphan Asylum (now Chapin Hall). He was a founder and supporter of the Humane Society. When in 1882 the Society extended its services to prevent cruelty to children as well as animals, Dr. Foster's wife contributed $10,000 in her husband's memory.

A great believer in public education, Dr. Foster served the schools first as a lay inspector, then as a member of the Board of Education for almost twenty years. For two of those years he was President of the Board and for fifteen years he served concurrently on the State Board of Education. In 1857, with a gift of $1,000, he had started the Foster Medal Fund. Its aim was to encourage academic achievement among grammar school students by awarding them gold, silver, or bronze medals. A grateful School Board named Foster School in his honor that year. Julia herself won a Foster Medal when she was thirteen.

Julia's mother is also remembered in a building's name. Foster Hall at the University of Chicago is named in her honor. Her gifts, totaling $100,000, were made in the 1890s, a critical time in the University's life.

So, although her father had died when Julia returned to Chicago in 1876, civic activity was taken for granted at 1012 N. Clark Street. It is not surprising, therefore, to find Julia one year later on the Board of Managers of the Chicago Nursery and Half Orphan Asylum. During her five years on that Board she served on four committees: North Side Investigating, Purchasing, Sewing, and in 1881, the Executive Committee.

The early months of 1881 were anxious ones in the Foster home. Maurice was very ill with a fever, considerable pain, and general debility. Dr. Truman Miller, a neighbor and the family doctor, diagnosed the illness as acute rheumatism. The family watched, helplessly, as Maurice died in March. He was thirteen years old.

A child had died and there was no hospital in Chicago devoted to the care of children. Those circumstances alone might well have suggested to Julia Foster Porter that she might establish a children's hospital as a memorial to her son. She had, moreover, sufficient money to carry out such a plan since her father had divided over half of his extensive real estate holdings among his three daughters back in 1869. There was a third reason as well. She knew, from experience, a great deal about opening a hospital. When her husband was rector of St. Luke's in Racine, he and several of his parishioners had established St. Luke's Hospital to provide free medical care for the indigent. Its first patient was admitted on Christmas Day in 1871. Within four years it had outgrown its four-bed cottage facility, and Julia herself had bought and given the land upon which a twenty-bed hospital had been built. Hard on the opening of the new hospital, the Reverend Edward Porter had been forced, by severe illness, to resign both as Rector of his church and President of the hospital. When he died a year later and Julia returned to Chicago, she committed herself to an annual contribution of $250 (one quarter of the annual budget) for at least a few more years.

It is tempting to believe, too, that she had seen a children's hospital in operation. In 1882 Children's Hospital in Boston had just moved into new modern quarters expanding its beds to sixty. It was the talk of Boston. Could Julia, who almost yearly visited New Hampshire to see her mother's relatives, have stopped to see the new hospital?

Whatever the motivations, a cottage hospital (eight beds)

dedicated to the care of needy children seemed to Julia a fitting memorial to her son. Its location was the southeast corner of Belden and Halsted, not far away from the Foster home on Belden and Clark, nor from 789 Fullerton Avenue where the household moved later in 1881. An advisor to the new enterprise lived close at hand too—Dr. Truman Washington Miller, the forty-two-year-old doctor who had attended both Dr. Foster and Maurice in their last illnesses. Although young, Dr. Miller was well established in Chicago's medical circles by the 1880s. In the seventies he had been on the staff at Cook County Hospital and an inspector for the Board of Health; in the eighties he had become a consultant at Augustana, St. Joseph's, and the German hospitals. Dr. Miller undoubtedly worked closely with Julia as she remodelled a dwelling at Belden and Halsted and equipped it as a hospital for about $13,000. The Maurice Porter Memorial Hospital opened its doors in May 1882.

During the next ten years (1882–1892) the Hospital was Mrs. Porter's Hospital. She appointed Dr. Miller Chief Surgeon. In the Episcopal sisterhood, she found a matron, Miss Calneck, not a professional nurse, but one with considerable experience in nursing and philanthropic work. Miss Calneck's salary was thirty dollars per month. Her two assistants were paid sixteen dollars each; one, Miss Fanny Baldwin, stayed with the hospital for thirteen years. These three women formed the first nursing corps. Dr. Miller donated his services.

It is impossible to say with complete confidence what the annual cost of running the Hospital was in this decade. Mrs. Porter left no records, nor was there a Board of Managers with Treasurer's reports. An anonymous typewritten *History of the Chicago Memorial Hospital*, written about 1915, states that the cost of maintaining the Hospital in 1883 was $2,034.82. This is probably an accurate figure, since Mrs. Porter was still living in 1915 and presumably had been consulted by the historians. The figure 82¢ could not have been wholly imaginative! Records in the nineties show that Mrs. Porter was then contributing $2,500, and later $3,000, per year for running expenses, so that the earlier figure seems in line.

More important, however, than the money Mrs. Porter gave to open and run the Maurice Porter Memorial Hospital were the ideals and standards at the base of its services. Undoubtedly, she relied on

Dr. Miller for medical standards, but the spirit of the institution, one feels, was Mrs. Porter's. The first pamphlet describing the work of the Hospital was published in 1886. It was designed to let the public know of the Hospital's expanded facilities at 606 Fullerton Avenue. Much had happened at The Maurice Porter Hospital in its four years of existence. Just one year after Mrs. Porter had founded the Hospital she bought several lots at the corner of Fullerton and Orchard for $7,950. Perhaps she was looking ahead to the need for a more permanent hospital than the adapted dwelling. Perhaps she remembered how quickly the Racine hospital had outgrown its first building. In 1884, at any rate, she began building a three-story brick hospital at 606 Fullerton Avenue, large enough to house twenty beds. Dr. Miller by this time had invited Dr. Frank Porter (not a relative) to become his assistant. Dr. Porter was a graduate of the Detroit Medical College; the doctors were fellow members of the Chicago Medical Society. Miss Calneck had been followed by two other matrons, neither a professional nurse; but in 1884 Miss Genevieve Gilmore, a member of the first class to graduate from the Illinois Training School for Nurses (established in 1880), was hired as Superintendent.

The 1886 pamphlet describes the new facilities as having "every modern improvement conducive to the welfare and comfort of the inmates." It also reflects the unchanging goal of the Hospital—"dedicated exclusively to the free care and treatment of children from three to thirteen years of age." Admission criteria are explicit: age limits three to thirteen years; no child with an incurable or contagious disease will be accepted. If the applicant has a chronic disease, or injuries of long standing, or deformities, he would be admitted if the surgeons felt after examination that they could give a course of treatment which would benefit him permanently. Applications must be addressed to the surgeons or Superintendent Gilmore; patients would be received "at all times without formality." The folder also emphasizes that competent nurses would be in constant attendance.

When the Hospital published its next pamphlet in 1891, it was still offering free care to children between the ages of three to thirteen, but there were many changes, both internally and in its relation to the city. The medical staff now numbered six. Dr. Miller

15

remained as President; Dr. George F. Fiske, an oculist and aurist, was staff Secretary. Dr. Porter was no longer on the staff, but Dr. William T. Belfield had joined Dr. Miller on the surgical staff. Dr. Charles Rutter, Dr. Frank Billings, and Dr. William S. Christopher were the attending physicians. The Superintendent was Miss Eva C. Cutler from the 1887 class of the Illinois Training School for Nurses. At the top of the page listing the Medical Staff, Mrs. Julia F. Porter appears as Patroness.

The title and content of the 1891 pamphlet reflect changes too. It is called an Annual Report, indicating that Chicago had become sufficiently aware of the growing hospital to be interested in a report of its work. "For Children" is added under the title, *The Maurice Porter Memorial Hospital*, to emphasize the institution's specialty. A general historical statement adds a few interpretations. One reads: "It is especially intended to reach those cases which require such attention on the part of surgeon, physician and trained nurse as cannot be obtained at home." Another: "There are no restrictions of race, creed or residence to bar admission to the hospital."

For the first time there is some description of the patients. Sixty-eight children were cared for in 1890; a total of 232 in the nine years since the Hospital had opened its doors. The report classifies them by nationality:

American	25	Polish	2
Swedish	11	Colored	2
German	10	French	1
Italian	10	Norwegian	1
Irish	3	Austrian	1
English	2		

It also lists the institutions from which patients had been received: The Humane Society, Children's Aid Society, The Home for the Friendless, The Half Orphan Asylum, The Glenwood Industrial School, and The Orphan Home in Andover.

A detailed medical report informed layman and doctor alike of the diversity of treatment available at the Hospital. In one year (1890) the physicians had treated twenty-six children suffering from twelve diseases: ten typhoid fever, four general debility, two each scarletina and varicella, and eight (one in each category) anemia, chorea, idiocy, mitral regurgitation, lobular pneumonia, acute rheumatism, thrombosis, and tonsillitis. Only two of the twenty-six had died. There were thirty-five surgical cases, some grouped as Deformities and Tuberculosis, others listed singly: R.R. injury, osteomyelitis, capitis, etc. The surgeons had performed fourteen operations: two amputations, two injections in tubercular joints, two paracentesis thoracis, two tenotomies, and one each of division of the plantar tissues and iridectomy.

The remaining pages of the 1891 Annual Report reach out to the community for financial support, an appeal entirely lacking in 1886. "With a view to increasing the efficiency of the Hospital," the report reads, "several generous friends have become responsible for the support of individual beds by giving annually to the Hospital the sum of $250 for each bed thus supported." There were three such beds in 1891, one by Mrs. Porter's sister, Adele Adams. Donations other than cash were also listed, undoubtedly with a hope of attracting more. They ranged from a telephone, a case of general operating instruments, and a sewing machine (from Mrs. Porter's mother, Nancy Smith Foster) to fruit, flowers, books, pictures, and ice cream. A group of little girls from Genesco, Illinois, had sent "a bundle of scrap pictures"; a gentleman had taken a few children for a sleigh ride; an "interested" lady had given them a picnic at Edgewater; and Adele Adams had taken them to see the Electrical Fountains (these must have been the fountains at the entrance to the Columbian Exposition, due to open in 1892 after two years of preparation).

The 1891 Report clearly shows that the Hospital for the first time was cautiously reaching out for public financial support. It reveals as well, in its list of donations, an interest, even in those early days, in the whole child. The small patients were to Mrs. Porter not just children in need of medicine and surgery. They also needed books, flowers, pictures, and enterainment. They were children.

The growth of a hospital treating children exclusively and its increasing importance in Chicago testify to a growing interest in pediatrics as a special part of medicine. Histories of pediatrics refer to the 1880s and even the 90s as a period of infancy, or of darkness before dawn, but there were stirrings then that implied a healthy child or a bright sunny day ahead. September 18, 1888, is an important day in the history of pediatrics. On that day the American

Pediatric Society was founded. Enthusiasm for such a society had been in the wind since the Ninth International Medical Conference a year earlier. Papers on children's diseases had begun to be read in separate meetings; the American Medical Association had officially recognized pediatrics by designating a Section on Pediatrics in its conferences; and *Archives of Pediatrics*, a periodical devoted exclusively to children's diseases, had been started by William Perry Watson in 1884. The founding of the Society itself followed naturally.

The founders were young men, most of them under forty; only four were over fifty. Membership at the outset was limited to one hundred. A year after its founding, the Society began to publish *Transactions of the American Pediatric Society*, thus making available to all interested doctors advancements in the treatment of children's diseases. The four papers in the first number of *Transactions* are typical: "The Place of Pediatrics in Medicine," "Treatment of Whooping Cough by Antipyrin," "Aneurism in Childhood," and "Clinical Studies on the Pulse in Childhood."

Medical education in the 1880s also mirrors the growing interest in pediatrics and, to some extent, the desire to separate it from women's diseases. Medical teaching in Chicago had by then almost entirely abandoned the apprentice system in favor of institutional teaching. But the latter was far from stable. Rush Medical College (chartered in 1837, opened in 1843) had failed to live up to early expectations of excellence. Dissatisfied with the training at Rush, seven young physicians had opened a new medical school in 1859 with higher qualifications for entrance, an extended term of three years, and clinical instruction in medicine, surgery, pathology, and diagnosis. To graduate after completing the course, one also had to be twenty-one years old and of "good moral character." This school, at first a part of Lind University, became the Chicago Medical College in 1863, and, while retaining its name, joined Northwestern Medical School in 1870. That was its status in 1891.

In the beginning, Chicago Medical College did not have a Department of Pediatrics. As usual this discipline was included in Obstetrics and Diseases of Women and Children. In 1883, however, Dr. Marcus L. Hatfield was appointed Professor of Pediatrics—the first in all of Chicago. By 1892 Rush Medical College also taught pediatrics as a separate subject.

The Maurice Porter Memorial Hospital, 1884.

Certificate Number **32654**

STATE OF ILLINOIS

OFFICE OF
THE SECRETARY OF STATE

To all to whom these Presents Shall Come, Greeting:

I, LOUIS L. EMMERSON, Secretary of State of the State of Illinois, do hereby certify that the following and hereto attached is a true photostatic copy of Articles of Incorporation of THE MAURICE

PORTER MEMORIAL HOSPITAL

Certificate of change of name to THE MAURICE PORTER CHILDRENS

HOSPITAL Filed May 6, 1899

Certificate of change of name to THE CHILDREN'S MEMORIAL

HOSPITAL Filed April 23 1904

Certificate of consolidation of The Children's Memorial Hospital

and The North Star Dispensary into and formed THE CHILDREN'S

MEMORIAL HOSPITAL Filed January 20, 1914

the original of which is now on file and a matter of record in this office.

In Testimony Whereof, I have hereto set my hand and cause to be affixed the Great Seal of the State of Illinois. Done at the City of Springfield this 21st day of September A.D. 19 27

Louis L. Emmerson

SECRETARY OF STATE

Articles of Incorporation.

	1895 Admt.	1896 Admt.	1897 Admt.	1898 Admt.	1899 Admt.	1900 Admt.	1901 Admt.	1902 Admt.	1903 Admt.	1904 Admt.	Total
January	2	8	11	11	13	13	18	14	34.	27	151
February	6	5	8	9	8	16	11	22	23	20	128
March	10	11	7	16	21	24	16	7	24	26	162
April	7	9	18	17	31	19	16	18	18	36	189
May	8	5	13	7	closed*	12	34	22	20	13*	134
June	7	15	13	11	" "	21	16	26	23	29	161
July	11	11	8	13	6	15	41	39	38	37	219
August	12	4	6	21	30	24	41	37	48	43	266
September	8	6	11	9	9	15	28	27	29	34	176
October	12	6	6	13	15	14	22	21	26	34	169
November	10	8	10	11	14	15	20	27	12	27	154
December	9	12	12	10	13	21	19	*	7	22	125
Total	102	100	123	148	160	209	282	260	302	348	2034
Monthly Average	8	8	10	12	13	17	23	21	25	29	16

*Quarantine

The Hospital reports to the public in 1905.

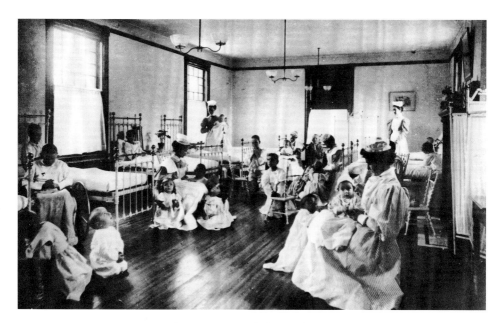

Saying prayers before bedtime.

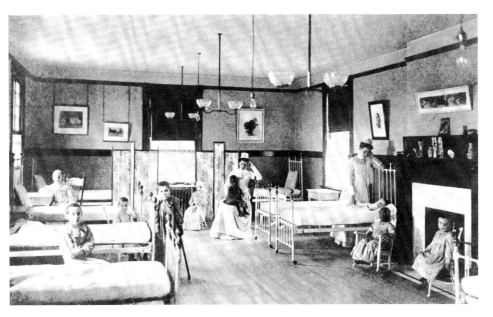

A ward in the Maurice Porter Memorial Hospital.

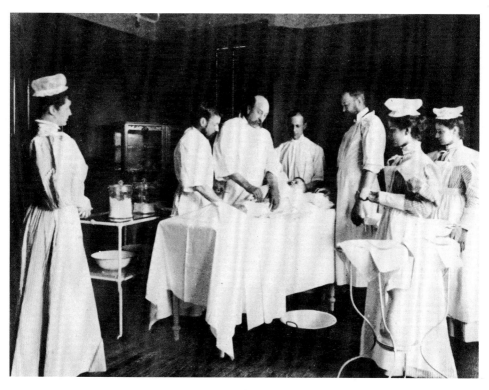

Dr. Truman W. Miller in surgery, 1886.

Aug 5th 1895

Being the first Monday in the
Month there was a meeting
of the board of Managers —
Mrs North — Mrs Adams — Mrs Mead —
and Mrs Taylor present —
The Meeting was Called to order
by Mrs North who presided in the
absence of Mrs Porter and Mrs.
McCagg —
Report of the Secretary was read
and approved —
The Report of the Treasurer Mrs. Adams
was read and approved —
Showing the Expenses for the
Month of July to have been
$323.13² — ~~balance on hand~~
982.83 balance $659.70
Report of Purchasing Committee,
Of the Kindergarten — (Miss Golding)
and Manor — (Miss Hewitt)
were also read and approved
— The Matron informed us
of 4 gallons of milk being
recd daily from Elmhurst —
from Mrs Bryan Lathrop and
a gift from the same source
of a tea set for the Nurses
Table —
It was moved and Seconded

A page from the Board of Lady Manager's handwritten minutes.

The Open Air Pavilion on the campus.

If it were difficult for a man then to acquire a good basic medical education, it was many times harder for a woman. Whether they should be educated as doctors was still hotly debated in the 1880s. Not too many years earlier, Rush had been censored by the Illinois State Medical Society for admitting a woman. Chicago Medical College had opened its doors to two or three in 1869 but at the end of one year the male students petitioned that the women be dropped. The men held that the faculty had omitted certain clinical material and observations because it was not proper to be shown or mentioned before women. Victorian mores prevailed. Mary Thompson Hospital then opened a medical school for women; after the Great Fire, it was enlarged and in 1890 it became The Woman's Hospital Medical College. In 1892 it was added to Northwestern as a Department; in 1902 it was closed and women were admitted to the Northwestern Medical School.

On the post graduate level, medical training in the early 1880s was completely missing. Many brilliant young physicians and surgeons had to travel to Europe to study new techniques, particularly in the relatively new, but rapidly expanding, field of bacteriology. Two of the members of Maurice Porter Hospital's medical staff in 1891 had followed that route: Dr. William Belfield and Dr. Frank Billings. Graduates of Rush and Chicago Medical College respectively, they had travelled to Vienna, Paris, and London for graduate work. And they had returned full of enthusiasm for bacteriology as an adjunct to medicine. Dr. Belfield showed slides of newly identified microorganisms—bacilli of cholera and tuberculosis among others—to the Chicago Medical Society, and Dr. Billings explained the new urine tests and the making of microscopic slides.

It was Dr. Truman Miller, head of Maurice Porter Hospital's medical staff, who helped found Chicago Polyclinic in 1886, the first post graduate center for medical training west of the Atlantic seaboard. Within a few years, three of Dr. Miller's colleagues at the Hospital joined him as teachers at Polyclinic: Doctors Belfield, Fiske, and William Christopher. The last was Professor of the Diseases of Children. He was to become a moving force at the Hospital. He was thirty-one years old when he joined the American Pediatric Society in 1890; from the beginning, he was one of its most vocal advocates for pediatrics as a special branch of medicine. When he became President in 1902 his opening speech was "Development, the Keynote of Pediatrics."

Another member of the Hospital staff in the early nineties, Dr. C. L. Rutter, brought the Hospital in touch with a unique service for children—the Chicago Floating Hospital. Organized in 1876, the Floating Hospital Association had rented a pier extending into Lake Michigan at North Avenue. Sturdy railings were put up and a shelter was built near the end of the pier. It was furnished with hammocks and cots. In July and August, five days a week, Monday through Friday, a boat made three round trips daily bringing children to breathe the fresh lake air and enjoy the sunshine. This service was thought to have restored health to thousands who lived in unsanitary, squalid surroundings in the city. Dr. Rutter was an active Board member of The Floating Hospital and for years served as its Secretary.

These stirrings in the field of pediatrics affected other Chicago hospitals. In 1885, Cook County Hospital assigned Ward 13 for the care of children exclusively. In 1890 Michael Reese Hospital opened a small children's ward of twelve beds.

And, across the board, a new note crept into Chicago's hospitals in the eighties. As the nature of bacterial infection became more widely understood, hospitals began to adopt antiseptic methods in the operating room. Disinfecting surgical instruments and using rubber gloves became common in the 1890s, but in the eighties a few hospitals began using some form of Listerism in their operating rooms. One of the oldest photographs in Childrens' Memorial Hospital's archives (1886) shows Dr. Miller in his surgery there. He is wearing rubber gloves.

CHAPTER III

A Board of Lady Managers and a Charter

1891–1894

THE WORD "patroness" describing Julia Foster Porter in the 1891 Report suggests a change in her position at the Hospital. It seems to underscore her financial responsibility, rather than her management of the day-to-day activities at the Hospital. While she was certainly still in close touch with Dr. Miller, her contact with the larger medical staff and the growing complexity of the Hospital's medical services must have been limited. Several of the early histories of the Hospital suggest that at forty-six, Mrs. Porter was not in very good health—her granddaughter says she had a hysterectomy about that time, one of the first in Chicago. Whatever the reason, or combination of reasons, Mrs. Porter in 1892 invited nine ladies to "act as an advisory board of Managers" for the Hospital.

The minutes of the Board of Lady Managers, as they were called, began November 15, 1892. Officers of the Board were Mrs. Porter, President; Mrs. Alexander C. McClurg, Vice President; Mrs. Orson Smith, Second Vice President; Mrs. Joseph T. Bowen, Treasurer; Mrs. Samuel J. Taylor, Secretary. Other Board members were Mrs. Robert North, Mrs. George E. Adams, Mrs. Henry Field, Mrs. Mahlon Ogden, and Mrs. Edward R. Mead. The composition of this first women's board is informative from several points of view. Mrs. Adams was Mrs. Porter's sister, already involved in Hospital affairs: she had endowed a bed, sent flowers and Christmas toys, and taken some of the patients to see the Electrical Fountains. Two ladies, Mrs. Bowen and Mrs. Orson Smith, were known in Chicago because of other civic activities. Mrs. Bowen was associated with many efforts to improve the lives of Chicago's poor.

When asked to join the Board, she accepted, but she was already deep in the work of Hull House, started by Jane Addams in 1889. Mrs. Orson Smith was making history in another sphere. In 1880, with several other public-spirited women, she had founded the Illinois Training School for Nurses from which the Hospital had drawn several superintendents. In 1892 she was Treasurer of the School and also busy putting together an exhibit of its work for the Columbian Exposition.

The motives behind the selection of other Board members are not hard to find if one examines the position and activities of their husbands, the usual route to information in the Victorian era when women were seldom featured for their own activities. In the 1880s, Mrs. Henry Field's husband had been a Director of the Relief and Aid Society and President of the Home for the Friendless. Mrs. Mead's husband was a doctor, a pioneer neuropsychiatrist in Illinois. He had established and directed an early hospital for the insane, the only one within several hundred miles of Chicago. Mrs. North's husband had been a Trustee of Hahneman's Hospital.

The new Board members touched money in the city. Mrs. Ogden's husband was active in real estate and a Director of Merchants' Loan and Trust Company. Mrs. Porter's father had helped found that bank and it was also the Hospital's bank. Mr. Orson Smith was Vice President of Merchants' Loan and Trust in 1892; he became President in 1898. Mrs. Samuel Taylor's husband was President of Chicago Chain Works, an important force in the city's industrial community. Mrs. McClurg's husband owned the famous McClurg bookstore, meeting place for Chicago's authors and journalists.

All of these men were prominent Chicagoans. In addition to promoting the city's financial and business interests, to a man they were backing its cultural institutions. They were members, trustees, directors and contributors to the Chicago Historical Society, The Art Institute, The Orchestral Association, the Newberry Library, and the Chicago Opera Festival.

Every member of this first Board of Lady Managers had, therefore, connections bound to spread the news of The Maurice Porter Memorial Hospital's work and to bring in financial support. Most of them also must have been acquaintances, if not friends, of Mrs. Porter. Several were fellow church members.

Business at the November meeting of the Board of Lady Managers included forming committees to insure the smooth running of the Hospital. Their variety shows the scope of the work Mrs. Porter had been carrying alone: Grounds and Building; Domestic Matters; Beds, Clothing, and Purchasing; Medicine and Delicacies; Auditing Accounts; Visiting Patients at their Homes; and Visiting the Hospital. All the ladies were members of the last committee—it came to be regarded as an informative and important duty. Mrs. Porter, Mrs. Adams, and Mrs. North were the committee to visit patients in their own homes, with an additional stipulation: "and all others who will." The first Monday of each month was set as Board meeting day; income was reported to be "at present" $3,000. Only one other piece of business is recorded: it was decided to arrange a Sunday School for patients.

The December meeting, the last for 1892, settled other Hospital routines: visiting hours 2-4 p.m. daily; and the use of the Harrison Street police station's ambulance to bring patients to the institution. The Secretary reported failure in organizing a Sunday School although a Miss Fanny Norton had volunteered to teach one class. The Superintendent reported on the patients, known to the ladies by name, so that they were grieved to hear that both Johnnie and his little sister Donna had died. The most important business was the Board's decision that, in spite of an increasing need of money, they would not take paying patients.

The minutes of 1893 (generally referred to as the first year of a woman's board) show a working Board, although only three or four showed up at some meetings and the summer exodus to country homes or travel began in June. Measles in the Hospital moved the March meeting to Mrs. Adams' home; chicken-pox in December took the ladies to Mrs. Porter's; and the opening of the Columbian Exposition postponed the May meeting one week. Necessary jobs, however, went forward. Mrs. Porter, at the Board's request, put in a new sidewalk on Orchard Street. The ladies began writing personal notes thanking donors; they were gratified by the increase in donations which followed. Miss Fanny Norton was still teaching one Sunday School class at the beginning of the year; by the end, Miss Forsythe had organized others. Through the Superintendent's monthly reports, the ladies had become interested in a little Italian boy, a deaf mute, and were delighted when a young lady volunteered to try to teach him.

The minutes are not very full: one is curious about the "delicacies" which supplement "medicines"; one wonders whether the heavy responsibility of purchasing supplies for the Hospital led to Mrs. T. Henry Field's resignation in June. And one longs to know what was in the letter from Dr. Sarah Hackett Stevenson which the minutes record only as having been read to the ladies in February.

The Board had slight contact with the medical staff at first, although they did buy an instrument case at the request of the surgeons. Mrs. Adams and Mrs. North undertook that commission hoping it would not be too expensive a purchase for the Board's scanty funds. A more important contact followed the Superintendent's report that four patients were under three years old. After discussion, Mrs. Adams was authorized to remind the staff of the rule forbidding admission of children under three. The minutes do not state that the doctors requested guidance on this point or on the readmittance of patients with a chronic disease, and little hope of a cure. Mrs. Porter, however, asked the opinion of the Board on the latter policy and they ruled that if "more acute cases" did not need beds, the Hospital could receive such patients. But a month later when presented with a request to admit an incurable, and "offensive" case, the President asked two Board members to consult Crippled Children's Hospital and The Half Orphan Asylum to find a home for the patient. He was not, they noted, an appropriate case for The Maurice Porter Memorial Hospital.

In the spring of 1893 the Board, led by Mrs. Porter, discussed informally the growth and welfare of the Hospital, but it was seven months later before they decided to invite the doctors to their January 1894 meeting to "confer on the best methods of extending the usefulness of the hospital." Only Dr. Miller and Dr. Christopher accepted the invitation; Dr. Fiske and Dr. Belfield regretted; no word came from the others. The only direction which seems to have come out of this discussion was to seek more publicity in order to increase the number of patients. Certainly the twenty beds had never been filled at one time in 1893, twelve was the highest reported day's occupancy. The ladies felt the Hospital was becoming better known— "more people are beginning to talk about [it] downtown" was the way the minutes put it. But they agreed that publicity was needed. They decided a new report should be published and the press should be courted. To accomplish the latter Mrs. North and Mrs. Taylor were asked to invite Mrs. William Penn Nixon to tour the Hospital and learn its needs. Mr. Nixon was business manager of the *Inter-Ocean*, the newspaper the Board hoped would be its "official organ." Mrs. Nixon herself was known to be widely interested in the conditions of working women and children.

Before the month was over a long article, "Little One's Home, Visit to the Memorial Hospital for Children," appeared in the *Inter-Ocean*. The subtitles: "The Patient Sufferers," "A Large and Excellent Medical Staff," and "Children Happy as in a Kindergarten—One Little Lad Cured of Hip Disease," suggest the tenor of the article. It states that because of the Hospital's "secluded situation and the founder's extreme modesty," it was not well known in Chicago. It emphasizes the pleasant homelike atmosphere; the excellence of the medical staff (all are listed); the prominence of many of the advisory members' board; and the cost of running the establishment. The ladies must have been highly pleased with their first attempt at newspaper publicity; later, similar articles appeared in *The Chicago Tribune, The Daily News, The Journal,* and *The Times.*

The Maurice Porter Memorial Hospital was emerging as one of the city's medical facilities, needing wider recognition and financial support. A brief statement in the February 1894 minutes, therefore, is not surprising: "The matter of taking out a charter was discussed and the names of several gentlemen suggested: Mr. Bryan Lathrop and Genl. McClurg." It is, on the contrary, rather astonishing that the Hospital had been in business twelve years without having been incorporated. Perhaps a specific impetus at this time was a bequest from Jane H. Green. Mrs. Green's will provided that her real estate be sold and the proceeds be divided equally among Presbyterian, St. Luke's, and The Maurice Porter Hospital. This matter had actually been pending since 1892, but without a legally incorporated institution bequests were difficult to accommodate. Early in 1894 the Secretary of the Board had written to the executor of Mrs. Green's estate about the bequest. If more money were to be sought from such sources, obviously the legal position of the Hospital needed definition.

In early March, Mr. Charles Norman Fay's name was added to the list of possible incorporators and on March 26 application was made to the State of Illinois for a Charter. Signers of the application were Julia F. Porter, George E. Adams, James W. Porter, and Charles Norman Fay. The purpose of the corporation was defined as the "care, treatment and cure of diseased or injured children." Seven directors were named: the four signers plus Bryan Lathrop, Orson Smith, and Alexander McClurg. Thus the Board of Directors consisted of three members of Mrs. Porter's family, Mr. Fay, and the husbands of three members of the Board of Managers, for during 1893 Mrs. Bryan Lathrop had joined the Board. Both she and her husband were prominent in the cultural affairs of the city. When asked to be a Director, Mr. Lathrop had stipulated that he should not be asked to raise money. If the ladies agreed, the promise was soon forgotten. General McClurg as well had a proviso: the Hospital could use his name but ill health would make it impossible for him to be active. Mr. Fay was a wealthy businessman, interested in developing Chicago's electrical industry and the telephone. He was active in the YMCA, serving on its Board of Directors in 1885.

The Charter was granted March 27, 1984. The Hospital now had a Board of Directors, a Board of Lady Managers, and a Medical Staff. But it had no Constitution and no Bylaws to define the election or appointments and duties of these bodies. To the ladies fell the task of writing those necessary documents, surely a new task to many of them. They set to work at once, "discussing" and "considering" over many months—the minutes carry frustrating, non-specific references to these conversations. They consulted similar documents from other institutions—Children's Hospital in Cincinnati was one. And they were successful. By the end of 1894 they had their own Constitution and Bylaws ready to include in the Annual Report. They were ready as well to enter a new stage in The Maurice Porter Hospital's development.

CHAPTER IV

From Incorporation to Mrs. Porter's Retirement

1894–1898

THE NEWLY formed Board of Directors (also called Trustees) elected Orson Smith President, Bryan Lathrop Vice President, George E. Adams Secretary, and Mrs. Joseph Bowen Treasurer. The new Bylaws required them to hold only one meeting annually, in December, when they would appoint a Board of "nine lady managers." The President, Secretary, or four Directors could request special meetings throughout the year. The Directors could fill vacancies on their own Board without reference to any other group. Extant minutes of the Directors' meetings begin in November 1908. Judging by references in the Managers' minutes, the Directors were in the earlier years a relatively inactive group, there to answer the questions, for the most part legal, of the Managers. Although the internal management of the Hospital was subject to their approval, that duty seems to have been largely ignored. It must be remembered, however, that Mrs. Porter (ex-officio) and Mrs. Bowen were on both Boards so that informal advice could easily be given and received. The role of the Directors changed dramatically at the beginning of the twentieth century when the Hospital faced a complete reorganization.

The Bylaws, however, set forth precisely the responsibilities of the Managers. They were to meet monthly and annually and have full charge of the internal management of the Hospital. They were to appoint and define the duties of the medical staff. They could if necessary enlarge their Board from nine to fifteen—with the approval of the Directors.

This tightening of organization gave the Managers a sense of a new start. They had three new members by 1895: Mrs. Cyrus McCagg (Mrs. Mahlon Ogden's sister-in-law), Mrs. Luther McConnell, and Mrs. Byran Lathrop. And they had lost three: Mrs. Henry Field, Mrs. Orson Smith, and Mrs. Alexander McClurg. They were still an intimate little group whose paths crossed in many places in Chicago's life, but they were not merely a social club. They were competent to meet the ever increasing tasks expected of them.

The upkeep of the Hospital of course never ended. Spring cleaning saw bedsteads repainted, beds "made over," and a dangerous veranda repaired. The fence received a new coat of paint and the grounds were put in order. Furniture was bought for a new operating room with a special gift of $250 from Clara Bass, another sister of Mrs. Porter. And Adele Adams paid fifteen dollars to repair and tune the Hospital's piano.

They solved, temporarily, the problem of religious education for the patients. That had concerned them from their very first meeting. At times they questioned whether they were responsible for running a Sunday School, but, good church members all, they could not ignore religion completely. Particularly at Christmas when a lighted tree, gifts, and a special dinner emphasized one side of the day's tradition, they felt there should be a religious service so that the children "may know why we celebrate the day." The Report of 1895 lists five Hebrew children among the patients but a religious service to the ladies meant a Protestant service. The Reverend William J. Petrie, Rector of the Episcopal Church of Our Saviour, is listed as Chaplain in 1895 and Miss Grace Golding as Sunday School teacher. Reverend Petrie had baptized two children in the Hospital in 1894, one just before she died. The question of baptizing children in the Hospital came to the Board's attention again when Miss Golding found four children in her Sunday School were unbaptized. Most of the Managers felt they could not assume a responsibility in that direction; they voted to leave baptism "up to the parents."

Secular education was also on their agenda. Late in 1894 the minutes noted that it might be good "to have some additional assistance in the hospital if not exactly a kindergarten, somebody who could act as a nursery governess." To carry out this idea they would have to raise special funds—the guaranteed income of $3,000 (from Mrs. Porter and the endowed beds) could not be stretched to cover

28

it. They were still debating "means" a month later, but Miss Golding, they found, was both qualified and willing to be a kindergarten, as well as a Sunday school, teacher. The Annual Report of 1895 lists her in both capacities. Committee assignments for the year also include a new committee, Kindergarten, with Mrs. Bowen and Mrs. Lathrop the members responsible. It was through their generosity that the Board was able to hire Miss Golding. The kindergarten lasted for at least two years; the committee was no longer included in the report of 1897.

Keeping the Superintendent and her staff healthy and happy was an ever present worry during those early years. The turnover was rapid; much was expected of them. They lived in the Hospital and were more or less on call twenty-four hours a day. There was no commitment for annual vacations; those were usually given when necessary to restore energy to an overworked employee. And the resultant extra expense for substitutes sparked many discussions of ways and means in Board meetings.

When the current Superintendent (Miss Marion Pollock) resigned in 1894 to take an easier job as a district nurse, the search committee suggested that the time was ripe for some changes. They recommended, at Mrs. Lathrop's suggestion, that Miss Catherine Hewitt (Illinois Training School 1886) be hired as Superintendent, and that an assistant be sought who could double as a kindergarten teacher. To relieve the Superintendent of excessive night duty, the committee suggested that an arrangement be made with German Hospital to supply night nurses.

The last suggestion was a sign of an enlarging world for the Board of Lady Managers. Community contacts were becoming more frequent. Newspaper publicity had spurred some of them. Many church groups and some secular ones were now sewing for the children. The Vassar Ten sent a box of "beautifully made garments"; the Lake View Women's Club a contribution because a child from their community had received "faithful care" in her last illness; and a lady from Ravenswood sent a portable bathtub (Dr. Christopher had requested one). As a result of the *InterOcean* article, children from all over the state had sent their pennies to the "little ones" in the Hospital—$26.24 was the grand total.

One community approach they rejected. The Children's Aid

Society proposed considering consolidation with the Hospital—the ladies replied, not "at present."

There is no record of the Medical Board's reaction to the incorporation of the Hospital nor of their having a hand in the definition of their duties as they appeared in the new Bylaws. They were empowered to make such rules and regulations as they "deemed necessary" for the health of the hospital. At least one staff member was required to visit the Hospital daily, inspect the children, exclude those suffering from contagious diseases, and give all necessary medical attention. They could also fill vacancies on their own Board. That permission was actually in conflict with the managers' stated responsibility to appoint medical staff members and, indeed, it did lead to difficulties in 1900.

These pivotal years in the Hospital's development—1894 and 1895—are marked by a change in the relationship of the doctors and the Managers. After Dr. Miller and Dr. Christopher met with the women in January 1894 to discuss the best way to extend the usefulness of the Hospital, the two groups seemed to have had little contact for the rest of the year. The minutes note only the request for a portable bathtub and a report from Dr. Christopher that two cases of whooping cough had necessitated isolating those children from the other patients. The Annual Report, however, expresses gratitude for the "faithful, skillful, and attentive" medical staff. And it notes that Dr. Miller, at his own expense, had entirely refitted the operating room: enameling the walls, adding "two surgical sterilizers of the last improved pattern, a new operating table, protecting screens, instrument stands and other articles." "Our operating room," the report concludes, "is now thoroughly equipped for modern surgery."

Dr. Miller's activity reflects the growing recognition among doctors of the importance of antiseptic conditions in operating rooms. But to what extent the doctors attempted to keep the women abreast of growing medical knowledge which affected their Hospital remains a moot point. Yet those years were marked by many advances in medicine, and their own Dr. Christopher was in the thick of them. He does not appear, for example, to have shared with the women a paper entitled, "Typhoid Fever in Infancy," which he delivered to the American Pediatric Society in 1892. Yet the Hospital treated typhoid patients every year and in 1890 they had formed over half of the patient load. Nor does he seem to have shared with them his continuing drive to have pediatrics considered a special branch of medicine. As Chairman in 1894 of the American Medical Association's Section on Pediatrics he presented his point of view once more in his lecture to them on "Pediatrics as a Specialty."

Changes in the relationship were on the way, however, and 1895 saw their beginning. The staff itself had changed: Dr. Billings and Dr. Rutter had left, Dr. William Quinlan had been added as House Surgeon. He was only twenty-eight and a recent graduate of Columbia University's College of Physicians and Surgeons. Pressure to admit more children was greatly increased as Chicago suffered from a serious economic depression following the Columbian Exposition. The Annual Report of 1894 estimated that there were 10,000 homeless children in Chicago and many more lacking suitable medical care. The Hospital's capacity was strained to the limits in spite of Mrs. Bowen's generosity in augmenting it with seven new beds with "all furnishings." The Managers refused to go into debt, so they were forced to refuse admission to some. In March they turned eight away in one week.

There was a sense of crisis when Dr. Christopher came to the May Board meeting and read a paper giving his views on what the Hospital needed. He urged building a new wing, thereby increasing the capacity to 100 beds, and then opening the Hospital to "physicians generally." He also advocated extending the Hospital's facilities to medical students, an extension important to medical education in the city and to the Hospital. He requested, for the first time, an infant ward—admission rules still set three years as the lowest admission age. Mrs. Porter asked Dr. Christopher to consult Dr. Miller about these ideas and to incorporate them into a new Report about to be published. The Managers were to hear much more from both doctors on the merits of admitting infants; the changes in the use of the Hospital did not appear in the next Annual Report.

In 1896, the doctors took a good look at the physical plant. There was no doubt that the Hospital needed to be enlarged, but until that happened some changes were imperative. They requested the Managers, for sanitary reasons, to close the laundry off from the rest of the house and they also pressed for an isolation facility. They asked for a better light in the operating room, and that drinking water be boiled and filtered. Closing off the laundry took considerable ingenuity, but the isolation facility was even more difficult to achieve in the existing building. Fortunately, a new Board member, Mrs. Henry Ives Cobb, offered help. Her husband was a well known architect; he had helped design, among other Chicago landmarks, the Potter Palmer mansion in 1882, and the new home of the Chicago Historical Society, dedicated in 1896. At his wife's request, he drew up plans for a separate isolation cottage. There was plenty of room to build it on the Hospital grounds, and the cottage itself could probably be built, he thought, for $2,500. The plan met with the approval of the Board, and Mrs. Porter offered to submit it to the Directors.

The idea of an isolation cottage disappeared, however, in the larger discussion of remodelling the whole hospital. A building committee was appointed to implement the more extensive plans. By the end of 1896 a large new wing had been added to the main building at a cost of $6,000. Bed capacity was increased from forty to fifty. The first floor provided nurses' rooms, the second a ward with ten beds, and the matron's old room was turned into a small ward, possibly for babies. On the fourth was the long desired isolation ward.

In 1896 the Managers were also meeting another situation which might lead to the admission of infants. Late in 1895 they had received a request from the *Chicago Daily News* Fresh Air Fund which maintained an open air sanitarium (not unlike The Floating Hospital) in Lincoln Park near Fullerton Avenue. From June to September (the dates depended on the weather) the Sanitarium received children and their mothers from the stifling hot tenements of the city and treated them to fresh air, sunshine, good food, and medical care if needed. The Fund's slogan was "10¢ keeps a baby one day at the Lincoln Park Sanitarium." The big Sanitarium pavilion, open on three sides, stood on a platform over Lake Michigan. Hundreds of infants' hammocks were suspended from supports in the airy interior. Usually the children went home at night but sometimes a critical case had to be kept for a night or two. Since the Sanitarium's dormitory facilities for such emergencies were limited, they wrote the ladies asking if the nearby Porter

Hospital would occasionally take a short term patient for them.

Their first request went unanswered, but when, a few months later (early in 1896) the Fresh Air Fund offered to support four beds at the Hospital for their patients, the ladies had to respond. They requested $400 for four months (June through September) for four beds. There is no record that the medical staff approved this decision, but since Dr. Storer (a new member of the medical staff in 1896) was an attending physician and Dr. Christopher on the consulting staff of the Sanitarium, one assumes they were pleased.

By July, however, the Managers were regretting their action. Nine patients had occupied the beds; three had been discharged, six had died. The death record of the Hospital was so distorted by these statistics that the women decided to keep a separate count of the Sanitarium's beds and to review their contract carefully. At the end of the summer they abandoned the whole arrangement "for the time being."

The Maurice Porter Memorial Hospital at the beginning of 1897 was a far cry from the small cottage hospital opened fifteen years earlier. Its physical plant was larger; its bed capacity had increased fivefold; and it had grown in importance in the city. Mrs. Porter and her Board of Managers were no longer responsible merely for internal management—from plumbing to decorating; they had policy decisions as well, for the doctors now came to them with problems and they had increasing contact with other institutions in Chicago.

All of these changes, as indications of growth, must have gratified Mrs. Porter, but perhaps she also found their challenge not to her personal liking. The reporter from the *InterOcean* had referred earlier to her "extreme modesty"; she is remembered by her grandchildren and friends of her later years as a shy, retiring person, almost a recluse. She was fifty years old in 1897; her health was not too robust; and she had in the 1890s taken into her home two little girls. Once again she made a decision which changed the Hospital's history. She would not continue as President in 1897. She became Honorary President and Mrs. Bowen moved into the President's chair. The Board enlarged its membership from nine to fifteen, increased the medical staff to nine, and lowered the age of admission to two. In the Annual Report of 1897, they dropped "Memorial" from the Hospital's name, calling it The Maurice Porter Free Hospital for Children.

CHAPTER V

Changing Times
Lead to Reorganization

1898–1903

THE HOSPITAL'S first venture in caring for babies had not been very encouraging. They were to face the problem again in 1898. Although they knew Dr. Miller did not approve of taking infants except in emergency, they invited him and Dr. Christopher to their January meeting to present the pros and cons of lowering the admission age to include them. Dr. Miller was firm: babies were often brought to a hospital in the last stages of starvation; they required wet nurses; and their stay in the hospital was likely to be long so that they tied up much needed room. Dr. Christopher disagreed: wet nurses were not necessary—he cited many cases where proper feeding by formula during the first year of a child's life had had lasting effect. As to the length of hospitalization, he felt it would be similiar to that of typhoid cases—about six weeks. Expense would be comparatively slight since the room reserved for them could accommodate six to eight cribs.

The Board's decision after this presentation was, as recorded, a bit vague: a "certain number" were to be admitted "with discretion," after being passed on by a representative of the medical staff. Discharge of these patients was to follow the same route.

Stating the role of the doctor in admitting and discharging patients was designed, at least in part, to reduce the authority of the Superintendent. The relationship of doctor, superintendent, and nurses was of growing concern to the Board of Managers, 1897-1900. For almost two of those years, from April 1898 to January 1900, Mrs. Bowen was not in Chicago. Mrs. Eliphalet Cramer and Mrs. Russell Tyson had to take her place and lead the Board as it faced the problems of its small school to train nurses for the special needs of a children's hospital. The School had been started a few years earlier at the time Miss Hewitt had become Superintendent. An efficient woman, she ran a tight ship. Since nothing in the Bylaws defined the management of the school, Miss Hewitt seems to have been largely in control.

Admission age for students was a minimum of eighteen years. Novice nurses were put on one month's probation; if satisfactory, they were paid eight dollars per month the first year, twelve dollars the second. Board and room were free since they lived in the Hospital but they provided their own uniforms. Formal training consisted of three lectures a week by the medical staff, one by the Superintendent. Examinations followed each stage of the course.

In mid-1897, Dr. Miller had attended a Board of Managers' meeting to discuss a number of policy questions about the school. Most important was the length of the course—two or three years? Dr. Miller favored two, based on the practices at the Illinois Training School and Polyclinic. He felt it unnecessary that nurses should have a "knowledge of bacteriology," or of mathematics, or be able to examine urine. A good English education was all that was necessary. He recommended a form to be filled out by applicants, and then sent to the Hospital to be signed by a physician or the Superintendent. He was firm in his belief that the medical staff should have a role in accepting an applicant; they should determine if she were intelligent and physically capable of being a nurse. He also recommended a two-year contract so that a nurse could not sue for wages if she left earlier, and a penalty of twenty dollars for breaking the contract. The Board of Managers, he felt, should have the final say if the Superintendent wished to expel a nurse.

After Dr. Miller left the meeting, the ladies discussed Miss Hewitt's feeling that her control of the nurses should not be interfered with. They decided to defer the Training School questions until they met again in the autumn. In October, at a special meeting to discuss financial straits, the Training School was again on the agenda. By this time Dr. Miller had sent the Board suggested rules for nurses and an application form. The Board appointed a committee to review Dr. Miller's suggestions and to consult with Miss Hewitt on a method for dismissing nurses.

It was unfortunate that nurses and finances were discussed at the same time, for in the stress of the moment, the ladies voted to reduce the nurses' salaries from eight dollars to four dollars per month for the first year, and from twelve dollars to six dollars the second. In November they reconsidered the reduction and restored the previous salaries.

They accepted without question Dr. Miller's seven Rules for Nurses. They were strict. The nurses were "subject" to the Superintendent, obeying without question her orders and the rules of the Hospital. Their shifts were 12 hours: 7 a.m. to 7 p.m.; 7 p.m. to 7 a.m. The day nurses were warned not to linger in the dining room after meals and were expected to retire at 10 p.m. They were never to comment on the treatment given their patients, nor to discuss with anyone that treatment or the nature of the disease of any child.

Another piece of business relating to the nurses was tidied up in these years too. The Hospital permitted, in fact encouraged, nurses to accept outside work when a temporary dwindling in the patient load made it possible. Miss Hewitt prepared a kind of report card to be filled in by their employers: had they been "neat, civil and obliging," "capable, attentive and trustworthy"? Had they made trouble in the household? And would the employer be willing to hire the same nurse again?

When the Annual Report for 1898 was published, for the first time it devoted several pages to the Training School. It outlined the course of instruction (contrary to Dr. Miller's ideas they *did* study bacteriology and the "testing and examination of urine"); the textbooks used; and all the minutiae of night duty, vacations, uniforms, etc. Dr. Miller's advice for a two-year course was followed. But the Superintendent was given "full power to decide as to the fitness of the applicant for the work, and to retain or dismiss her at the end of the month of probation."

Discussion of the Training School was minimal for a while but there was still tension between Dr. Miller and Miss Hewitt. Her request to the Board in the spring of 1898 that she be allowed to adopt a baby abandoned at the Hospital foreshadowed her intention to leave. She resigned readily in 1899 after Dr. Miller told the women that the staff felt "the interests of the Hospital were no longer best served by Miss Hewitt as Superintendent."

Dr. Miller then requested that the doctors have a hand, with the Board, in selecting the new Superintendent. That too was granted and a joint committee selected Miss Grace Watson (Illinois Training School 1892). For the moment peace reigned.

The Board of Managers, however, could not relax; they had plenty to keep them busy. They bought new laundry tubs, a mangle, and six rocking chairs. They scrutinized gas bills and grocery bills, and investigated purchasing drugs wholesale—all with a view toward saving money. They mended cement and renewed insurance. They ordered a daily paper and electrified the whole hospital. They took Dr. Christopher's advice and began getting Gurler's milk, the purest in the city. They made the isolation ward a self-sufficient unit by adding a bathroom (plumbing $100, nickel fixtures a gift). They planned treats for patients and celebrated Christmas with a glittering tree, presents, and a huge dinner. They arranged to send one of their patients who needed long-term care to the Home for the Friendless, another to the Feeble-minded Children's Home.

They took a good look at their own Board's composition and conduct. One result was the appointment of an Executive Committee to carry on business in the summer; another, a rule that three consecutive unexplained absences would remove a member from the Board. After a few months that rule seems to have been ignored. And they changed the meeting day to the second Monday of the month. Membership remained at fourteen to fifteen; faces changed, but enthusiasm and hard work did not.

The burden of money raising was heavier each year as expenses rose. Back in 1896, with work on the new addition going forward, they had faced their first deficit (ninety dollars) and had not liked it. Out of a meeting to discuss ways and means a new idea was born. Mrs. Dunlap Smith, a new member, suggested the sale of Associate Memberships at five dollars each. The first year, 144 men and women responded. Greatly encouraged, the women continued this money-raising scheme. The 1898 Annual Report lists 231 Associates. The Board continued as well to encourage the endowment of beds at $250 each, but at the end of 1897 they had only two. Donation Day (Easter Sunday) had been established in 1895; the ladies varied this appeal—cards one year; paper bags to be filled with groceries and money, another. The Day brought in a steady, if not spectacular, amount of money each year. A box at the entrance hall of the Hospital, labelled "Help the little ones," added four dollars to six dollars per month to the income.

One December, Adele Adams gave a birthday party. Three members of the Board made ribbon bags which they sent to 1,000 persons, asking that they fill the bags with as many pennies as they were old. That effort netted $600. A second birthday party, held at the Hospital, featured colored envelopes instead of ribbon bags. It too was successful.

To reach a wider public, they sponsored an Open House at the Hospital in December 1897, accompanying each invitation with a tiny Christmas stocking and a bit of doggerel:

> This tiny sock makes mute appeal
> Suggesting how you may,
> By filling it from toe to heel
> Bring joy on Christmas Day.

The Managers much preferred these routes to money raising to sponsoring entertainments. But they tried that a time or two as well. It is a pity that their efforts to arrange first, a baseball game between Lake Forest and Wheaton Golf Clubs, and second, a football game between the Bankers Club and the Chicago Athletic Club, were frustrated. The minutes, disappointingly, do not record why these imaginative efforts failed! They were more successful in sponsoring an exhibition of the Robert Hall McCormick's art collection; but there is no record of how much money that raised.

Their most spectacular success, by far, came in 1900 when they sponsored a lecture by Ernest Thompson Seton on "Personalities of Wild Animals." The Managers went all out on this one: publicity in newspapers and on street cars; circulars sent to a long list of names culled from the Social Register, churches, clubs, schools, and the ladies' friends. There were even souvenir programs decorated with little bears (from wood blocks donated by Scribner's and the Century Co.). Although expenses, including Mr. Seton's fee of $500, came to $1,000, the benefit netted the Hospital $1,641. The ladies came of age in the benefit world with this venture.

Nineteen hundred was another pivotal year for The Maurice Porter Children's Hospital. Mrs. Bowen was back in the President's chair after almost two years' absence. She focussed the January meeting on conditions at the Hospital as she found them on her return. They were now paying $215 a month to nurses, but many beds were empty—only thirty-one were occupied in January. The Managers were convinced that only by enlarging the medical staff would they attract more patients and widen the knowledge of the institution. It was a "delicate matter," the minutes note, to find fault with doctors who had given time and service, free, for years. But the Hospital's welfare must come first. The Managers proposed that two physicians be added to the staff and Mrs. Bowen asked two of the ladies to discuss the Board's feelings with Dr. Miller and Dr. Christopher.

The Medical Board met promptly after this interview and agreed to enlarge the staff. In eight days the names and positions of the staff were in Mrs. Bowen's hands. The full complement of doctors was fifteen (an additional six); only one position remained open—House Physician. New positions included a neurologist and a pathologist; there were some promotions and two resignations. The staff, in turn, had a request for the Managers: restrict visiting hours to parents and guardians—mothers on Wednesday, fathers on Sunday from 3-4 p.m. on each day. Too many visitors had been a worry for doctors and nurses for a long time.

Mrs. Bowen reconvened the Board a few days later. She was not entirely pleased. In his zeal to enlarge the staff, Dr. Miller had forgotten Bylaw XI which gave the Managers authority to appoint the Medical Board, subject to the approval of the Directors. A letter with this reminder was sent to Dr. Miller and the ratification of the new staff was postponed to February. When the dust finally settled, the Managers had added two names and the Medical Board had a new look. Dr. Miller's rule for visitors was accepted with the deletion of "mothers on Wednesday, fathers on Sunday."

But the struggle was not over. Mrs. Bowen again left the city in March and did not return before November. Mrs. Cramer and Mrs. McCagg shared the responsibility of guiding the Board during a few anxious months. A number of letters went back and forth between the Medical Board and the Board of Managers in March and April. The doctors claimed the privilege, given in other hospitals, of filling their own vacancies; the Managers clung to Bylaw XI. But in the end, the two names suggested by the women were withdrawn and two new nominations by the doctors were approved. In the minutes of the annual meeting of the Board of Managers in December is a statement explaining this action: "since Staff and Board were equally anxious for the best interests of the Hospital, after looking over the matter very carefully, the conciliatory course was considered the wisest, and it was thought best to revise the Bylaws."

Discussion of admission problems and the need to segregate some patients led to the doctors sending the following document for the Managers' consideration in May:

RULES FOR ADMISSION AND DISCHARGE OF PATIENTS

1. Patients under two years or over thirteen years of age are not admitted.
2. Contagious and incurable diseases are not admitted.
3. All medical cases must be examined by one of the physicians connected with the hospital before being admitted.
4. Surgical or Emergency cases, when necessary, may be admitted by the Superintendent without examination.
5. When a case for any cause is denied admittance the reason therefore must be stated on a blank provided for that purpose, which blank shall be given to the one bringing the case.
6. When a patient on admission is dangerously ill this fact must be stated on a blank provided for that purpose, which blank shall be given to the one leaving the patient.
7. No patient shall be discharged except with the knowledge and consent of the Medical Attendant in whose care the case may be.

A letter accompanying the Rules stressed the need for a receiving room in which incoming patients could be kept for two or three days until physicians were sure no contagious disease was being brought into the Hospital. Doctors Christopher, Storer, Houston, and Walker, who signed the letter, thought the isolation ward could be used for this purpose; it could always be restored to its original use if there were an epidemic in the Hospital. The women approved the Rules and began plans for a receiving room.

The Managers must have felt they could relax a bit after the May meeting, but June brought a blow—Dr. Miller, only sixty years old, died unexpectedly. Mrs. Porter came to a special meeting on June 4 to present a resolution of appreciation for his faithful services as surgeon and President of the Medical Board for eighteen years. She praised him too as a most interested and generous friend of the Hospital.

It was the end of an era for Mrs. Porter. Her active participation had dwindled since she had resigned from the Presidency in 1897. Her attendance at meetings of the Board of Managers fell from six that year to two in 1899. The special June meeting was the first one she had attended in 1900. She still carried a few committee assignments—Auditing, and Building and Grounds. These were key committees for Mrs. Porter, for she still contributed annually to running expenses and had a stake in the expansion of the Hospital. But she was letting go. That was demonstrated when in 1898 she had given the Hospital building and the land on which it stood to the Directors. Many of her family were still active: George and Adele Adams, James W. Porter, and in 1900, her son James F. Porter was made a new Director. In 1901 her daughter-in-law Ruth (Mrs. James F. Porter) would join the Board of Managers. But she herself was no longer a constant visitor and participant.

With the death of Dr. Miller, new questions arose about the future of the Medical Board. The ladies noted that the staff "should be left unbiased in the election of a new President," and before June was over confirmed the selection of Dr. M. L. Harris. While he settled into his new post, the ladies returned to coping with plumbing crises, helped Miss Watson dismiss—gently—an overly nervous nurse, and ran their successful Ernest Thompson Seton Benefit. The year ended on an upbeat note. They received an unexpected gift of $5,000 to endow the Stanley Bed; returns from the benefit gave them a cushion in running expenses, and for the first time, the Hospital had treated more than 200 patients in one year (100 medical, 101 surgical).

Mrs. Bowen, reelected President in 1901, headed an active, experienced Board of fifteen. It was a year for decisions. Several problems, unresolved in earlier years, were solved in this one. Lincoln Park Sanitarium applied again for service. This time, after two Managers conferred with the Director of the *Daily News* Fresh Air Fund, and consulted Dr. Christopher, the Board voted to admit and treat Sanitarium referrals. That meant of course lowering the age of admission. But with a forty-three bed capacity, often eight were empty at one time, and Dr. Christopher felt the doctors could handle younger children. Dr, Miller, of course, was no longer there to object. Admission age was lowered to include infants.

Training School problems were harder to solve. Many of the nurses under the present course objected because they had insufficient training with adult cases. A plan to exchange nurses with Polyclinic proved unworkable. In the end the Boards voted to discontinue their Training School and hire all of their nurses from Polyclinic. One advantage of this plan was the release of the rooms then housing nurses. That space could be used for an examining room or a laboratory, or both. The Hospital's Dr. Harris was chairman of the Polyclinic Training School that year so that the change was made smoothly. By June it was agreed that Polyclinic nurses, after nine months' nursing experience, would come to Maurice Porter for six months' duty. The Hospital would pay Polyclinic for their services.

In 1901 change was in the air, and it was not long before the Board of Managers was in the thick of reorganization. Often this year they held two meetings a month to air ideas. In March, the Managers, led by Mrs. Bowen, asked the medical staff, in view of the coming reorganization, to elect its officers for 1902 early. They also proposed, since reorganization would call for extra professional help, that Dr. A. J. Ochsner be asked to be President of the Medical Board. He had an excellent professional standing, had built up German Hospital in the neighborhood, and was a personal friend of some Board Members. In their zeal, the ladies seemed to have forgotten that the doctors wished to have a free hand in their own affairs. Dr. Fiske and Mrs. Bowen conferred and a joint reorganization committee was appointed: Mrs. Tyson, Mrs. Smith, and Mrs. Nelson from the Women's Board, Dr. Christopher and Dr. Henrotin from the Staff. Dr. Henrotin had joined the Hospital in the spring of 1901; although new, he knew Maurice Porter Hospital well, for he was President of Polyclinic.

The next move of the women is difficult to understand; it certainly did not promote cordial relations: they asked the entire medical staff to resign. Then the Board wrote to Dr. Christopher asking him "to form with Dr. Ochsner a staff of physicians and surgeons" for The Maurice Porter Hospital. Because of Dr. Christopher's long and valued services and knowledge of the Hospital, they felt he, with Dr. Ochsner, would choose staff "who will best serve its future." The staff *did* resign but Dr. Christopher refused to organize a new staff.

When the Managers received Dr. Christopher's refusal, they retreated from their position, reappointed the entire old staff, added the names of Dr. Henrotin and Dr. Ochsner, and gave the Medical Board power to go ahead and elect its own officers.

Dr. Christopher was in close touch with the Managers the remaining months of 1901. He came to many of their meetings to answer questions and list needs. Among the latter were an ambulance, or carriage with wide seats; a microscope ($150); a two-tube tester (for urine); scales with a metric and avoirdupois beam; and a stadiometer—an instrument for measuring standing and sitting height. He got into trouble with the last item because he bought it without the Managers' explicit consent. Since it was expensive, the ladies tried for months to return it or sell it second hand!

The ladies' medical education advanced materially in these years—sometimes with humorous overtones. Apparently the word "orthopedic" and its exact meaning was new to them. They were anxious about the standing of their Hospital, their minutes record, because it had no "authopedists" on the staff. It took a visit from Dr. Christopher to assure them that almost all of the doctors were orthopedists—the Secretary still, however, spelled it "authopedists."

At another meeting in 1901, Dr. Christopher read them a short paper on the use of a hospital for treatment and study. Perhaps this was the paper he had written that year for the American Pediatric Society. In 1901 he was President of the Society and also Professor of Pediatrics at the College of Physicians and Surgeons (Medical college of the University of Illinois). The paper examined the progress of medical education over, roughly, the period from 1880 to 1901. The latter year Dr. Christopher defined as a "boom time," ripe for pushing the clinic as a basis for medical training, research, and action. His words fell on fertile ground; a few months later when he returned to talk again about the use of a hospital, the Managers voted "that students be admitted to the Hospital for clinics with any member of the Staff."

It is this kind of policy decision which points up how far the Board has travelled in nine years. Its focus was no longer kitchen stoves and laundry tubs, new paint and more sheets, and repair of the ever needful plumbing. Not that those chores were forgotten—

they were, after all, part of any good housewife's life, but the women were also aware that they were running a *hospital*. They wrestled, for example, with the problem of long-term patients with incurable diseases. They decided such children did not belong in a hospital but they could not just discharge them. If such a child could not return to his own home, the women found an institution for him: The Home for Incurables,The Nursery and Half Orphan Asylum, The Home for the Friendless, The Crippled Children's Hospital, and others. They felt a deep obligation to place these children in good care, but not to nurture them over long years themselves. Hospital beds had other uses. Many times the minutes refer to discussions of the length of time a child should be kept in the Hospital. They never faltered in their concern for the whole child while he was there, the quality of care he received, from the purest milk and water to picnics and excursions, was always important to them. If they floundered a bit as they moved into decisions on medical matters, their intelligence, ability, and background of civic involvement carried them through moments of crisis.

The year ended on a sad note with the death of Mrs. Porter's mother, Nancy Smith Foster. A bed was endowed in her honor. After her mother's death, Julia Porter, with her little girls, moved to Lakeside (later renamed Hubbard Woods, now a section of Winnetka). Her son James, trained as an architect, had built two houses there on a bluff overlooking Lake Michigan. He and his family occupied one; the other, designed as a summer cottage, was remodelled and became Julia's year-round residence. Cousin James W. Porter moved to the Union League Club.

Dr. Henrotin was elected President of the Medical Board in 1902, heading a staff of sixteen distinguished surgeons and physicians. Dr. Henrotin was fifty-five years old, well known in Chicago's medical circles as one of the founders of Polyclinic Hospital (later Henrotin) and as a consultant gynecologist at St. Joseph's, St. Luke's, and German Hosptials. A few years earlier he had been President of the Chicago Medical Society.

As soon as Dr. Henrotin assumed office the Board of Managers requested a conference with him and Dr. Christopher. Building a new hospital was high on the agenda for that meeting. Epidemics of scarlet fever and measles once more highlighted the need for more rooms generally, and, in particular, for isolation facilities. Mrs. Bowen mentioned that she had heard of patients dissatisfied with their treatment. Was it adequate? Did they need a bacteriologist on the staff? There was much to discuss.

The doctors agreed that more attention should be given to isolating patients with contagious diseases—they had urged that for a long time. They recommended the use of bed screens for some cases. They asked the Managers' permission to hire an extern (salary fifty dollars per month) to devote his time to the Hospital. They agreed to have an oculist examine and treat patients one day a week.

From discussion of expansion came a new idea: could the present hospital be used as a convalescent home, an adjunct of a new children's hospital built near Polyclinic on LaSalle Street? Dr. Henrotin, for obvious reasons, liked that location; he urged it again a month later when a site became available near Polyclinic. He stressed the benefit of a convenient location for patients, doctors, nurses, and students.

The women never showed much interest in a "downtown" location. Mrs. Bowen on the contrary advocated a new building on the old site—"with small wards, the best plumbing and hygienic outfit, rooms for the nurses, a detention ward and an isolation ward." They could continue to hire nurses from Polyclinic or some other Training School. Finding the right doctor to head the new hospital was of utmost importance. The women shared the feeling that many of the staff were too busy with private practices, teaching, and serving as consultants for other hospitals to concentrate on the needs of The Maurice Porter Children's Hospital. Mrs. Bowen spoke out vigorously on this point. She felt the work of the Hospital was standing still or possibly deteriorating. Two things were necessary: 1) a head interested in the progress of the institution and able to give time to make it work efficiently; and 2) money to remodel or build a new building satisfying modern requirements. Remembering, perhaps, former unfortunate, hasty approaches to the Medical Board, the women wrote and rewrote a message conveying these beliefs to the staff. In the end, the letter stated merely that the Board realized the inadequacy of the present building and, since they were now in a position to do something about it, they asked the Medical Board to appoint one of their members to a Committee of Reorganization, which would also include one Trustee and two Managers. The staff appointed Dr. Henrotin; Mrs. Bowen appointed Mrs. Cramer and Mrs. Tyson; the Trustees asked Mr. Adams to be their representative. Dr. Christopher also joined the Committee when it first met in December 1902.

At this first meeting on a Sunday morning at Mrs. Tyson's, the Committee on Reorganization came to grips with present conditions and future goals. First they listened to a report on cases treated at the Hospital in 1902. In spite of having to close at intervals for diphtheria, measles, whooping cough, and scarlet fever, the hospital had admitted 256 children. Of these, 213 had been discharged, 43 had died. More could have been admitted, particularly typhoid patients, if detention and isolation facilities had been larger—an old song, but one emphasizing the absolute necessity for adequate space for these facilities in a new or remodelled hospital.

Discussion of finances followed this review. The Committee was unanimous in its belief that an endowment fund must be raised before improvements could begin. Two decisions were necessary before plans could be drawn up: whether to have private rooms for paying patients, and whether the Hospital should include a dispensary under its roof. It was imperative also to fix a location for the new hospital if it were not to be on the old site. Mrs. Porter's wish to have both location and name remain unchanged was discussed.

The women repeated their belief that money could not be raised unless the doctors took more interest in the Hospital, and they asked that a young man be appointed to act as liaison during the reconstruction years ahead. Dr. Christopher suggested Dr. Samuel Walker whom he described as "conservative, and careful, scientific and up-to-date." He also promised to outline a policy to help in making changes in plant and management (he sent one within a few weeks). The doctors had priorities, too, in addition to the overriding need for enlarged detention and isolation wards. They wanted room to separate medical and surgical cases; and they needed a resident intern. The extern, hired in the wake of an earlier conference was proving very useful.

The committee also discussed using nurses' aides: Dr. Rotch's Hospital in Boston, Dr. Holt's in New York, and the Baby Hospital in Milwaukee were reported to be finding their use productive. Dr.

Christopher also promised to give bedside lectures to nurses and to visit the Hospital every Thursday morning.

The way ahead became a little clearer as the meeting ended with some basic decisions. They agreed that a building fund of $50,000 and ten endowed beds would assure a successful children's hospital. Fifty free beds and possibly a few private rooms for paying patients would be a reasonably sized hospital. The question of paying patients had tempted them over the years when money was tight, but they had clung to free care, perhaps at Mrs. Porter's insistence. There should be enlarged detention and isolation facilities; an up-to-date card catalog system; good patient records; and regular, systematic doctors' services.

Mrs. Bowen's term as President ended in 1902; she remained on the Board one more year, serving on the important Reorganization and Finance Committees. Mrs. Tyson became the new President for 1903, another critical year for the Hospital. Mrs. James F. Porter joined the Executive Committee that year, a key place for a Porter in a transition year. The election of Miss Martha Wilson to the Board of Managers in December 1902 and her immediate appointment to the Reorganization Committee in 1903 marked the beginning of a long and fruitful relationship with the Wilson family.

At the annual meeting of the Trustees and Managers on January 27, 1903, further decisions were made. The Board of Managers was empowered to draw up a plan of reorganization and to submit it to the new Board of Trustees. The latter was expanded to fifteen: the nine former members were reelected and the names of Mr. Harold Fowler McCormick and Mr. Wilson A. McIlvaine were suggested as possible additions to the Trustees' Board. Behind this expansion, as became amply clear in the following months, was a desire to make this Board more active in Hospital affairs.

A spirit of let's-get-things-done permeated both Boards in 1903. Action followed quickly on needs expressed. An intern was appointed to the satisfaction of all. His daily reports to the doctors moved patients out of the Hospital more quickly. "We no longer look like a home for incurables," the women noted in their minutes. The doctors became more strict in their admission policies for orthopedic cases— only those who might benefit from operations. In these policies from the beginning, this restriction had apparently been relaxed over the years. In 1903 as well, the medical staff, with the approval of the Managers, designated one ward as a detention place for incoming patients until they were pronounced free of contagious diseases.

Repairs on the Hospital were kept to a minimum in 1903 since the future of the building was uncertain. They had to repair the roof and calsomine some interiors for sanitary reasons, but those were the biggest maintenance costs except, of course, for the ever-present plumbing bills.

They made a great effort to attract more associate members and they sponsored a benefit performance by Mrs. Patrick Campbell who, hearing of the work of the Hospital, had offered her services. The benefit brought in $2,617.34 helping to swell the income and pay the bills.

Raising money, however, became increasingly difficult with their antiquated building. In 1903, Trustees and Managers took a decisive step. Two events served as catalysts. The first was a letter from Mr. John B. Wilson, father of Martha, and legal advisor to the Merchants' Loan and Trust Co. (Mr. Orson Smith was the President of the bank). He offered to raise $20,000 for the Hospital if a fireproof building for contagious diseases be built free of debt and ten beds be endowed for $5,000 each. He stipulated further that of the $20,000, $5,000, possibly $10,000, could be used for the building, the balance for the endowment of the beds.

The second catalyst was a generous offer from the architectural firm of Holabird and Roche to draw up some plans (free) for a new building. That offer the women accepted at once but how they could meet Mr. Wilson's challenge needed further consideration. Caught between a deteriorating plant and a tantalizing financial offer, the Managers in March decided to write Mrs. Porter a letter. Its contents, carefully studied by Trustees and doctors as well as by the women, go the the crux of the problem.

Chicago, Ill.
March 9, 1903

Mrs. Julia F. Porter
Lakeside, Ill.

Dear Madam:

The undersigned members of the Board of Managers and Board of Trustees of The Maurice Porter Children's Hospital ask your consideration of the situation in which they find themselves with relation to the Hospital.

After several years of faithful endeavor to administer the generous trust confided to us by you, and in the attempt to obtain during that period the necessary support from others, our experience has lead us to the following conclusions:

"We believe that the people of Chicago wish to have a well equipped modern Children's Hospital. We find from experience that the public hesitates to contribute to the support of a hospital named after an individual. So long as the Maurice Porter Children's Hospital bears a name indicating to a certain extent private and other than public interest, we think that the family whose name it bears rather than the public, must largely be depended on for its support. We feel, therefore, that the time has come for us to adopt one of the following plans.

(1) To ask Mrs. Porter to donate a sufficient sum to erect a building adequate and effective and to provide an additional fund to maintain it in the name of Maurice Porter.

(2) To ask that Mrs. Porter donate $75,000 to be used to erect a new building. Said building to be known as Chicago Children's Hospital. A cornerstone to be inserted bearing the inscription "Built in Memory of Maurice Porter." The undersigned to work for the Hospital as heretofore, with the assurance to Mrs. Porter that an endowment sufficient to maintain 10 more beds can probably be obtained in the immediate future.

(3) To reconvey the Hospital property to Mrs. Porter and resign our trust.

We hope that the third plan will not be the one chosen by you for our interest in the subject matter and in this particular hospital is very great and accordingly we earnestly ask consideration of the second plan which recommends itself to our best judgment.

We feel that the present hospital building on account of the risk of epidemics, and particularly of fire, is a menace to those entrusted to our care; and although the work which we do now is to a certain extent beneficial, it is not scientific and cannot be in the present building, and therefore, has not the enthusiastic cooperation of the doctors.

We submit these conclusions to your kindly consideration, and hope for a reply before a special meeting of the Board of Managers to be held on March 30th.

Assuring you of our entire sympathy in your purpose, even if we should find ourselves unable to carry it out, we remain,

Very truly yours,

The letter was signed by all the Trustees and Managers except the members of the family.

Mrs. Porter's unfaltering interest in free care for sick children is evident in her reply. She would agree, she wrote, to plan two if she were assured that an endowment, which would maintain a hospital with the current number of patients, had been raised.

In April, the Board of Managers accepted Mrs. Porter's proviso, asking only that she give them the income from the $75,000 until such time as the Board could ask for the principal. At the same meeting they reviewed Holabird and Roche's plans but thought them too large. Mr. and Mrs. James Porter were appointed to confer with the architects, asking them to alter the building plans so as not to exceed $85,000. It should accommodate seventy-five children and have a main building so constructed that wings or stories could be added. The women accepted the fact that they would have to raise money for both the endowment and a building.

Those obligations were heavy; on the plus side, however, they were able to inform Mr. Wilson that with the $75,000 promised by Mrs. Porter, they now had $81,000 pledged for a new fireproof building and the promise of eight endowed beds. They would soon be able to meet all of his conditions.

Succeeding months saw hospital building plans reviewed and discussed. Comparisons were made with children's hospitals in the east—Mrs. McCormick even visited Dr. Holt's Hospital in New York when affairs took her there. At one point they must have felt they were losing touch again with the doctors, for they suggested a woman, Dr. Katherine Rich, be appointed to the staff—to keep the Managers better informed. The idea was tabled by the Medical Board until reorganization was accomplished.

Meanwhile, with a new building assured, the women faced two other questions: (1) should they merge with Crippled Children's Hospital—about to expand its patient capacity, and (2) how could they obtain purer milk for the children?

The first was not new—a suggestion to consider a merger had been made six years earlier. This time it was more seriously considered. But, after a few conferences, both hospitals agreed the time for a merger was "not ripe."

To answer the second question the women turned to The Children's Hospital Society. The Society had been founded in January 1903 to facilitate care for Chicago's sick and crippled children. Dr. Henrotin had encouraged establishing such an organization, hoping it would become a clearing house for placing children, a setter of standards, and an evaluator of child care institutions. In the summer of 1903 the Society had formed a Milk Commission to organize a laboratory to test milk, and depots to distribute it. Dirty milk was still a scandal in Chicago and a principal cause of infant death. Superintendent Watson appealed to the medical staff in September to secure certified milk from one of the Society's depots (at 4½¢ per quart). Unfortunately, demands on the Milk Commission had become so heavy that there was not enough milk to go around. The Hospital was told to raise its own milk standards as much as possible. Mrs. Cramer took on the job of talking to H. B. Gurler Co. and the Milk Commission to achieve the desired pure milk.

When the Corporation Board (Trustees and Managers) met at the end of 1903 it faced up once more to the question of ways and means. "The sense of the meeting," as recorded in the minutes of the Annual Meeting of the Board of Managers for 1903, was "that a Board of Men Managers would work more harmoniously with the Medical Staff, would be able to raise an endowment and building fund more easily and would be more practical and efficient in building than a board composed only of women. The women, as in most other hospitals, to act as an auxiliary board to attend to the internal management and help in the raising of funds as heretofore."

Thus the pattern was set for the Boards which would govern the Hospital in the years ahead. For twenty-one years women had carried the primary responsibility; Mrs. Porter alone for eleven years, a Board of Managers (together with a relatively passive Board of Directors) for ten years. During this time approximately twenty-one hundred children had been admitted and treated by a medical staff which had grown from two to eighteen physicians and surgeons. Admission ages at the beginning were three to thirteen years; in 1903 babies to fourteen years were admitted. The Hospital had been housed in a dwelling (eight beds), a small building (twenty-two beds), and an enlarged and remodelled building (forty to fifty beds). One policy remained the same for all of this period: the Hospital provided free care to needy children regardless of color, creed, or place of residence.

PART TWO *1904–1940*

"Children's personality is conveyed in the word 'memorial.' With one exception every building had been erected as a memorial, emphasizing a background of human interest and sentiment."

Overleaf: Social Work staff and volunteers hear from a physician.

CHAPTER VI

From Reorganization
to World War I

1904–1917

THE Boards of Directors and Managers edged into 1904 with big dreams and big plans but a good deal of uncertainty as to their implementation.

One obvious task at hand, however, was reorganizing the Boards. That meant rewriting the Bylaws. If the Directors were to become more active they needed more members. The new Bylaws permitted them to enlarge their group from nine to fifteen on a three-year rotating basis (but for years they renominated the same men). They also established four standing committees: Executive, Finance, Medical Staff, and Site of New Building and Proposed Improvement. Their officers were John P. Wilson, President; Charles Norman Fay, First Vice President; William B. McIlvaine, Second Vice President; Charles B. Pike, Treasurer; and James F. Porter, Secretary. Filling out the roster were Orson Smith, Eliphalet W. Cramer, J. Medill McCormick, Bryan Lathrop, Russell Tyson, Thomas Davies Jones, Dr. Samuel J. Walker, Morton D. Hull, George Packard, and Morrill Dunn. Two of the old guard were missing—George Adams and Colonel McClurg. For the first time a doctor was included; the others were powerful bankers, lawyers, businessmen, and an architect. All were friends and associates of earlier members.

The name, Board of Managers, was felt not to describe accurately the status of the Women's Board in the new line up. It was changed to The Auxiliary Board. Although permitted to increase its membership to twenty-one on a rotating basis, it remained at fifteen for years and resignation only removed anyone from the Board.

Like the men's Board, the Auxiliary Board had a familiar look: Mrs. Russell Tyson, President; Mrs. James F. Porter, First Vice President; Mrs. E. W. Cramer, Second Vice President; Mrs. Charles Pike, Secretary; and Miss Martha Wilson, Treasurer. A few women, active since the nineties, did not continue on the new Board: Mrs. Bowen, Mrs. Smith, Mrs. Adams, and Julia Porter herself. But Mesdames Tyson, Cramer, McCagg, Lathrop, Wilson, and Walker were an experienced nucleus; and new willing hands belonged to Mrs. John Jay Borland, Mrs. Harold Fowler McCormick, Mrs. Thomas B. Marston, Mrs. James S. Harlan, Mrs. W. J. Chalmers, Mrs. R. F. Howe, and Mrs. Samuel J. Walker.

On the two Boards there were six husbands and wives, and Mr. Wilson and his daughter—providing plenty of cross reference. A Corporation of forty men and women, drawn chiefly from the two Boards, met formally once a year to approve reports of the Hospital's work; it did not initiate policy.

There remained only the adoption of the new Bylaws and the formal renaming of the institution to finish the basic outward changes in the Hospital. Honoring its founder, the Boards named the building under construction The Maurice Porter Pavilion. For the Hospital itself they chose a more general name, The Children's Memorial Hospital, to emphasize the public nature of the institution and to invite Chicago's support. As The Children's Memorial Hospital, it faced its first great period of expansion, both physical and medical.

At the time it must have seemed to the Auxiliary Board that its role had not changed even though its name had. The women still spent hundreds of hours managing the internal affairs of the Hospital. They accepted—or seemed to—as a matter of course that they would buy much that was needed: an ice chest, new rugs here and there, a clock for the operating room, braces for a needy patient, a gas "apparatus" for administering anesthesia, ventilators, rubber sheets, carpet sweepers, and a fire extinguisher. Needs were never ending and money was never budgeted to meet them. The women were good managers but always kept a personal touch. They insisted, for example, that Miss Grace Watson, Superintendent from 1899 to 1907, establish a petty cash account and keep accurate records; then assumed a few extra duties themselves so that she could have a vacation—with a fifty-dollar gift from the Board. They encouraged Church Guilds to make garments for the patients, but, after inspecting several ill-fitting ones, hired a sewing woman for one morning a week at 75¢ and carfare. When a janitor departed with all the keys, it was a Board member who saw to it that locks were changed.

Over their heads as well always hung the obligation to raise money for building funds and endowment. Soon after the Board of Directors was elected in 1904, they had purchased a triangular piece of land on Fullerton Avenue, opposite the original building (606 Fullerton). The triangle was bounded on the east by Orchard Street, on the south and west by Lincoln Avenue. A residence, Dow House, was the only building on the plot. As plans evolved, the Directors decided to build two pavilions on the unused portion of the triangle: a main one, The Maurice Porter Pavilion, with Mrs. Porter's gift; and a smaller one, Cribside (for babies only), with money to be raised by the Boards. Construction of Maurice Porter began at once; Cribside had to wait until funds were in hand.

The Auxiliary Board, ever creative, thought up a new approach to money raising. They invited a group of young women to form The Cribside Society. Its objectives were to support the babies' free cribs in the new Pavilion and to furnish amusement for convalescent children throughout the hospital. Mrs. Stanley Field was the Society's first President. Under her leadership it quickly sponsored a Francis Rogers recital and a Burton Holmes travelogue, with combined receipts of $1447.51. By the time the *Annual Report for 1904* was published, the Society had formed eight chapters in the city and suburbs and had 112 members—among them many women from the Auxiliary Board.

For seven years, The Cribside Society worked hard to carry out its mandate. Their money raising efforts ranged from a concert at Orchestra Hall (with the proceeds divided between the Hospital and the Theodore Thomas Invalid Fund) to selling tickets for an amateur production of *The Bunny and the Stylish Dude.* But the peak of their success, both in money and publicity for Children's Memorial Hospital, was *A Kirmess,* a musical extravaganza in which Board members danced and sang. An elaborate program explained how the word "Kirmess" had come to mean "gift," a far cry from its original meaning, "church ale," referring to the "brew and vintage" given as a tithe to churches in the Middle Ages. The Society imported a producer from New York, persuaded most of the eligible young men of Chicago to take part, and with a cast of 148 performed tirelessly for three nights in January 1906. From the Grand Tableau and Procession, led by Mr. Honoré Palmer, through a bewildering succession of national dances (Italian, Dutch, Spanish, Indian, Irish, etc.) to the closing Triumphal March, the spectacle was—according to the newspapers—"the jolliest and most brilliant event of the winter season." A gourmet supper, supplied by the Auxiliary Board, brought each dazzling night to a close. And the Cribside Society's treasury swelled by almost $25,000.

The Directors decided a few months later to begin construction on the Cribside Pavilion. In addition to housing fifteen babies, the building would contain a well-equipped milk laboratory and a large room where mothers could be instructed in the feeding and care of their babies.

Entertaining the small patients was an appealing part of the Cribside Society's responsibility. At first they assigned regular visiting hours to their active members, but soon realized that the children needed more than story reading, coloring books, and cutouts. Should they perhaps hire a kindergarten teacher? Mrs. Lathrop undoubtedly told them of the Board of Managers' experiment in that direction eight years earlier and their regret at ending it. At any rate, Cribside Society decided to try again. They hired their first teacher for the summer months when volunteers were limited as many Board members left the hot city for summer retreats. Her work was so successful that in the fall they extended her job to a year-round one and voted that each Chapter in turn would pay a month's salary.

After the Cribside Pavilion opened formally in June 1908, the Society felt some letdown. It turned to the Auxiliary Board for help in setting new goals. Eager not to lose good money raisers, the Board suggested it start an endowment fund for Cribside. To simplify its organization the Board proposed that it disband its chapters (ten by this time), reclassify the members as active or subscribers, and have one set of officers. For a closer tie with the Auxiliary Board, those officers would become members of that Board.

The Society accepted these suggestions and Mr. Joseph Field

started the Endowment Fund with a gift of $5,000. The Directors, now actively involved in the Hospital's financial affairs and its building program, assumed responsibility for investing and managing the Fund.

Reorganization, however, did not spark the Society as the drive for building funds had. Even a visit from the eminent Dr. Roach of Boston's Baby Hospital and his statement that Cribside Pavilion was the best equipped infant hospital in the country gave only fleeting pleasure. Mrs. Field, still the Society's President in 1909, informed the Auxiliary Board at the end of that year that Cribside Society would disband unless it were given definite work.

This time the Board turned to its Visiting Nurse, Miss Kreer, for ideas. The women had hired their first V.N. from the Visiting Nurse Association in 1905. Her job was to see that children dismissed from the Hospital received proper care and treatment at home during convalescence. Hired on a half-time basis, she soon worked full time; and now Miss Kreer, the current V.N., had much more work than she could handle alone. She had dozens of suggestions for the Cribside Society: (1) increase the corps of volunteers who read to and played with the children; (2) collect old clothing for the needy families from which most of the patients came; (3) help get jobs for fathers, mothers, sisters, and brothers to relieve the families' financial stress; and (4) arrange guided tours of the Hospital. Further afield, she pointed out the need to investigate the work of other hospitals and institutions to which children were referred. A really new idea was to arrange for a course in social service at Children's Memorial. Dr. Richard Cabot of Boston was suggested as the teacher.

At a special meeting a few days later, to which the new Superintendent, Bena Henderson, Dr. Frank Churchill, and Visiting Nurse Kreer were invited, the Cribside Society accepted these ideas and the Auxiliary Board offered to help arrange the social service course. In effect they were giving recognition to social service work at Children's Memorial Hospital.

In 1910 the Cribside Society gave $6,400 toward maintaining the baby pavilion—largely from the dues of its eighty-odd members. But its real enthusiasm was for its new work. A Clothing Committee distributed 514 new and 644 used articles of clothing to needy families; a Milk Committee provided pure milk for sick babies during a long hot summer; and an active Visiting Committee, under the supervision of the V.N., visited the homes to which patients must return and began to investigate city institutions to which some children had to be referred for temporary or permanent care.

In January 1911 the Cribside Society ended as an independent organization and the Social Service Committee was born. Mrs. George Taylor, a Cribside member, was its first Chairman. Those Cribside Society members who wished to remain active were absorbed by the Social Service Committee, the Auxiliary Board, and the fledgling Junior Auxiliary.

As the Cribside Society's work changed directions, the Junior Auxiliary had been organized to carry on some of the tasks the Society was dropping. Their mandate was rather vaguely worded: "to render personal service" to the hospital. That service translated into responsibility for the kindergarten; sewing and mending for the children; entertaining them—with special emphasis on Christmas and Easter; and giving an occasional party for mothers and nurses. The Junior Auxiliary committees were Sewing, Old Clothes, Vegetables and Flowers, Visiting, Toy and Kindergarten. Many families that later had a long connection with Children's Memorial made their first contact through the Junior Auxiliary: the Swifts, Counselman, Cyrus Adams, Chandler, Cudahy, Cooke, Keep, Ranney, and Wetten, to name but a few.

From the outset the Junior Auxiliary attracted many young women eager to serve their community. Some of them had heard about Children's from their mothers, aunts, and even grandmothers. Others had come as Junior League provisionals doing their required term of service. Many of the latter remained as volunteers because they felt they were doing "real" work—as one of these women expressed it to this author in an interview. The Junior Auxiliary's membership grew steadily—from 75 in 1910 to 119 in 1917. Miss Julia Cummins, Mrs. Joseph Cudahy, Mrs. Gustavus Swift, Jr., Mrs. James C. Hutchins, Mrs. Emil Wetten, and Mrs. Augustus Maxwell served as Presidents during these years.

The Auxiliary's service to the Hospital grew too. In 1909 there was one kindergarten teacher, in 1917 there were four, two full-time and two assistants. Helped occasionally by Auxiliary Board members, the Junior Auxiliary paid the teachers' salaries during all of those years, for although there had been a long period of demonstrating that teaching was indispensable to the happiness and well being of the children, Children's Memorial Hospital seemed still to consider it a luxury and to regard it as a non-budgetary item. To Mrs. Julius Rosenwald (a new Auxiliary Board member in 1910) belongs much of the credit for the expansion of the kindergarten's work. Not only did she, with five other Board members, underwrite the salary of the second teacher for a few months, but she also started a Fund for Kindergarten Work in 1912 and insisted that the activity continue year 'round. Junior Auxiliary members assisted the teachers every day and bought necessary school supplies.

The Junior Auxiliary members did not vanish in the summer—at least not all of them. Some of them met once a week in Lake Forest where they sewed and mended for the children, and drove back to the city loaded with flowers and fresh vegetables for the wards.

Their holiday parties became famous: Christmas began with carol singing in predawn darkness and ended only when the patients, dazzled by a visit from Santa, stockings bulging with toys, and a dinner of turkey with all the trimmings (gift of Directors or Auxiliary Board members) were tucked in bed at dusk. Easter featured ice cream for all; a plant, fruit, or jelly for every ward; and a frieze of sentimental and humorous bunnies to catch the eyes of even the sickest child.

Although the Cribside Society and the Junior Auxiliary attracted hundreds of young women into work for Children's, the senior Auxiliary Board expanded slowly after reorganization. Many meetings lacked a quorum. Valuable new members were recruited: Mrs. Mason Bross (Julia Porter's niece, daughter of her sister Adele Adams), Mrs. Cyrus McCormick, and Mrs. Richard T. Crane; but additions were frequently offset by resignations—Mrs. James Porter, who found Winnetka too far away for meetings, Mrs. Harlan, Mrs. Howe, and Mrs. Harold McCormick. The twenty-one-member limitation was removed, but it was 1908 before the Board numbered thirty-seven—after electing twenty new members in one year. Mrs. John Jay Borland became President of this enlarged Board in 1909: she was supported by Vice Presidents Miss Martha Wilson and Mrs. Edmund Burke, and Secretary Mrs. Bross. Its officers changed—Miss Wilson became President in 1911—but the Board still numbered thirty-seven in 1917 when the Hospital began to feel the impact of World War I.

Their work during the fifteen years from reorganization to World War I was challenging and difficult. As they dodged around construction trucks to hold meetings in odd corners of the Hospital or retreated many times to Mrs. Tyson's home, they were grappling with the everyday problems of administration and internal management as well as policy questions which were to determine much of the future of Children's Memorial Hospital. In all they were increasingly supported by the Board of Directors—particularly in financial matters.

They mourned the death of Dr. Walter S. Christopher whose advice had helped them through many a crisis. They marked Dr. Henrotin's death with appropriate resolutions and memorials. When Superintendent Watson left in 1907 the Directors hired a male Superintendent, Dr. J. F. Waugh, a former Superintendent of Presbyterian Hospital to succeed her. His uneasy regime lasted only 2½ years. His replacement was the former head of the Children's Hospital Society, Miss Bena Henderson. Perhaps because the Managers once again reviewed and redefined the authority of the position—this time with a committee from the Board of Directors—they were able to work closely and happily with Miss Henderson for the next fourteen years. In the beginning her salary was $1,800 ($700.00 less than Dr. Waugh's), but within eight years she was earning $3,500, had an assistant, and was regarded by Directors and Managers alike as a mainstay of the institution.

These years saw a single Visiting Nurse become a Social Service Department. That development went hand in hand with the rapid growth of the Outpatient Department. Begun tentatively, as an experiment in 1905—with its adjunct, the Dispensary—the outpatient work had been tucked into a few rooms in Dow House. No one anticipated the tremendous community response; demand from the beginning outran the Hospital's ability to supply. To the V.N., who had her station in the Department, the doctors referred cases for home visiting; they also expected her to keep records of patients and see that children returned for treatment.

In 1908 the Outpatient Department was bulging at the seams

and the Directors were looking at Dow House for nurses' housing. The Department and The Dispensary were moved to larger, refitted, and redecorated quarters in the basement of 606 Fullerton. That year they treated 1,068 patients (2,006 treatments); the V.N. reported 1,437 visits, and work on 207 cases. Doctors, Directors, and the Auxiliary Board considered the work so important that they prepared a card to be sent to all "public schools, charities, and druggists in the neighborhood," announcing free examination of sick children from 10–12 daily except Sunday.

Other parts of the Hospital needed more room as well. Before Maurice Porter Pavilion and Cribside were completed it had become obvious that a new laundry and heating plant would be needed for the larger institution. The women recommended that it be added to the building program and that Dow House be thoroughly remodelled for the nurses. Where to put the sorely needed detention and isolation wards was a subject discussed over and over by the Directors' Committee on Building, Dr. J. P. Houston, the new chairman of the Medical Board, and James Porter who represented his mother as well as the Directors. Fitting all Hospital services into three new buildings—a remodelled original hospital building (606 Fullerton), Cribside, and a renovated Dow—was a bit of a jigsaw puzzle, but the last piece was in place early in 1909. Children's Memorial Hospital now had 108 beds.

More remarkably, the Board of Managers had, in one way and another, raised money to pay for all. The women had used every device they could think of to increase annual memberships and the number of endowed and supported beds—even though they raised the price of those to $10,000 and $500 respectively. They managed to get 33 percent of the annual Charity Ball proceeds one year— working through Mrs. Watson Blair who knew Mrs. Potter Palmer, Chairman of the *secret* committee! They approached the City Council, reminding it of the Hospital's free care for 300 of Chicago's children in one year. What would the Council do for them? To Mr. Julius Rosenwald, head of Associated Jewish Charities, they spoke of care given to many Jewish children—could they have a contribution? Both appeals were successful. (The City Council's contribution was the first tax money the Hospital received. The Managers evidently regarded it as *quid pro quo*, and it did not worry them as "public" money was to do twenty years later.) A special circular, broadcast to 15,000 persons, yielded $21,710. The women also put mite boxes here and there throughout the city, and once more when money was very tight they discussed accepting pay patients. That question was referred to the Directors. A few months later the men moved a little closer to such acceptance when they voted to allow the Hospital to charge a "reasonable" fee for services if parents could afford it. But even this action seems from the treasurer's reports not to have been implemented at that time.

The Directors took another step in 1908 to enhance Children's prestige in Chicago. They signed a contract with Rush Medical College (once again enjoying a top reputation in medical schools), putting the entire medical and surgical work under its "care and direction." That meant Rush would nominate the medical staff and instruct Children's nurses in training. The Hospital, as "means" permitted, agreed to provide laboratories as needed and teaching facilities.

The year was a busy one. Singly, or in groups, members of the Auxiliary Board, Cribside Society, and the Junior Auxiliary furnished the new Maurice Porter and Cribside Pavilions and the remodelled Dow House. In 1908 they also equipped new operating rooms with modern sterilizers. A nurse who came to take charge of the Milk Laboratory in Cribside that year described the early sterilizer as a tub with two openings to which rubber tubes were attached. The end of each tube was put in a pitcher of boiling water; then the entire equipment was put in the tub and covered. Steam coming through the tubes did the sterilizing. In the same year Mrs. John Jay Borland gave the Hospital its first X-ray machine.

By the end of 1909, the Endowment Fund had reached $57,500, twelve beds were endowed and twenty-nine supported. Hull House and the Children's Hospital Society accounted for two of the latter.

Perhaps in response to the ever widening circle of Chicagoans who knew about Children's Memorial Hospital, the 1909 Annual Report for the first time includes essays on the work of various departments. One describes the Pathology Laboratory, another a case of meningitis treated with Flexner serum—a new treatment. The principles and techniques of pediatric surgery, particularly in infancy and early childhood, are set forth with illustrations of apparatus used during recovery. An article on the Orthopedic Department features a child strapped to a frame—he is recovering from tuberculosis of the spine. The article also alludes to the increase in polio cases at Children's since 1907. Statistics in the Report show an almost doubled patient load: in one year 841 children—2,063 if one included those seen in the Outpatient Department—had been cared for.

Meningitis, tuberculosis, and polio were discussed in many papers read to The American Pediatric Society in these years. Dr. Frank Churchill was the author of one, just a few months before he joined the staff of Children's Memorial Hospital. His focus was the bacteriology of meningitis; he relied heavily on laboratory work. With the staff's pathologist, Dr. C. P. Clark, he wrote on the importance of blood cultures in diagnosis. Since it was the custom in Chicago then to pay house pathologists a salary, Dr. Clark was the Hospital's first doctor to receive remuneration—seventy-five dollars per month for half-time. It was not until 1915 that Dr. Richard Austin became the first full-time pathologist on the staff. By that time the Hospital could not manage with less—in 1914, for example, the laboratory had made 2,155 throat cultures, 644 nasal cultures, 1,497 vaginal smears, 174 Wasserman tests, 3,648 urine, and a small number of other tests.

In 1912 laboratory work at Children's was further enhanced not only as a tool for diagnosis, but also as a springboard for research. The Hospital that year provided facilities for the Chicago-based Otho S.A. Sprague Memorial Institute to pursue its research in the diseases and physiology of childhood. Founded in 1910 for "the relief of human suffering," the Institute boasted that it had no buildings, no laboratories, and no paid administrative staff. The first Board of Trustees in 1911, which included Dr. Frank Billings, consultant at Children's, and John P. Wilson, had decided that all money should go for research. Since a Carnegie Foundation Report had called Chicago's medical education a "plague spot in the country" and characterized ten of its fourteen medical schools as mere diploma mills, the Trustees had decided to focus on building the city's medical reputation. Their method was to support "investigators" working in laboratories provided by hospitals or medical schools. Children's was very eager to provide such a laboratory. Dr. Henry

Helmholtz, new on the Hospital's staff in 1911, was one of the first investigators. The main thrust of the Institute's work in the first five years was the chemical aspect of medical problems—Dr. Helmholtz's research dealt with sugar metabolism in infants.

Mr. Albert S. Sprague, founder of the Institute, joined the Board of Directors in 1914. Ties between the Hospital and the Institute have remained close: Directors Thomas D. Jones, John P. Wilson Jr., and Hughston McBain have served on the Institute's Board over the years; in 1982 Children's is still receiving research grants from it.

The importance of sunshine and clean air in treating and preventing disease enjoyed top priority among doctors in the early 1900s. United Charities, aided by the Board of Education and the Elizabeth McCormick Fund, was experimenting with open air schools for tubercular children. Becoming increasingly concerned with preventive medicine, the American Pediatric Society turned its attention to the physical conditions in schools. It found them generally lacking in proper ventilation, adequate light, and well constructed desks. They were also behind the times in planning physical recreation for the children. Some of these criticisms could also be leveled at Hospital facilities. Children's Memorial's answer was, in part, to study the ventilation of the wards (with particular attention to cross infection) and, in 1909, to convert a sunporch into a pneumonia ward. Here the children in cloaks, caps, and mittens received "open-air" treatment. A year later, Mrs. Hubbard Carpenter give the Hospital a large tent for summer outdoor work with all patients. It is typical of the women's extra touch of concern that they knitted the mittens and caps in every color of the rainbow.

Nine years earlier Dr. Christopher, as a member of the Board of Education, had worked through the school to improve conditions for physically handicapped children. Now it was Dr. Churchill's turn. He agreed with the American Pediatric Society's charge that public schools had inadequate education in sex, alcohol, and narcotics (this was in 1908, not 1982!). Dr. Churchill was working with children from the Juvenile Court at that time. Noting the rising incidence of venereal disease in Chicago, he insisted that several hundred girls (clients of the Juvenile Court) be given Wasserman tests; and then, if necessary, he treated them with salvarsan, whose efficacy in treating congenital syphilis had been discovered a few years earlier. With another doctor he presented a long paper describing the medical work of Chicago's Juvenile Court. Children's Memorial usually saw one or two cases of gonorrhea or syphilis a year, but in 1910 there were fourteen.

With ideas going back and forth between the American Pediatric Society and Children's Memorial Hospital, it seemed only natural that an interim meeting of the Society be held in The Maurice Porter Pavilion in 1909. After a tour of the Hospital Society members were served brunch—by the women as usual.

The expansion of the Hospital facilities to 108 beds and the increasing specialization in pediatrics led naturally to a scrutiny of the Hospital's nursing, long recognized as a basic element in a "good" hospital. Even before the new beds were ready for occupancy the Auxiliary Board had set up a powerful committee (Mesdames Tyson, Borland, Pike, Bross, and Miss Wilson) to consider reopening the Training School for Nurses. Word of this possibility got around; while the Committee was still debating, Miss Rena Wood, a veteran of five years as head of nursing in Philadelphia's Children's Hospital, applied for the similar job at Children's Memorial. Perhaps her application tipped the scales; at any rate, the Directors hired her and the new Training School opened in December 1908 with a Principal, two assistants, eight graduate nurses, four "experienced" nurses, and twelve pupils. In addition to students taking the full three-year course, others from carefully selected affiliated schools (six at the outset), were accepted for a short intensive course in children's nursing.

The School grew slowly—by 1911 there were twenty-five full time and eight affiliated students. To attract and to hold young women, successive heads of the Training School (Miss Wood, Miss Gregory, and Miss Burks) gently pushed for improvement in the nurses' living quarters and in the quality of their life. Successive Auxiliary Board committees, investigating the requests, recognized their validity. In addition to the usual refurbishing with bright chintz, paint, and new rugs, the women stocked Dow House bookcases with fiction as well as technical books, added a few magazine subscriptions, and hired a chaperon of "good character and dignity" to escort the girls to the movies, concerts, and plays. The number of concert tickets listed in donations increased materially at this time.

Clay tennis courts on the Hospital campus and bridge lessons were popular with the nurses. So too were ballet lessons offered a few years later. The Committee, however, had a hard time convincing the Board that these lessons were not introduced in a spirit of frivolity but as exercise well known for strengthening back and legs.

Graduation was a high point of the year. It was held at the nearby Chicago Theological Seminary. The President of the Board of Directors presented the diplomas, the Auxiliary Board President the pins. She also usually gave the address. Music was an important part of the exercises; but one year, the selection of a soloist caused a flurry. The singer invited turned out to be a Christian Scientist; when, the minutes record, the ladies could not "overcome this trifling objection," Mrs. Frederick Upham leaped into the breach and provided a string quartet. The elegant luncheon following the ceremony was supplied by the Social Service Committee and served by a number of butlers "offered freely," the minutes note, by Board members.

The cry for "more room" was addressed in 1911 when Children's Memorial was off again on another building program. Every department needed more space: the surgeons, the burgeoning Social Service Department, the Outpatient and Dispensary (their waiting room was described as the Black Hole of Calcutta), Ear and Eye, and Dermatology; above all, *adequate* observation and isolation units had never been established.

Once again John P. Wilson started the ball rolling: he pledged to give $100,000 (later raised to $125,000) if others would give or raise $300,000. Part of the total—$250,000—he stipulated must be added to the Endowment Fund, the remainder could be used to erect a new building. Directors Jones and Morris immediately pledged $50,000 each and Mrs. Borland $25,000. Within three months the Finance Committee had secured $11,000 from Martin Ryerson and a pledge of $50,000 from Ogden Armour. By June the building money was assured and ground was broken in October. Planned as a main building with two wings, the Pavilion opened a year later with only one wing. Costs had risen too rapidly to be covered by the projected $150,000 to $175,000. President Wilson yielded to the Boards' wishes that the building be named The Agnes Wilson

Memorial in honor of his daughter Agnes. When it was completed, the Directors built new brick walls around the campus to protect the outdoor tent, playground equipment, and nurses' and interns' tennis courts. Mr. Lathrop assumed the task of landscaping the whole campus. That was one of his last services for the Hospital; after twenty-years as a Director he died in 1916.

The Agnes Wilson Memorial was in a sense the climax of this surge of building before the United States' entry into World War I in 1917 stopped physical expansion for a time. Only one other task was attempted, basically a remodelling one. There were 176 beds when The Agnes Wilson Memorial opened late in 1912. But the Training School could supply only enough nurses to take care of 128. One difficulty was lack of housing. The Directors' Building Committee bought two small three-story apartments adjacent to Dow and turned the three structures into a "perfect" Nurses' Home. By 1915 it was completed with all the amenities of a sitting and an assembly room, kitchens for snacks and tea, a suite for the Principal, and attractive rooms. The Junior Auxiliary furnished it.

Building ended for a time, in spite of the surgeons' desire for a separate surgical building, the Outpatient Department's warning that it would soon outgrow its quarters again, and the ophthalmologist's murmuring that the converted coal storage room, while functional, was not exactly a dream come true as an Eye Clinic.

The most striking growth at Children's during the years 1912–17 was that of the Social Service Department. When former Cribside Society members became volunteers under the V.N. in 1911, service horizons expanded. The Auxiliary Board responded by hiring its own visiting nurse whose work would not be divided between the Hospital and the parent organization. Miss Adelaide Walsh, R.N., became the first Director of the Social Service Department in 1911. Within five years she had five assistants and a Ford Sedan to speed up home visits and bring children to the clinics. Yet hospital social work was barely understood when Dr. Richard Cabot of Boston was invited in 1911 to give a series of lectures on the subject at Children's Memorial. Dr. Cabot, at his own expense, had established the pioneer program in social service at his hospital, Massachusetts General. The work there became the prototype for Children's. Four Social Service Committees visited and reported on thousands of patients' homes; they made or bought thousands of garments, and they helped plan for the children who could not go back to their own houses for convalescence—or sometimes never. That last task necessitated a thorough knowledge of government and private social agencies and institutions in Chicago and adjacent areas. An impressive number of reports on these facilities are attached to the Social Service Committee reports: Henry Booth House, Chicago Commons, Gad's Hill Center, Northwestern University Center, Jewish Aid Dispensary, United Charities, Cook County Welfare Agent, Mother's Pension, The Home for Disabled Children, Bethel Home for Convalescents, St. Vincents' Orphanage, The Foundling Home, The Municipal T.B. Sanitarium—the list is long.

In the Hospital itself, the Social Service volunteers became recorders in the clinics. There were never enough hands, although the Social Service Committee by 1917 had 26 active and 125 sustaining members. Dues from the latter substantially underwrote the work of the Committee. Very little of this money (never more than $250) was assigned to their Emergency and Relief Fund, which was to be used only in extreme emergency cases. It was feared that the sheltered young volunteers, seeing need for perhaps the first time in their lives, might give money hastily and unwisely. Through the early records of the Social Service Department runs an underlying theme: we must "teach resourcefulness and self-help," not undermine a family's self respect by just giving relief. Money, on the other hand, was spent freely to pay for dental work and to buy braces, crutches, and eye glasses for those who could not afford even the low fees of the Outpatient Clinic and the Dispensary.

The fame of the Department spread—the Chicago School of Civics and Philanthropy sent two students for field work in hospital social service; Miss Walsh was made a probation officer of the Juvenile Court and President of the Illinois State Association of Graduate Nurses. From that office she spearheaded an effort to pass a state Senate Bill requiring a three-year course in nurses' training schools and making registration of social service cases mandatory. In that drive she enlisted the Auxiliary Board. "Write your senators," was a new cry to the women in 1913, but supported by Miss Wilson, it was heeded. The bill passed.

Summer camps for those able to go, picnics for the less able—
they were managed by the Social Service Department too. And a
circus party for thirty-five children; the women were somewhat star-
tled to learn that ten of the boys came from one family!

It all took money and so the Rummage Shop was born, not full-
fledged in 1914 and 1915 when Hat Sales were held at the Black-
stone Hotel. The first netted $381.50; the second $805.13. The 1916
sale lasted for several days and swelled the treasury by $1,331.36. In
1917, with a new name, The White Elephant Rummage Sale, and a
variety of merchandise it netted $2,500. A subsidiary sale at
Charlevoix that summer brought in another $516.38.

Members of all of the women's boards were expected to give
some time to the rummage sales and for a long time it was an activity most members enjoyed. There was no trouble by this time in
securing Auxiliary Board members; in fact the membership committee was warned by Miss Wilson one year always to keep one
place open in case a "candidate of extraordinary and superlative
ability turned up."

In part through the work of the Social Service Department, the
Auxiliary Board became much more a part of Chicago's public and
private social agencies and institutions. They had to cooperate. The
minutes record with some exasperation that filling out reports for
Chicago's Health Department necessitated hiring three extra clerks
for two or three days a month. They were partners of the Association of Commerce in its efforts to register the city's social service
cases, although they could not afford $7,000 to become a permanent
member of the Bureau of Social Service Registration. They were
asked—and accepted—an invitation to prepare a model infant's
hospital room for a 1911 Child Welfare Exhibit at the Coliseum.
Jane Addams was President of that important event. The women
decided to add a replica of their Milk Laboratory, unique in
Chicago. They sent delegates to the opening of a new building housing The Home for Crippled Children. And they cooperated with the
summer work of the Elizabeth McCormick Memorial Fund. On a
more personal level, Miss Wilson herself stormed the city's Building
Department to point out the expensive folly of adding a fire escape
to a building temporarily housing a few nurses. She won!

Some of this cooperation was, of course, imperative, as the work of the Hospital grew and as the welfare of children began to be laid on the consciences of government agencies. From Washington itself came increasing pressure. The voice of the United States Children's Bureau, a brain child of the first White House Conference on the Care of Dependent Children (1909), was heard throughout the nation. Authorized in 1909 by President Theodore Roosevelt, the Bureau began to exert a real influence by 1912 when Congress voted it an appropriation of $25,640. It addressed the health of children from school programs of immunization to child labor laws. And it pressured medical organizations to do the same. The A.M.A. in turn urged the schools to instruct the children in hygiene and sanitation, and to step up their programs of immunization and detection of infectious disease. It also supported child labor laws specifying an eight-hour day, a minumum working age of sixteen, and better working conditions.

Some leaders in The American Pediatric Society, like Children's Dr. Frank Churchill, wanted the Society to take part in anything affecting children's health. Others, however, felt the Society's mission was to encourage scientific work to relieve children's diseases. A paper read at its 1913 meeting bore, indirectly, on this question. For the first time the importance of social service as an ancillary to clinical pediatrics was emphasized. The meeting also went on record as favoring the regulation of midwives, day nurseries, and orphan asylums. And among other committees appointed that year was one to cooperate with the Children's Bureau. That Committee, in 1915, stated unequivocally that if pediatricians were concerned with preventive medicine, they must support slum clearance, playgrounds, hot school lunches, and proper diet.

President Martha Wilson was keenly interested in all of these movements and ideas which influenced hospitals. Not only was she President of the Auxiliary Board, but also an active member of the Social Service and Training School Committees. She felt responsible for educating the women in hospital matters. At its last meeting in June 1912—before the summer hiatus—she suggested some "light summer reading" for the Auxiliary Board: *Hospital Management, The Life of Pasteur, A History of Nursing,* and *Social Service in the Art of Healing.* She recommended as well that the women subscribe to *the American Journal of Nursing.*

The Hospital was thirty-one years old in 1913. Miss Wilson felt someone should write an up-to-date history of its development. Mrs. Bross and Mrs. Cramer volunteered, but when they faltered a few months later because so much had happened, Miss Wilson offered her help and that of a secretary to do the clerical work. The history is not mentioned again in the minutes but it is probably the anonymous ten-page document in the archives. Very likely it was also the basis for a one-hour lecture on "The History of Children's Memorial Hospital" which Miss Wilson gave to students in the Training School for Nurses from 1917 until her death in 1923.

References to World War I begin to creep into hospital documents in 1915. A nurse in the X-Ray Department was granted a leave of absence for "nursing in Europe." The Directors sent word to the medical staff that there were too many heated discussions about the war in Europe—would they "refrain from arguments" in the Hospital? By 1916 four more nurses had gone overseas. In 1917 the Annual Report featured a picture of Major Frank Spooner Churchill, M.R.C., President of the Medical Staff, The Children's Memorial Hospital.

CHAPTER VII

The War Years
and Their Aftermath

1917–1930

WORLD WAR I had a direct impact on Children's Memorial Hospital. Both the years of the nation's active participation and those immediately following the return of the armed forces had their problems. The watchword at home was "holding the line" in quality of service as doctors and nurses left for the front, expenses skyrocketed, and demands for service increased.

The picture of Major Frank Churchill in the 1917 Annual Report was prophetic. The Training School felt the war at once. Sixteen doctors and nurses joined the armed services in 1917, leaving the heavy burden of sustaining quality education on those who stayed behind. Many of them, moreover, were merely marking time until their departure. By the autumn of 1918 over half the staff had been called for service. (It was in this period that many women came to Children's as interns and attending staff members.) Dr. Henry Helmholtz, named Attending Physician and Chief of Staff late in 1918, held the medical group together for almost two years—he left in 1920 for a position on the University of Minnesota's Medical School and to further pediatric research at the Mayo Clinic. He was followed at Children's by Dr. Joseph Brennemann.

The situation called for constant adjustment. Out of that necessity rose three suggestions in nursing education: (1) establish a "close relationship" with "some great university" which would be responsible for such basic courses as chemistry, physiology, anatomy, bacteriology, etc.; (2) establish scholarships for graduate work at Columbia University's Department of Nursing and Health; and (3) open the doors of the Training School to nonresident nurses.

With these changes the teaching load at the School would be materially reduced and the nursing corps of the Hospital greatly expanded.

The way was paved for affiliation with the University of Chicago in 1919—not a merger, as the Hospital carefully stated in describing the terms of the arrangement. Students would take courses in "fundamental scientific material" at the University, probationary work at Children's and adult nursing at a general hospital. Affiliated hospitals were invited to send interested nurses to Children's for a three month's course, theoretical and practical, in the nursing of children.

The contract with Rush Medical College was cancelled—it had never been as productive an affiliation as the Hospital had wished. The University of Chicago now assumed the duties of nominating medical staff and instructing nurses.

These changes did not, however, solve all of the Training School's problems. Applications were sparse: some felt the calibre of the University's courses intimidated the young girls, others that the three-year training was too scattered. By 1923 the Auxiliary Board, on the recommendation of its School of Nursing Committee, decided to discontinue the three-year Training School and offer in its place a four-month's post graduate course in pediatric nursing. One focus of the course was the importance of child welfare work in that field of nursing. That year Superintendent Henderson began teaching a five-hour course on "The History of Nursing." Included in its consideration was "Social and Philanthropic Movements and their Influences on Nursing."

This shift in Children's role in teaching nurses was more productive than previous changes had been. Applications picked up; in 1928 they gave certificates to 147 students and two postgraduates. The School joined the Central Council of Nursing Education, cooperating actively with it on keeping high standards of education at all levels.

Offering shorter terms at the Hospital did not, however, relieve the institution of its housing problems. Children's still had to take care of the students who came for specialty training. In the war years, the Auxiliary Board tried to make life as pleasant as possible for the nurses, inadequate though the housing was. It must have done a good job, for a nurse accepted for the postgraduate course in pediatric nursing in 1924 recalls her initial impression of sunshine, fresh air, flowers, green grass, and clean and attractive rooms. She remembers a vivacious Director of Recreation serving afternoon tea in pretty tea cups in the Nurses' Lounge.

There were, however, still not enough rooms; thirty-six graduate nurses had to be provided with room and board off campus. That meant a monthly item of $900 in the budget. A new nurses' home on hospital grounds was a priority; so too was a home for interns, nine in number by the late 20s. The latter lived in a building referred to affectionately by them as "Green Mansions"—the Managers described its plumbing as "beyond repair." The Directors' Committee on Building began looking for a convenient site—that of the original Hospital at Orchard and Fullerton seemed most promising.

It is probable, however, that physical expansion from 1917 to 1930 at Children's Memorial would have been confined to remodelling existing structures if it had not been for the death of Miss Martha Wilson on Christmas Eve, 1923. Before that date Mr. Thomas Davies Jones had stated firmly—and more than once—"no physical expansion now." The Agnes Wilson Memorial Pavilion was only a few years old when Mr. Jones took over the presidential chair from his old friend John P. Wilson. They had a similar approach to the conduct of the Hospital. It was said that for years they had lunched together daily at one or another of their clubs; undoubtedly Hospital policy had often been discussed.

Both men were generous and deeply interested in Children's Memorial, particularly in building up the Endowment Fund. When Mr. Wilson died in 1922 after eighteen years of service to the Hospital, he left $333,333.33 to the Fund if $666,666.67 could be raised by the Boards within two years. Income from an additional million helped meet ongoing expenses but it fell far short of solving all problems. And it did not provide money for building.

The war years were plagued by a sharp rise in expenses: food, salaries, patient care, and medical equipment. In the post war years, as thousands of men returned to Chicago, they too met those high prices and, often, no jobs. Unemployment to the Hospital meant more demands on the Outpatient Clinics and the Dispensary. A depressed Chicago economy meant many lean years at Children's

Memorial. References like the following became common in Auxiliary Board minutes in the twenties: a thank-you note was sent to Directors Jones, Crane, and Wilson for meeting the deficit this year, or Directors Crane and Jones, Miss Wilson, and Mrs. Upham met the 1921 deficit of $33,000.

It was obvious why expansion was kept to a minimum. Yet the Directors approved building an Open Air Pavilion in 1921, funded as it was by Rummage Shop proceeds. There was a Rummage Shop by 1921, not just rummage sales. The great flu epidemic of 1918 had made the old crowded four-day sale in temporary rooms unwise, so the Committee found permanent housing in 1919 at 27 East Ohio Street. They opened the new shop with a flair. There was a circus in town, advertised with a traditional parade up Michigan Avenue. It was led by a huge white elephant. Mrs. Upham borrowed the elephant, tied a large flowered hat on its head, and had it led around the neighborhood to call attention to the White Elephant Shop! In their new quarters the shop could stay open every day with volunteers helping a few paid clerks. As the fear of flu subsided, the Shop organized special sales throughout the year: hats, furniture, books, home dressmaking, clothing. They bought a Ford truck, sporting white elephants on its sides, to collect rummage from Lake Forest to Hyde Park for sorting and pricing in the Shop. Profits increased every year; 1921 saw an extra boost when Miss Wilson bought 27 East Ohio Street for the Hospital and rent was no longer an item in the budget.

Under these circumstances, when the women proposed to the Directors that an Open Air Pavilion be built they met with no resistance. Holabird and Roche designed the Pavilion; it was opened in May of 1921 with a huge garden party—food, courtesy of the ladies, free ice cream from Gapers. Mrs. D. Mark Cummings was Chairman of the Social Service Committee that year; Mrs. Joseph King head of the Rummage Shop Committee.

A month following this opening an Auxiliary Board Committee, which had been studying the benefits of Heliotherapy (direct sun) treatment, recommended the construction of a Heliotherapy Room on the roof of the Agnes Wilson Pavilion. It would house eight to ten children and would cost, even with an adjoining bathroom, only about $4,000. Plans were approved and construction, which was to be plagued by labor strikes and long delays in getting materials, began. The Heliotherapy Room received its first patient in 1922.

These additions, however, called for relatively small financial outlay. Then Miss Wilson died. Her life had revolved around the Hospital since 1902; she had served as President of the Auxiliary Board since 1911. Now, as residuary legatee, Children's received $700,000 from her estate. While the Directors and the Auxiliary Boards considered how best to spend the money—it was *not* given as Endowment—the women started a Martha Wilson Memorial Nurse Fund of their own under the leadership of Mrs. Upham. Following Miss Wilson as President, Mrs. Upham reminded the Board that a fund for special nurses had long been a dream of her predecessor. Within a year the goal of $30,000 was reached and an additional special nurse was hired early in 1924.

By then the Directors, with the approval of the Auxiliary Board, had decided to build a Martha Wilson Memorial Pavilion at Orchard and Fullerton to house administrative offices, general wards, and rooms for a few private pay patients. Provisions for the last had been a request (but not a mandate) in Miss Wilson's will. Her motive was not to secure income for the Hospital but to coordinate the work of the doctors. Under existing rules they had to take their private patients to other Hospitals. The staff, except for a few technicians, was still unpaid, and as Miss Wilson and others had pointed out, the doctors still had to earn their living. In her frequent tours of other hospitals Miss Wilson had always investigated arrangements for private patients and had reported on them to the women. Dr. Brennemann, head of the medical staff by this time, thoroughly approved of the plan. Ground was broken for the new Pavilion in the summer of 1925; it opened for service in 1926. It made available thirty-six beds for private patients in sixteen rooms and six wards.

That year Mr. Jones resigned as President of the Directors' Board but stayed on as a member and Chairman of the Executive Committee. Mr. John B. Wilson, Jr. was elected President.

There remained only a few changes in Cribside (cubicles were built to help control cross infection) and the construction of an elevator on the outside of the Maurice Porter Pavilion, with an entrance to the Martha Wilson Pavilion, to complete the physical expansion of this period. Plans for more adequate housing for nurses and interns, perhaps a separate building for patients with contagious diseases, even one for minor surgery—all had to wait for consideration in the thirties. A residence for convalescent children was occasionally talked about but always as a dream for the future.

The twenties saw not only the acceptance of pay patients at Children's but also the beginning of fees in the Out Patient Department. The number of children treated there during the war and post war years had skyrocketed: 18,000 in 1917; 27,372 in 1920; 47,465 in 1930. That rise helped push up total operating expenses at the Hospital from $150,000 in 1920 to just under $350,000 in 1930. On the other side of the ledger there was higher income from a growing Endowment Fund. It had increased from $443,550 in 1919 to $4,516,437 in 1929. Bequests from many old friends had contributed to this growth—not only the Wilsons but also, among others, Mr. Byran Lathrop, Mrs. Russell Tyson, Mrs. John C. Black, Mrs. Charles Pike, Mrs. Cyrus McCormick, Mrs. Potter Palmer, Mrs. E.A. Valentine, Mrs. Victor Lawson, Mrs. James Deering, and Mr. Watson Blair. Yet it was necessary to scrutinize every expenditure if deficits were to be kept at a minimum or avoided entirely and, of course, essential to search for new sources of income.

A powerful joint committee of Directors (Mr. Jones, Wilson, Cramer, Morris, and Packard) and Auxiliary Board members (Mesdames Wilson, Borland, Spoor, Cramer, Martin, and Bross) examined the question of fees for services from every angle: parents, doctors, contributors. With some trepidation they made their recommendation a few months later: parents who could should pay one dollar per day. Consultation with a social worker and the Out Patient office at the time of application would establish clearly the status of each parent. If necessary, free service must never be denied.

The fee system began with no apparent difficulty. Small amounts were collected in the first months, but by year's end in 1921 the Treasurer reported $11,000 from fees. By 1929 fee income reached $34,616. From private patients that year the Hospital received $31,630.30. By that year, as well, the cost of endowing a bed in the private area had been fixed at $12,000 each in a one-bed room; $10,000 in a two-bed room. In 1929 there were two of the former, one of the latter. In other areas there were thirty-four endowed beds and forty-one supported memorial beds.

The Boards could curtail physical expansion and try to cut operating costs, but medical services in the twenties could not be confined. Their astonishing growth was due to the specialized clinics. Before he left for military service in 1917, Dr. Frank Churchill had established the first—the Infants or Baby Clinic. Its chief task was advising mothers how to feed their children, for it was thought that diet underlay most infants' illnesses. Fewer admissions to Cribside and reduced infant mortality among patients soon attested to the success of the Clinic. After the war it was open three mornings a week, always with a waiting room full of patients.

Other clinics followed in the next decade. An Orthopedic Clinic under the direction of Dr. Edwin Ryerson drew surgeons from all over the country to observe his techniques. Dr. Stanley Gibson's work on heart disease in children led to the establishment of the Cardiac Clinic. Children's Memorial Hospital began to be considered an authority on pediatric cardiac treatment. In 1922 there were thirty cardiac patients in the Hospital, two hundred under treatment in the Clinic. Dr. Gibson demonstrated the use of a cardiograph for the Auxiliary Board that year and talked to them about the heart work in the Hospital. He inspired them to find places for some of the cardiac patients in special summer camps, like Sunset Camp, and also to allow a social worker to study how heart disease affected the personality and behavior of children. With a nurse, another specialist, Dr. Harold A. Bachman, demonstrated the operation of a Cardiac Clinic for the Illinois State Association of Graduate Nurses.

Other clinics specialized in Nutrition, Syphilis (rising sharply in Chicago), Nephritis, and Quartz Light treatment. After some difficulty in financing, a Neuropsychiatric Clinic was opened by Dr. Ralph Hamill in 1924. It was not firmly established, however, before 1927, when a former patient gave Dr. Hamill $200 to hire a psychiatric social worker. At first the Clinic seemed something of a stepchild. The Auxiliary Board, when appealed to for more room in 1928, noted, with almost an audible sigh, "only a whole building will satisfy that Department." But when the Clinic did move to expanded quarters late in that year, the Superintendent reported enthusiastically on its work with retarded and disturbed children.

Pediatricians nationwide were becoming more aware of the needs of these children in the twenties. Dr. Emmett Holt's presidential address to the American Pediatric Society in 1923 stressed the pediatrician's responsibility for caring for "various types of mental instability and disease." He asserted that their foundations were "often laid in childhood and there not understood." In 1926 Dr. Herman Adler, an invited guest, read to the Society its first paper on child psychiatry. It was Dr. Adler who a few years later congratulated Dr. Hamill on establishing the first Psychiatric Clinic in a children's hospital in the United States.

One of the last clinics established at Children's in that period was the Speech Clinic. It opened to care for the needs of children who had been operated on for cleft palates and hare lips. For years Children's Memorial had referred these children to other hospitals, but in 1929 it operated on sixty-seven. The Speech Clinic offered help in post operative speech training, muscle training, and massage.

While the work of these new Clinics was expanding, so too was that of the older Eye and Dental Clinics and, supplementing all, the Drug Department. Patient loads of all soared in the twenties.

After 1921 Dr. Joseph Brennemann was an important factor in supporting and encouraging all of this growth. Although he did not officially become Chief-of-Staff (with a salary) until 1930, in effect he carried that responsibility from his joining the staff in 1921. Superintendent Henderson reported to the Auxiliary Board that year that it was necessary again to reorganize under "the Hospital's new Chief of Staff." Dr. Brennemann himself a few months later, addressed the women on the three functions of a hospital: (1) to care for the sick; (2) to prevent sickness; and (3) to teach. He noted the change in focus of pediatrics from surgery to medical treatment. And in the numbers of doctors choosing pediatrics as a specialty—"Nearly everyone now," he said, "wants to be a pediatrician."

Dr. Brennemann loved teaching and he was an inspiring and magnificent teacher. The year he joined the staff, the University of Chicago and the Hospital organized postgraduate courses in pediatrics at Children's. They were largely clinical, covered recent advances in the field, and were supplemented with lectures. For Dr. Brennemann the Out Patient Department with its Clinics was the best classroom. He lectured and wrote eloquently of the unique op-

Caring for patients included playing in the fresh air.

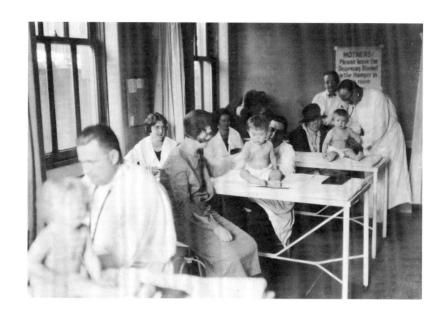

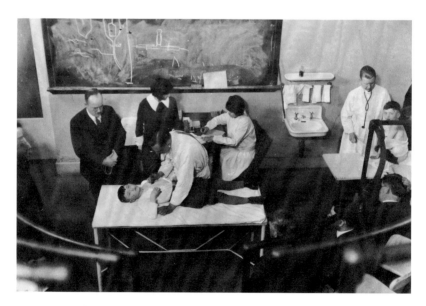

Outpatient care was begun as an experiment in 1905.

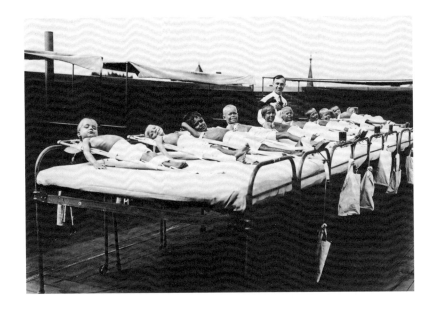

Children enjoyed sunshine as part of their treatment.

Response to outpatient and social services rapidly exceeded expectations.

The first White Elephant Shop at 27 E. Ohio Street, 1919.

Nurses carolling at Christmas, 1934.

The Bambino.

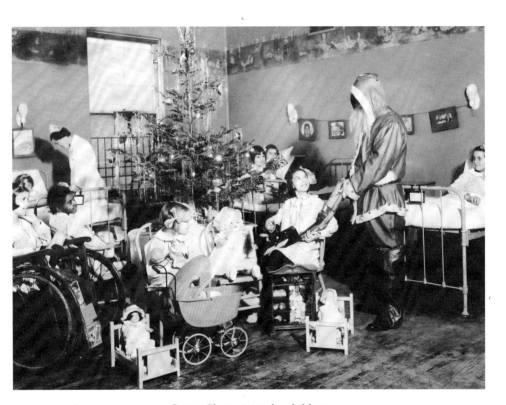

Santa Claus visits the children.

Taking time out to wrap Christmas gifts.

Children and staff are entertained by a circus elephant.

portunity it offered in teaching clinical efficiency. He pleaded constantly for more room and was therefore delighted when the Out Patient Department moved to spacious new quarters in The Agnes Wilson Memorial Pavilion in 1926.

The need for volunteers grew in direct ratio to expanding services. With more patients the Junior Auxiliary needed more volunteers to carry on its traditional tasks: occupational work with ward patients, entertainment, assisting the kindergarten teacher, and making surgical dressings. The kindergarten grew from one teacher at the beginning of the twenties to three in 1929—one for retarded patients. Two volunteers assisted each teacher every day. The Surgical Committee had to be enlarged to meet demands: they made 2,000 dressings in one meeting, 9,000 in 124 hours of work, and 52,800 in one year.

A Clinic Committee was added to the Junior Auxiliary in 1925, and a Psychiatric Committee in 1927. They helped in the expanding O.P. Department. Not only did they work in the Clinics themselves, but they also spent hundreds of hours driving children to and from the hospital and home for treatment. After a polio epidemic, the Junior Auxiliary hired a physiotherapist to work with afflicted children and then found volunteers to work under her guidance.

Many who came to Children's Memorial Hospital as volunteers in these years became Board members and worked for the Hospital for years. Mrs. William Lawlor, Jr., is a good example of this type of volunteer. She came to Children's as a Junior League provisional in 1928. Fifty years later she was given the Bambino Medal to honor her long service. (The Bambino is a replica of Andrea della Robbia's bambino which decorated Cribside Pavilion's entrance and had been adopted by the Auxiliary Board as the Hospital's symbol in 1922.) Mrs. Lawlor's service encompassed membership on the Junior Auxiliary Board, the Social Service Committee and the Woman's Board. She worked tirelessly on most of the committees of these boards—certainly the ones that demanded activity. During World War II, for example, as a member of the Surgical Dressings Committee, she made 100,000 dressings in one year!

Volunteers were also channelled into work in the Clinics through the Social Service Committee. The source of help was unimportant; there was always room for more.

Every Board member helped with The White Elephant Shop, the profits from which supported many parts of the Hospital's work. During the twenties it became a very important source of annual income. Mr. D. Mark Cummings, Mrs. Augustus Maxwell, and Mrs. George H. Taylor were among those who guided its work in early days. Although they were presidents of the Auxiliary Board, Miss Wilson and her successors, Mrs. Upham (1924–28) and Mrs. Cummings (1929–32), were also active workers at the Shop. Monthly reports from the manager, Miss Hanna Schmidt (not a volunteer), record the hundreds of hours the women spent sorting, pricing, and selling the merchandise that was collected at three teas a year held at members' houses—Mrs. McCormick, Mrs. Gustavus Swift, Mrs. Upham—and after a few years, also at a huge annual party at the Casino. One year the annual party was dubbed "The Gimme Tea." White elephants "poured in": beautiful gowns from Edith Rockefeller McCormick; mink coats and ermine stoles; boule furniture from an estate; a player piano and several uprights; jewellry; doll houses; a motor boat; a 1917 Packard; a large bronze temple incense burner; and, once, a real milk wagon! The ladies decided *that* might prove to be a real "white elephant." There was less valuable "rummage" too, but most was grist to the mill. One year a group of women prisoners at Marquette Prison sent several dozen handmade doilies. Neckties and hats arrived in a steady stream and always found customers.

The women showed endless ingenuity in attracting donations. They sent bags to their dressmakers asking for remnants of cloth for the home dressmaker sale. When stocks were low they stripped their own and their husbands' wardrobes ruthlessly. At the start of the fishing or hunting seasons there were always tales told of irate husbands looking in vain for favorite fishing hats or comfortable old tweed jackets. One year the Rummage Committee sent a special letter to bachelors and widowers reminding them to send the Shop their discarded clothing.

The White Elephant truck travelled the length of the city and suburbs picking up items from collecting points in members' homes. During the war a volunteer took a motor driver's test so that she could replace a man driver called up to army service. Although she was the first Chicago woman to take such a test, she passed with the highest grades. The Shop Committee threw an ice cream and cake party in her honor.

Sometimes the women had to reject goods. "No more gas stoves" was the plea month after month one year from the manager of the Shop to the Auxiliary Board. A glut of baby carriages took up too much space another time. Mah Jong sets with missing pieces left something to be desired even though the handyman tried to carve substitutes. Sometimes the women kept valuable articles in their homes: a large Aubusson rug, a marble statue, or sizable oil paintings. Patiently they made appointments with customers to view the articles.

It was hard work, but fun, and an unmistakable rallying point for the women. There were always stories to tell, pathetic, funny, and bizarre. There was the woman who bought three voluminous mourning veils for her daughters to wear at her funeral. When city authorities took the mistreated children away from her, she tried to return the veils. There was the immigrant who made a point of buying something now and then because Miss Wilson had been kind to him when, newly arrived, he had sold Cluny lace from door to door. There was the girl who tried to exchange a winter suit off her back for a spring one she "fancied." There were the customers who slyly exchanged tags or just marked down prices themselves during a sale. And there was an oft repeated tale of the Lake Forest chauffeur who had been pressed into helping shift heavy furniture in the store. He made the mistake of slipping into comfortable old shoes for the job —his smart black ones were sold for 50¢ while he was working!

The stories were endless but, working together day after day, exchanging tales over lunch (often hard boiled eggs and sandwiches brought by the women) drew them close together and built up a strong morale. Profits dwindled as the economic depression deepened at the end of the twenties, but the women only worked harder. There were always a dozen places to use the money which they turned over to the Hospital month after month. The receipts from 1924–29 reflect this ongoing support as well as the state of Chicago's economy; $24,265.75; $26,265.70; $25,765; $20,339.26; $20,700; and $16,200.

Three large portraits hung in Children's Memorial Hospital by 1930. A friend presented Louis Betts' study of John P. Wilson soon after his death in 1922. To it in the next year was added Leopold Seyffert's portrait of Miss Martha Wilson, given by Thomas D. Jones. Both Directors and Managers felt the picture of another benefactor should be added to this gallery. They requested and received a portrait of eighty-year-old Julia Foster Porter painted by Paul Trebilcock. The three subjects spanned the almost fifty years of service which Children's Memorial Hospital had given to children.

CHAPTER VIII

The Brennemann Years

1931–1940

As WORLD WAR I had affected the growth and policies of Children's Memorial Hospital in the twenties, so the Great Depression influenced its actions in the thirties.

Physical expansion was a case in point. The site for the desperately needed nurses' and interns' housing had been selected in 1929. And it was one of two items on the Building Program approved by the Board of Directors early in 1930. The other was a new power plant and laundry. Perhaps it was the inefficient, and hence expensive, operation of these units which gave them priority; for more and more the question became not can the Hospital afford a new power plant and laundry but can it afford not to modernize and expand these facilities.

Ground was broken in March 1930, and construction proceeded rapidly. But, with each month, the price of engines, boilers, and laundry machinery rose alarmingly. As Miss Mabel Binner, the new Superintendent (1929), with the architect and Mrs. Joseph King, an Auxiliary Board member (she became President in 1933) visited nurses' homes and laundries to see the latest and best in both, they began to fear that the cost of the latter, already begun, would postpone once again residences for nurses and interns. Certainly Children's could not rise to some of the amenities they were shown in Pittsburgh, New York, and White Plains: swimming pools, bowling alleys, shampoo facilities with hair dryers and curling irons, a kitchenette and laundry on every floor. Not when laundry washers and presses would probably cost $50,000.

Both power plant and laundry were operating by the spring of 1931, the former proving its value by saving $3,800 in a three-month period as compared with a similar time in 1930. But it was July 1931 before the original Maurice Porter Memorial Hospital building was torn down to make way for the Nellie A. Black and James Deering buildings. The bronze name plate on the first hospital, carefully protected, was later embedded in the sidewalk outside the new buildings. The impetus to build the nurses' home was the receipt of $700,000, the residue of Mrs. John A. Black's estate, which the Hospital had not expected for another ten years. For the interns' residence, the Directors reached back to the largest gift the Hospital had received to that date—James Deering's bequest of $500,000 in 1926.

The interns moved into James Deering in September 1932; three floors of Nellie Black were ready for nurses in November. But the buildings were not formally dedicated until January of 1933. Chicago was deep in the Depression by that time so that the Directors felt it best not to have a big celebration; the Hospital "family" only was invited.

A minimum of repair and repainting and small alterations for convenience (a passageway to Cribside and remodelling the former nurses' home for the hospital help, for example) reflect the mood of the Building Committee in the years that followed. Constant reshuffling of quarters solved problems temporarily by providing a larger record room, a more convenient drug room, or an infirmary for the help. But that was all. The Hospital was caught in a dilemma. On the one hand, the Depression brought a soaring demand for free care as prices on everything from food to wheelchairs climbed sharply. On the other, income and the number of contributors declined. The market value of the Endowment Fund fell in the thirties from $4,482,113.71 in 1930 to $2,265,386.55 in 1934. A slow climb of the market in the later years of the decade, plus sizable additions to the Fund following the deaths of Thomas D. Jones, Richard T. Crane, Jr., Mr. and Mrs. Eliphalet Cramer, Mrs. Frederick Rawson, and Mr. Bryan Lathrop brought the total up to $3,693,794.22 by 1940. These bequests, if unrestricted, were usually added to Endowment; the Directors thought times too uncertain to spend money freely on building and unnecessary refurbishing. Approval of buying new beds and sterilizers was delayed several months, for example, while requests for more assistants in X-ray and the Eye Clinic didn't even make the first priority category one year.

To tighten the business management of Children's, the Directors paid Arthur Young and Co. to reorganize the accounting system and hired Mr. William Slover, an accountant, as Assistant to Miss Binner. His firm hand was soon felt. He tightened the Hospital's belt by many small measures: using one light instead of three in a corridor; substituting twenty-five-watt bulbs for sixty watts when possible; using less gas to burn the rubbish in the incinerator; and reducing the amount of whiskey dispensed in the drug room—he cut that from 143 to 94 gallons in five months! He also persuaded the Lincoln Park Commissioners to haul power plant ashes and large rubbish away free—the Hospital had paid sixty-five dollars per month for that service. And he saved another fifteen dollars a month by no longer sprinkling dusty Fullerton Avenue in the summer months. Competitive bidding on coal saved $3,000; on printing $500. No item of expense went unexamined.

In these minor economics Mr. Slover was ably supported by Superintendent Binner. Because of her experience as Director of the Dispensary and of Social Service under Superintendent Mary Stewart (Miss Henderson's successor 1923–28), she knew that small expenditures could grow to large items in the budget. She first turned a critical eye on the nurses' personal laundry procedures. She discarded the old lengthy laundry lists which still included corset covers, gingham petticoats, and drawers—"extinct," Miss Binner labelled them. She established new regulations for delivering and picking up personal laundry, saving time and money in the change. A year or two later she asked for a study of time spent in ironing nurses' uniforms. Straight skirts and non-bib aprons she discovered, would, on the basis of 100 uniforms washed three times a week, save 22½ hours per week of ironing time. Since laundry wages were rising, a new type of uniform was gradually introduced. She also installed a mending machine to prolong the life of sheets, towels, etc.; the 8,000 new pieces of linens put into circulation in the new laundry had hard usage and could not last indefinitely.

The Directors were, of course, acutely aware of economic conditions in Chicago and in the Hospital. They met frequently in these times of crisis, often three or four times a month. New men, replacing those who had died, were elected to the Board during the thirties: Bruce Borland, Frederick Scott, Arthur Cable, Samuel Insull, Lester Armour, and Frank McNair. Mr. Wilson came to talk to the Auxiliary Board in June 1931, presenting three ways to meet the Depression: (1) cut salaries; (2) lower standards; or (3) limit intake. The first he thought impractical since everyone was overworked and only seven persons in the whole Hospital were paid more than $200 a month. The second he rejected as counter to the determination of the institution to develop the highest standards in the care of sick children. The third would need definite suggestions from Dr. Brennemann and the Medical Staff and probably policy changes. It was obvious to all that a fourth option was raising more money.

All of these discussions and reports brought home to the Auxiliary Board the gravity of the Hospital's problems. They were further shaken when a little later the Social Service Department had to borrow money to meet ongoing expenses. This heightened realization was undoubtedly behind their recommendation to the Directors in 1932 that the Psychiatric Clinic be closed. This had never been a very popular Clinic with the Boards—psychiatry for children was still a new idea—and closing could save $5,000 to $6,000 a year. The Directors agreed and the Clinic closed admissions and began tapering off client treatments. Then Mrs. Robert Wheeler, a new Board member in 1932, offered to underwrite the salary of the Clinic's one paid social worker. The Clinic was saved—at least it was until the end of 1935. At that time, more hard pressed than ever, the Directors decided to close the whole Neuropsychiatric Department.

In spite of Mr. Wilson's stand on salaries in 1931, salaries were cut twice in the thirties: 10 percent in 1932, a further 5 percent in 1934, with appropriate variations for those who lived inside or outside the Hospital.

The women, for their part, redoubled their efforts to attract new contributors, keep the old, and reinstate those whose contributions had lapsed. Several small benefits brought in modest sums: Mrs. James Thorne's exhibit of miniatures and a few of her "little rooms" netted $477.25 in 1932; the Junior Auxiliary's sponsoring of special sales at Tatman's or selling tickets to see Colleen Moore's Doll House at the Fair added a few hundred dollars to their resources. Later in the thirties, the women tackled their most ambitious benefit in years: John Barbirolli's conducting the New York Philharmonic Orchestra in a spectacular concert. The favorable publicity surrounding the event, a social climax for the year, brought new contributors to the Hospital; the concert itself netted $10,762.87.

Everyone, of course, pitched in to increase the profits at the White Elephant Shop. Monthly reports of this vital source of income were made to Directors and Auxiliary Board and a special year's report to the Annual Meeting of the Corporation. Mesdames Spoor, Cummings, Johnson, Maxwell, Martin, Chase, King, and Foster served as Chairmen of the Rummage Shop Committee in the thirties. Stock was hard to get as the Depression continued, but they hit upon new sources. Appeals to retail stores brought two truck loads of curtains and three manikins from Marshall Field's; lace, shoes, and underwear from Carson, Pirie, Scott. Then they tried the packing houses. Armour & Co. sent one hundred cases of creamed chipped beef and two cases of soap; and Swift & Co. white coats and trousers. The women found that furniture, china, bric-a-brac, and clothing from estate closings sold well. Items from the Jep J. Dau and Mrs. Harry Shearson estates swelled income for several months. So did the sale of the beautiful furnishings from Mrs. Cramer's Drake Hotel apartment, and from Mrs. McCord's home—both women had given hundreds of volunteer hours to the Shop. And, as always, there were amusing individual items which added money to the profits and stories to the treasury of Rummage Shop anecdotes. A lorgnette was snapped up within hours by a fortune teller to assist her in "reading" her globe; an Indian suit was bought by a real Indian, Chief Short Wing. Quaint bonnets and gowns from Mrs. Eames MacVeagh's mother found their way to a theatrical costume shop. A donation of rifles and shotguns was unusual; the Committee enjoyed the donor's warning—"Do not sell to racketeers"!

Yearly income from the White Elephant Shop varied from a high of $22,077.66 in 1931, to $10,275 in 1935—probably the lowest point in the Depression. A cloud hung over the enterprise in 1932 when illness forced their efficient manager, Miss Hanna Schmidt, to retire. Her death in 1939 was noted on the Memorial Page of the Annual Report.

It was inevitable that hard times should bring public money into Children's coffers. No one was very happy about this turn of events, but they were powerless to refuse in the face of their commitment to free care. The problem was obvious even in 1930. Superintendent Binner reported then the Hospital's serious financial situation; per capita care had risen from $3.64 to $5.10 per day; overall expenses for the year were $47,392 more than in 1929, although there were only 264 beds instead of 272. In the Clinics the financial picture was even more gloomy as the patient load rose 46 percent. An index of trouble ahead was the drain on the small Social Service Department fund used to provide free drugs, glasses, braces, X-ray, etc., for those who could not afford even the smallest fees. In the first ten months of 1930 the Department spent $4,000 more on these items than they had in 1929. The Auxiliary Board tried to build up the Brace Fund, essential to the work of the Orthopedic surgeons; and they tightened up the screening of applicants, but the problems could not be solved by these measures. The fact that the social agencies which referred many of their clients to Children's were increasingly unable to pay for these medical services compounded the difficulties.

A conference convened by the Council of Social Agencies late in 1932 placed responsibility on public bodies to relieve the situation. For Children's, the question was what state, federal, or city funds were available for hospitals? It was willing to try all of them rather than cut down on free care as many Chicago hospitals were doing in the crisis.

In August 1932 the Illinois Emergency Relief gave $1,045 to the Out Patient Department and promised $1,000 more in September. A month later it agreed to pay 90¢ a visit for a limited number of families. Bookkeeping became a nightmare but the money bind loosened slightly. The next year brought financial help from the Emergency Welfare Fund of Cook County for glasses and orthopedic appliances. That year a new statement was inserted in the Annual Report; "Substantially all of the medical and surgical care at the Hospital is free, and the income from endowment and receipts from patients are so inadequate that the annual budget of the institution can only be met through the generosity of its friends, and during the depression the work could not have been carried on without help of the relief agencies." This statement, with slight modifications, was repeated throughout the thirties. In 1935, in bold black type, the percentage of free care was added: 91 percent that year, then 89 percent, 87 percent, 92 percent, and 88 percent (1939). Graphic charts were published to illustrate these figures, in part, certainly, to answer a common attitude that the Hospital's money raisers met as the voluntary dollar dwindled—"Children's Memorial Hospital has a large endowment, why should we give to it?"

A new type of patient began coming to the Clinics—the child of the middle class, blue collar worker, who earlier would have been treated by a private physician. The child of the indigent came too, but—another anomaly of the period—often lack of carfare or even money to telephone delayed his arrival until he was critically ill and had to be hospitalized. Malnutrition and tubercular pneumonia, companions of inadequate food and housing, afflicted hundreds of the children and accelerated the course of the usual childhood diseases. It was difficult, too, to send convalescent children back to homes where nourishing food and special diets could almost certainly not be provided. The need for convalescent care facilities, long a dream of Children's Memorial Hospital, became acute.

The Bank Moratorium and an epidemic of chicken pox arrived simultaneously at Children's. They found the Hospital in the throes of coping with relief funds. Relief dispensing was a roller coaster, with Children's having little or no control of its ups and downs. State and county funds were, understandably, cut when employment became available, however temporary. That happened in 1932–33 when the Century of Progress opened up a few jobs, and again in 1935 when a slight building boom provided work for carpenters and masons. But when these jobs ended it took a long time and much red tape to get families back on the relief rolls. Again the Hospital was caught in the dilemma—it carried 40 percent of those relief families. Letters setting forth the institution's plight were sent to Governor Horner, Wilfred Reynolds (Executive Secretary of the Illinois Emergency Relief Commission) and Harry Hopkins (Federal Relief Administrator). Often these letters were unanswered.

An unexpected gift of $8,750 from the city government balanced the budget one year, but there was no assurance that it would be repeated. Joining the Community Fund had been a consideration for several years but was rejected because the Boards feared inroads into its own list of contributors. In 1934, however, Children's joined the Fund and received its first share, $1,211.52. By 1939 their allotment was $63,731.62. The Boards worried about their increasing dependence on this type of support but they saw no way to replace it.

Troubles were compounded in the mid-thirties when the federal WPA program was launched. With it came new regulations for relief eligibility. Too often these cut off relief from the indigent months before the much publicized work program could provide jobs for those able to work. Inevitably the Clinics received these families, bewildered and unhappy. Mrs. Babette Jennings, Director of the Social Service Department (1929), recalled nostalgically the early days—twenty-five years ago—when Dr. Cabot had come to lecture on social service and the Hospital had hired its first Social Service nurse, Miss Walsh. Goals had seemed clear then, and within reach. Now in 1936, with eight professional social workers, five clerks and stenographers, and dozens of capable volunteers, the Department struggled with situations beyond its control and perhaps insolvable. She urged the Auxiliary Board to support the Social Security Act passed in January 1936 because of its provisions affecting children: Mother's Aid and Care for Dependent Children, extensions of Public Health Service into areas of infant and maternity help and control of syphilis, and vocational rehabilitation of the handicapped.

Sometimes the problems and complaints of the unemployed were a little too much to bear. Invited to a luncheon forum on "The Emotional Difficulties of the Unemployed Woman," Miss Binner responded irritably that she was too much employed to find time for luncheons. And she shared with the Auxiliary Board some verses on Employment Blues:

Lines indited by a relief worker all hot and bothered from keeping up with daily job, transferring clients from work-relief to CWA, distributing salt pork, eggs, dried apples, blankets and what not and doing anything else that Harry Hopkins & Co. *think of.*

> Pity, my friend, the poor employed
> Who, though by early hours annoyed,
> Still must raise daily with the lark

To give the unemployed their pork.
Replete with beans and lollypopkins
From dear old Santa Harry Hopkins,
The unemployed may lie at ease
While those with jobs go out and freeze.
At Midnight when they're snug in bed,
The poor employed creeps home half dead
And on a couch her corpse is flung,
Unwashed, unpowdered and unstrung.

Improvement in the economic situation in the last few years of the thirties brought, ironically enough, further trouble. Frustrated by years of low wages and long hours of work, the blue collar worker demanded redress. Strikes and attempts to unionize workers were the order of the day. Labor's demands and problems dominated meetings and conventions of social workers and hospital administrators. Returning from one in 1937 Miss Binner called all the Hospital's employees together. She discussed the situation and distributed pamphlets from the Chicago Hospital Council which bore on the problem. There was little doubt in her mind, she reported to the Auxiliary Board, that the help would join a union, and indeed she felt some of their grievances were justified. In the meantime she advised the Board to keep an open mind, not just fight organization.

Shortly after, union officials called a city-wide mass meeting of hospital workers. The invitation listed their grievances: no rise in wages although cost of living was going up, long hours, bad meals. "You are overworked," the list ended.

Five of the Hospital's workers went to the meeting (attendance was estimated at 300–500) and came back disgusted. One reported to Miss Binner that he'd rather be loyal to Children's than to some unknown union boss. She felt that such loyalty, which could resist rabble rousing approaches, was built on her and her predecessors' years of insisting that everyone in the Hospital from the Chief of Staff to the woman who mopped the floors was an integral part of a high standard of care for sick children. Everyone felt important.

In the meantime the Hospital tried to improve living conditions and took a hard look at the help's food, hours of work, and salaries. At the direction of the Department of Labor, women employees' hours were cut from an average of sixty hours to forty-eight hours per week (six eight-hour days). A new, more liberal vacation plan was started, and salaries were gradually raised. In 1938 the Auxiliary Board appointed a Personnel Practices Committee—a sign of the times.

The Depression had some positive results for Children's Memorial Hospital. It became a strong and influential member of Chicago's social agencies and institutions which planned for the welfare of the city's children. That, in itself, led to constant examination and reevaluation of its work. When, in the thirties, it was one of thirty-five children's hospitals chosen for a study by the American Academy of Pediatrics, it participated gladly in answering long questionnaires and setting aside time for interviews. The American Academy, founded in 1930, was a larger and more activist organization than the American Pediatric Society. The Academy was interested in social reform, in establishing high standards for pediatric education and practice, and in strengthening hospital administration. Dr. Isaac Abt was its first President; Dr. Aldrich was an influential member of the Executive Board of Region IV (Midwest).

Children's waited eagerly for the results of the study, published in *The Journal of Pediatrics* in 1934-35. The Hospital came out well in the study's ratings. It was lacking in only a few respects: its training course for pediatric nursing was short according to Academy standards; it did relatively little in preventive medicine; and it had inadequate provision for care for convalescent children.

Miss Minnie Howe who had been appointed Principal of the Training School and Director of Nursing in 1929 when Miss Binner became Superintendent, had been urging an extension of the training course to six months—and eventually a year—for some time. The study strengthened her request.

The Hospital sadly admitted that it was not a forerunner in preventive medicine, much as it agreed with its aims and methods. Top priority had been given to preventive medicine in the country after the 1930 White House Conference. The Hospital's slight venture had been to equip a dental room and secure interns from Northwestern Medical School to staff it five mornings a week (in time it offered field work for all of the School's oral hygienists). But lack of room prevented the Hospital from developing an extensive preventive medicine program. For that, they would need a new clinic building. It was difficult to turn down the Chicago Health

Department's request in 1931 to join in a community program for immunization against diphtheria and innoculation against small pox. But how could the Clinics accommodate more children? Impossible!

Children's had a better record in the field of syphilis. When in the thirties Chicago became agitated over the prevalence of syphilis and turned to hospitals to test and treat cases, Children's could point to its pioneer work in this field. In 1924 it had begun to treat syphilis from its social as well as its pathological side. It had opened a Syphilis Clinic then and had never flagged in its efforts to identify and treat the disease. In the crisis of the mid-thirties, the number of patients in its Clinic rose 1000 percent in four years, but it was able to cope. With a grant from the Public Health Institute it also hired a technician to determine the incidence of syphilis in all patients admitted to its wards and clinics.

As for convalescent care, no study was needed to tell the Hospital it lacked facilities there. It had experimented briefly with running a convalescent home in 1917 when Mrs. Arthur Ryerson had offered her home on Lakeview Avenue for convalescing children for the summer. Fourteen children with serious heart trouble had been cared for from June to September. The experiment had demonstrated clearly the benefits of a separate convalescent care facility, but had also shown that it was an impractical undertaking for the Hospital. Members of the Auxiliary Board had given $1,000 for upkeep; Mrs. Cramer had provided necessary equipment.

In 1934-35 Children's had tried a different road. They had persuaded Chicago Orphan Asylum to provide convalescent care for a few children under two. Twelve had been cared for in several of the agency's foster homes—and at its expense. Again the experiment was highly successful but Chicago Orphan Asylum was reluctant at that time to expand its convalescent work.

Children's, however, encouraged by success, continued to press the community to find more foster homes for their use—a job beyond the scope of hospital work. In October 1938, the Chicago Junior League, aided by the Council of Social Agencies, launched a three-year Convalescent Care Project. The League offered to pay the board and general expenses of patients if Chicago Orphan Asylum would find and supervise homes to receive them. In keeping with their principles of direct service, the League would also provide volunteers to visit children in the foster homes, provide recreation and tutoring for them, and transportation to the Hospital for treatment and check ups. In the first year ten children were carefully selected for the project by Dr. Brennemann and Miss Jennings. It was a delicate task; the type of disease and probable length of convalescence were factors in selection; so too was the ability of the parent to accept the fact that his child needed a foster home rather than his own when he left the Hospital. Convalescent care for babies had its peculiar problem, it had to be on an emergency basis; at the moment when the acute stage of his illness was over, a baby needed to be removed from the dangers of cross infection in an institution.

The Convalescent Care Project was highly successful. When it ended in 1942 the Community Fund picked up board expenses and, after some hesitation, Chicago Orphan Asylum opened a Department for Convalescent Care in 1945.

As the Hospital drew closer to other child caring agencies in the thirties it also strengthened its ties with national, state, and county professional organizations. Miss Binner, Miss Jennings, and Miss Howe attended meetings and conferences indefatigably, returning with deeper insight and renewed vigor to tackle the problems they found common to all. They shared with the Auxiliary Board, the School of Nursing Committee, and the Social Service Committee the emphasis and trends learned from the American Association of Hospital Social Workers, the National Association of Social Workers, the state and national Councils of Nursing Education, and the Chicago Hospital Association. In particular they were alert to suggestions for implementing the recommendations of the 1930 White House Conference on Child Health and Protection. When it was mentioned, mildly, by the Auxiliary Board that all this travelling to meetings was expensive, their response was that without such outside stimuli they did not know how they could bear the daily frustrations of hard times.

While at times in the Depression it seemed virtually impossible to run a top-quality hospital, that same period saw quality care, joined to love and concern for the "whole" child, become the hallmark of Children's Memorial Hospital. That had been the purpose of Julia Foster Porter in simpler days in 1882; magnified, it is the stamp of the Hospital today in 1982.

No small part of this achievement in the thirties belongs to Dr. Joseph Brennemann. He was at the height of his career when he was appointed Chief of Staff on a full-time basis with a salary in 1930. For ten years he had been observing sick children, talking with their parents, and learning their backgrounds. Over the same period of time he had watched the discipline of pediatrics grow—he knew its concerns, discoveries, and advances in treatment—he had himself contributed to those advances. Now in the thirties the Hospital was his forum from which he could share his great clinical knowledge and his firm, forward-looking convictions. The crammed O.P. Clinics of the period were still his favorite classrooms, for he was first and foremost a clinician. He tried to develop in his students the ability to diagnose accurately from what they saw—and smelled—at the bedside and in the examining room, and what they heard from parents. Laboratories he regarded as important ancillary aids.

Dr. Brennemann was not one who rushed into wholehearted endorsement of new drugs and new treatments; he waited for proof of their validity. When the sulfa drugs were discovered in the thirties, he praised their effectiveness in treating pneumonia but urged "caution, caution" in their use. This characteristic earned him the reputation of being a "therapeutic nihilist." With his witty pen he seemed to enjoy debunking some of the favorite theories of the day. His address as President of the American Pediatric Society in 1930 illustrates this trait. *Vis Medicatrix Naturae in Pediatrics* urged doctors *not* to overmedicate, to let nature take its own healing course. Its qualifying subtitle was "A Plea for the More Extended Use of Conservatism and of Common Sense in the Practice of Pediatrics." "Resist," he said in his speech and preached to his medical students at Children's, resist the all too human urge to "do something active from without, preferably from a bottle." Wait for "a restoration from within . . . supported by measures that promote comfort and insure rest and proper hygiene." He was careful to exclude from his remarks diphtheria, scarlet fever, malaria, syphilis and other diseases for which there were specific remedies. In fact, at this time, he was in frequent consultation with Dr. Gladys Dick of the McCormick Institute on the efficiency of the Dick test for scarlet fever and he recommended it for use in the Hospital.

In 1931 Dr. Brennemann's target was psychiatry. *The Menace of Psychiatry* was the catchy title of a paper he read to the New England Pediatric Society that year. He confessed to premonitions that he would be accused of premature critical evaluation of a movement still gathering momentum. He accepted the value of psychiatry (he included in the term psychology, mental hygiene, child study, and parent education); what he deplored was unthinking acceptance of an unfamiliar and still highly experimental field of work—particularly as its precepts trickled down to anxious young parents. He repeated his warnings in other speeches and articles —adding as well his thoughts on the touchy subject of the relationship of pediatrician and psychiatrist. He urged mutual respect and inter-education.

The Menace of Psychiatry became a classic—often quoted. It called forth an entertaining appreciation from Dr. John Ruhräh of Baltimore, an earlier President of the A.P.S.:

> In ancient days long since gone by
> When Solomon was king,
> The erring child who strayed from God
> Was straightway brought back by a rod
> It seemed the proper thing,
> And sanctioned by the Holy Writ
> The psyche was not hurt a bit.
>
> One hesitates to cast a doubt
> Upon the tale as voiced,
> The child to elders showed respect
> His conduct was most circumspect
> The heavenly hosts rejoiced.
> They could not pass such angels by
> Which made the death rate very high.
>
> Those days were really wondrous days
> It scarcely seems 'twas true.
> Whate'er the parents chanced to say
> The child was taught he must obey
> Or else the hour he'd rue.
> The ego, in between the id
> And superego, smoothly slid.
>
> . . . .
>
> But times have changed, as proverb says,
> Old things are obsolete,
>
> . . . .

Before the parent dares to chide
The wise guys take the child aside
    And psychoanalyze.
They probe his every hope and fear
And wonder why the child is queer.

The clinic doors are opened wide
    Professors sit within
The more they strive with their advice
To make the wee one mild and nice
    The more the young ones sin.
They wonder what it's all about
And so do I, which lets me out.

The fact that the Psychiatric Clinic almost closed a year later (1932) cannot, in spite of his views, be laid at Dr. Brennemann's door. The Hospital continued to include "Psychiatric Conditions in Children" in the curriculum of the School of Nursing—it had been taught first in 1930 by Dr. Bert Beverly, a psychiatrist on Children's staff. Dr. Ralph Hamill, head of the Psychiatric Clinic, had joined him in teaching the course until he left the Hospital in 1935. Dr. Beverly continued teaching it until he retired in 1939 when Dr. Byrd Smith, a psychologist on the staff became the instructor. Dr. Brennemann, however, never failed to include a child guidance clinic whenever he discussed the essential services of a first rate children's hospital.

For him, however, the essence of a good hospital lay beyond the services it provided. He described it in his presidential address to the Children's Hospital Association in October 1931: "The children may be well cared for; the medical staff may be made up of able clinicians and investigators; the superintendent may be as wise as Solomon and as "just" as Aristides, and may see that the whole machinery of administration is well oiled and the physical equipment faultless; the board of trustees and the women's board may be actively interested and may do all that could be desired in other ways; the nurses may be intelligent, faithful and well trained; the interns and residents may be well schooled and prepared for their duties, ... and yet the vital spark will be lacking if there is not back of it all an all-pervading spirit of cooperation and of kindliness or, as Emerson has so beautifully expressed it, 'an element of love that permeates it like a fine ether.' "

Tradition, Dr. Brennemann felt, established a hospital's "personality." If there was a tradition of kindliness, attentiveness, thoughtfulness, flexibility, and cooperation, the hospital's personality would be warm and friendly, inviting to patient and parent. Children's personality, he wrote, in an article about the Hospital for the *Journal of Pediatrics* in 1934, is conveyed in the work "memorial." With one exception (power plant and laundry), every building had been erected as a "memorial," emphasizing the background of "human interest and sentiment." He further defined Children's personality as primarily a clinical rather than a research one. Unless a doctor showed initiative or interest in the latter, Children's did not stress it as an essential part of its work. This emphasis was entirely compatible with Dr. Brennemann's interests and he fostered it at the Hospital for twenty years.

His common sense approach also helped change theories of infant feeding, still a hotly debated subject in the thirties. Dr. Brennemann deplored the rigidity of feeding schedules, the anxiety of the mother as she weighed and measured her baby with a book of "standards" in one hand. "No child should ever be made to eat," he preached. This point of view he shared with Dr. Andrew Aldrich and Dr. Clara Davis, both colleagues at Children's. The former wrote widely on the subject; Dr. Davis conducted an experiment in free selection of food with thirteen babies—six to eight months old. Her report of this experiment to the American Pediatric Society, and the support of Drs. Aldrich and Brennemann, raised many questions about a pediatrician's usual exact instructions: one egg yolk, one-quarter ripe banana, one quart of milk, etc. Dr. Brennemann called her study one of the most fundamental and far reaching pieces of work of his time.

At the Hospital in 1932, Dr. Davis introduced the idea of serving patients food from a cart, allowing each (within his diet restrictions) to select what and how much he wanted. Seconds were always available. Appetites picked up; Children's became noted for its method; and wasted food dropped from sixty-three pounds to eleven in one week. That saved money too!

Crowded though it was, Children's did manage, at the insistence of Dr. Brennemann, to fit in a new Department of Bronchoscopy in 1935–36. Endoscopic work in Chicago was in its infancy then, more or less a by-product of otolaryngology. At Children's it was limited largely to removing foreign bodies from the bronchi and esophagus. But when Dr. Paul Hollinger returned to Chicago from his training in the clinic of the famous endoscopist Dr. Chevalier Jackson, Dr. Brennemann was eager to secure him for the Hospital. Setting up an endoscopic clinic was expensive; it required a special operating room, unique x-ray machines, two special nurses, and several thousand dollars worth of unique instruments. The project hung fire until Mr. and Mrs. Preston Wells, old friends of Children's, came to the rescue with a gift large enough to equip the clinic and maintain it for two years. Space was made by using rooms reserved for tonsil and adenoid patients. This move reduced the total number of beds from 264 to 252, not a popular move with everyone. Before the year was out Miss Binner reported to the Auxiliary Board that the new Clinic was tying up all special nurses, and the high humidity required in the operating room was peeling the paint from the walls. But Dr. Hollinger charmed the ladies by explaining his techniques and showing them his strange instruments; they forgot the inconveniences, and remembered that the publicity generated by the new Clinic was valuable in money raising. Dr. Brennemann called the Clinic an important item in the progress of Children's since it opened up a new field of work not possible before.

Space was, fortunately, not needed to broaden and deepen two other important areas of hospital work in the thirties: recreation and occupation. They developed hand in hand. Education was in the hands of the Junior Auxiliary in the thirties; in some ways it was an easier job than in earlier days. The Board of Education no longer needed to be convinced of the value of hospital schools. There were four teachers and several assistants at Children's in the thirties— one year they requisitioned $107.83 worth of books from the Board of Education to carry on their work. The schoolroom on E floor was equipped with blackboard, desks, and bulletin boards. When new bedside tables were needed in an older boys' ward, they were bought with an eye to convenience for homework. The Sunbeam League, a service organization, supported a new kindergarten at the Hospital in 1934.

In this decade the Chicago Public Library also stepped up its services to two half-days a week. A library cart was bought (with

$500 from Director Richard Crane) to carry books from ward to ward for the children's selection. That project grew like wildfire. Before long the Junior Auxiliary was calling for volunteers to catalog books, mend them, or replace them when small hands had put them beyond repair. Board members loved to contribute books, outgrown by their own children, or new. The Children's Library boasted 1,036 volumes by 1935, exclusive of school books and 10¢ paper books.

Then a teacher from a conservatory of music was persuaded to give classes in singing and to develop a rhythm band. As each of these ideas succeeded, often beyond expectation, the conviction grew that the Hospital needed a trained occupational worker to develop a plan for education and recreation and to guide volunteers. The Junior Auxiliary offered to pay her salary—up to $100 per month. The women turned to Miss Binner and Miss Howe to find a qualified worker. With the help of Miss Neva Boyd, Assistant Professor of Sociology at Northwestern and Instructor in Recreational Therapy in Children's School of Nursing (after 1930), Miss Anne Smith was hired as the first Supervisor of Recreation in 1932. And the Auxiliary Board appointed a new committee: Occupational Therapy.

The Hospital's commitment to play therapy for its patients deepened as the years passed. It increased instruction to nurses on how to play with children (singly or in groups) together with courses on child development. The climate of the times after the 1930 White House Conference encouraged education in child psychology, behavior, and recreation. Miss Howe felt the School had much to offer in these fields—courses were lengthened to six months; the goal was fourteen months.

New lines of work developed: pre-operative and post-operative play with tonsil and adenoid patients; group work with children under 4½ years. The nurses were enthusiastic; so were the Hospital's social workers. In fact, the Chicago chapter of Social Workers held a three-day Play Institute to which Children's was invited to discuss its work. The Hospital put together a demonstration, "The Practical Application of Play to Hospital Work." They gave the program to the superintendents of their affiliated nursing schools, to the Illinois League of Nursing Education, the Central Council of Nursing Education—and of course to its own Auxiliary Board.

Miss Smith carried the message as far as the National Conferences of Social Workers in their 1935 meeting in Montreal.

Other avenues of work opened. A display of books, games, and craft equipment for a Hospital Day exhibit at Children's was repeated for the Chicago Association of Settlement Houses' annual meeting. Similar material was shown to parents during visiting hours—with volunteers demonstrating their use. The Hospital wondered if older bed patients could do woodwork with simple tools. Mrs. James Thorne (a new Auxiliary Board member in 1931) bought some good tools and the children began turning out bookends, puzzles, and circus animals.

Caught up in the enthusiasm for play therapy, the Auxiliary Board not only made generous gifts for work materials, but also began to include more frequently chalk talks and puppet shows in their traditional parties: Mrs. Patrick Valentines's Valentine Party, Mrs. Paul Healy's Birthday Party, Mrs. William Greenlee's Spring Party. A flood of drawings and paintings followed the first; making their own puppets was a natural outgrowth of the second. The children became adept at handling puppets to act out favorite stories. Sometimes they wrote puppet plays themselves. After Mrs. Thorne gave the children an exquisite doll house, she found herself giving lessons in making doll furniture and accessories. Creative play heightened the children's appreciation of the Winnie the Pooh mural with which Mrs. Thorne brightened an unattractive basement wall.

Recreational work was second only to clinic work in popularity with volunteers. Obviously, in its new form, it required more training than had been needed for reading a story or helping a child with a puzzle. Good intentions were not enough. A course of training was arranged—it was opened also to Cook County Hospital volunteers and to the Gray Ladies. Some volunteers even elected to attend the nurses' class in play therapy. Mrs. Ira Couch, the vigorous chairman of Volunteer Services (Social Service Committee) in 1933, with her Vice-Chairman, Mrs. H.W. Sanborn, wrote a pamphlet "Dos and Don'ts for Volunteers." Mrs. Couch's goals were to restrain enthusiastic but untrained volunteers from doing the wrong thing, and to channel their talents into work they could do. The booklet helped.

Only the construction of a new Out Patient Building remained to satisfy the great need of Children's for more room in this period. That had seemed within their grasp in 1935 when Miss Gwethalyn Jones (new Auxiliary Board member in 1933) gave almost $600,000 in memory of her uncle Thomas Davies Jones, who had died in 1930. Friends had added to the memorial gift so that it had soon reached $635,052.29. Dr. Brennemann regarded the money as an answer to prayer. It could open the way for erecting a five-story building on Orchard Street large enough to house all the usual O.P. and Social Service needs, together with X-ray facilities, record rooms, pharmacy, electrocardiograph, a dental department, a room for basal metabolism determination, a photography department, an amphitheater, and isolation rooms for contagious diseases. Eventually Dr. Brennemann hoped to see all the laboratories on the fifth floor, and animal quarters on the roof. The opportunity to plan the building exactly as they wanted it was heady. They poured over blueprints; and once again, visited children's hospitals all over the East. They sent questionnaires to all doctors whose departments would be housed there and consulted daily with the architect. Dr. John Bigler was drawn into the planning; since 1931, when Northwestern Medical School had begun sending senior students to O.P. medical clinics at Children's, he had been organizing, facilitating, and supervising all student work there. Dr. Isaac Abt, then head of the Department of Pediatrics at Northwestern Medical School had also begun to conduct a clinic at Children's in 1931; he too was asked for suggestions.

For a time this planning was an exciting and positive activity in the worst period of the Depression. But lack of money postponed building once again. There was enough money to build, but as Mr. Wilson, Dr. Brennemann, and Miss Binner studied the cost of equipping, maintaining and operating the vast new plant, they were forced to admit that the Hospital could not afford it. In 1936, therefore, they began studying once more the possibility of remodelling the old Clinic building to meet growing needs. That proved impossible too; it was obvious that clinic work could not be expanded; it would be difficult not to curtail it.

But in 1939 the financial picture changed. Sparked by a bequest from Mrs. Eliphalet Cramer (she died in March 1938 after serving on the Women's Board since 1897) of almost $350,000, Mr. Wilson appointed a new committee to reconsider a new O.P. building. An unqualified "yes" by November 1938 set all in motion. "The shovel," Dr. Brennemann wrote, "has . . . taken its place beside the blueprint." For him the new O.P. building would symbolize his belief that inpatient and outpatient work were co-equal. The more efficient the latter, the less need for hospitalization—always the goal at Children's.

To make way for the new building, Cribside was moved to a new location fronting on Lincoln Avenue. The babies were housed temporarily in the nose and throat wards, thereby reducing tonsillectomies from 1333 in 1938, to 868 in 1939. They were back in a rebuilt Cribside complete with an up-to-date Milk Laboratory by the end of the year.

The new O.P. building was in almost full operation by 1940. Laboratories were not yet housed on the fifth floor but the space was ready when the Hospital could afford to resettle them. Having seen his dream come true, Dr. Brennemann chose that year to retire.

In his last annual medical report he selected the O.P. building and the Doctors' Library as two outstanding developments at Children's in the thirties. He had encouraged the growth of a medical library for years, using fees from the graduate course in pediatrics to add to its resources. A trained librarian in 1935 had brought order to the mass of books, articles, reprints, etc., which had been purchased or given to the library by doctors, medical societies, and Board members. The Junior Auxiliary subscribed to fourteen medical journals as their contribution. A bibliography by subject and author added materially in the late thirties to its usefulness as a reference library. One of the ways the Directors and Medical Staff chose to honor Dr. Brennemann on his departure was to name it The Joseph Brennemann Library.

At the formal opening of the O.P. building—The Thomas D. Jones Memorial Building—the Directors presented Dr. Brennemann with a gold watch and chain; the women gave him a leather case containing a clock, barometer, thermometer, hydrometer, and compass. In one of his last talks to the Auxiliary Board he said he had had little to do with the physical changes during his twenty years at Children's but had helped with the "pattern" of the Hospital. He urged the women to keep stressing the human side of the

Hospital and the use of the clinics for teaching as well as treating. He also recommended that doctors be allowed to bring as many of their private patients to Children's as they wished.

Familiar faces were missing as the calendar was turned to the 1940s. Julia Foster Porter, ninety years old, had died in 1937. James Porter had left the Board of Directors when his term expired in 1930. He had served thirty years. Both Mr. and Mrs. Eliphalet Cramer had died within three years of each other, the former after thirty-one years as a Director, the latter after forty-one years on the principal women's board. His portrait was hung in the Board of Director's room; hers, by request, in the living room of Nellie A. Black. Death had also removed Directors Jones, Crane, Rawson, Simpson, and Rockwell.

It was difficult to replace Miss Minnie Howe, Director of the Department of Nursing and Principal of the School of Pediatric Nursing when she died in 1939. She had held the school together during the difficult years of the Depression when low pay and long hours had accelerated the turnover of nurses. She had consistently emphasized high nursing standards, promoted scholarships for special work at other schools, and installed a good health program for her nurses. She was a moving force in forming an excellent nurses' library. As a memorial to her, doctors, nurses, board members, and patients established the Minnie Howe Scholarship Fund.

Once again in Children's history, war was just around the corner for the United States—it had started in Europe. Miss Binner had sensed a first small impact; silkworm gut and ephedrene (an alkaloid used in fighting asthma) came to the Hospital from China. War had already slowed delivery of these important materials; it might make them unavailable.

PART THREE *1941–1960*

---

*"The Children's Memorial Hospital
will continue as an indispensable
medical institution, and as we have
been required to grow in the past, we
will be required to grow in the future"*

CHAPTER IX

World War II
Hampers Progress

1941–1950

T HE STILL distant war was not, however, foremost in the thoughts of the Hospital family as it gathered to open the Thomas D. Jones Memorial Building. Settling-in problems worried Miss Binner. Moving day in a hospital was never easy. Several problems had been anticipated: all records before 1927 were to be microfilmed and then filed in cabinets—mountains of paperwork could then be destroyed and space gained for other purposes. Tablets commemorating donors of $10,000 or more were to be framed and hung in the lobby of the new building near Dr. Brennemann's portrait—proper recognition of large contributors was always a knotty problem.

Most important of all, a new Chief-of-Staff had been selected, Dr. Charles Andrew Aldrich. Dr. Stanley Gibson was appointed Assistant Physician-in-Chief and Dr. John Bigler Medical Director of the O.P. Department. There was no doubt that Dr. Aldrich would stress the "human" side of the Hospital; Dr. Brennemann used the word to characterize his successor: "a stimulating thinker, interested in experimentation, human, and a good organizer." Before moving into his new post (January 1, 1941), Dr. Aldrich left for a two-week's tour of eastern children's hospitals to study ways to improve Children's.

The Board of Directors used the transition period to study its organization and its problems. Money as always had top priority. Only $3,000 was left in the building fund after the last bills for Thomas D. Jones Memorial had been paid. Income from patients, contributors, and a few government grants had risen but so had expenses. A half a cent more per quart for milk didn't sound like much, but it added $1,149 to the annual budget. With an enlarged physical plant the Board could delay no longer in adding an assistant housekeeper to the staff; she had, in fact, been needed since 1929. It also raised residents' salaries: $100 per month for the head resident; $50 for other full-time residents, and $10 for assistants. (In the midst of war manpower shortages a few years later, these salaries were raised to $125, $75, and $30, respectively.) Pressure for free care in the clinics increased when Illinois passed a three-year residency requirement for eligibility for relief, and declined to pass the Aid to Dependent Children Act, thus cutting off federal funds for indigent children.

Small items, perhaps, in themselves, but inevitably operating expenses climbed up. Miss Binner responded with increased vigilance over small expenses. Would the ladies bring cosmetic jars and screw-top bottles for use in the drug room? They would: 1,412 jars and 1,218 bottles later they figured they had saved the Hospital $400 in eight months. With her thoughts on money as she turned over the presidential gavel to Mrs. James C. Hutchins in 1941, Mrs. William Greenlee urged the ladies to think of a benefit "amusing and irresistable." The Junior Auxiliary saved money by streamlining the Christmas stocking procedure. They discontinued letters to Santa Claus and bought all the Christmas presents themselves.

Personnel problems loomed as large as money problems. Miss Alice Morse, the new head of nursing in 1941, struggled to stabilize her staff, but a large turnover became a recurring problem as the war drew closer. Nurses were restless; the war seemed imminent as they listened to speeches on the role of the nurse in a democracy or raised money for the Red Cross Relief Fund by passing canisters in local theatres. And after a Red Cross worker visited Children's to talk about enrolling for service, knitting for the boys was a familiar sight in Nellie A. Black's lounge.

By the time the United States sent its first troops abroad in 1942, every part of the Hospital was feeling the impact of war. Four Directors had joined the armed services: Lester Armour, Dexter Cummings, Nelson Morris, and John B. Wilson, Jr. Thirty-three doctors left for the front in seven months, although medical students were urged to complete their education before joining the medical corps. Blackout curtains were fitted to 1,600 windows at a cost of $1,000. To brighten the dismal after-dark look for the children, the nurses pasted colorful cutouts on the curtains—balloons, clowns, trains and dolls. Employees from kitchen, laundry, and maintenance crew, as well as nurses and social service workers, were drawn to war industries by patriotism and the lure of high wages. The Department of Social Work reported a 300 percent staff turnover, the Department of Nursing a steadily decreasing cadre of graduate nurses. For the first time the Hospital considered hiring black nurses. A special recruitment campaign was organized by the Nurses' Council of War during acute shortages in 1943, and the Red Cross intensified its drive for nurses' aides. In addition, volunteers were eagerly sought for dozens of hospital jobs from answering the telephone to recording in the clinics.

After the United States declared war in 1941, the Directors invested some of Children's resources in war bonds. The women bought defense stamps, promoted the Victory Exchange (war stamps for articles to be sold to further the war effort), and the Do-Without-Club. Small patients participated in the last, proudly displaying a large button after they had "earned" one dollar in stamps for "things-they-did-without."

Dr. Aldrich characterized the chief problem at the Hospital in 1943 as maintaining the "remarkable progress in medicine and surgery" with a "frightening shortage of staff." He made that statement shortly after twenty-two more doctors had left for service and the Radium Clinic had had to be closed because of lack of personnel. Even an attempt to start a first-aid class was thwarted by the lack of staff to teach it. More serious was the threatened lack of blood serum as war hospitals demanded tremendous quantities for the wounded. Children's responded by opening its own blood bank. Volunteers manned the donors' rooms; thirty persons, largely Board members and staff, gave blood on the opening day.

The Hospital kindergarten was another victim of war—the women were forced to close it when the Sunbeam League decided to buy war bonds instead of paying the teacher's salary.

Scrap rubber entered their lives. The Hospital collected 285 pounds of tired and worn rubber for the rubber drive. The White Elephant Shop, however, did appeal to the rationing board for extra coupons to enable Mrs. Royal Vilas to buy much needed tires for the car with which she collected stock for the shop.

The Chicago War Commission Board installed a fully equipped casualty station in Thomas D. Jones, and sent a man to show the staff how to deal with incendiary bombs. The women passed to the men the vexing question of who was responsible for civilian defense kits!

Rationing hit the Hospital hard. When the sugar ration was cut 50 percent, the dieticians were hard put to make trays attractive to patients. Even more difficult to handle was a drastic cut of 25 percent in processed foods. High priced fresh fruits and vegetables had to replace canned varieties. Canned goods had always been used to extend shortages of fresh food and to create appetizing dishes. The cooks complained that without them it would be impossible to vary menus, maintain minimum standards of nutrition, and keep the cost of meals within reason. Fifty-seven boxes of fresh fruits and vegetables from suburban victory gardens helped one year. So did a bushel basket of tomatoes brought by a truck farmer grateful for Children's care of his small son years earlier.

While the war hampered and frustrated normal day-to-day operations, it did not paralyze the Hospital. Even the physical plant was improved: Martha Wilson was redecorated for the first time in sixteen years; Agnes Wilson was redesigned to include Cribside babies and an infirmary for employees. Cribside itself was turned over to brace, carpenter, and paint shops. The ever-expanding Brennemann Library was relocated in larger quarters on the ground floor of Maurice Porter—displacing seven department offices which had to be fitted in here and there in other buildings.

Space was found as well for enlarged medical services: an expanding dental clinic, a reorganized nutrition clinic, and a newly established research project in renal diseases. A sharp rise in polio in 1943, coupled with a flare of enthusiasm for Sister Kenny's treatment, led the Hospital to admit more polio patients for aftercare. Since none of the Children's nurses had used the Kenny treatment, a physiotherapist trained in that method was added to the staff.

Funding these developments in war time was not easy. President Wilson's request to the Auxiliary Board that it raise $100,000 in 1943 led them to accelerate their efforts to find new contributors and to consider that "amusing and irresistible" benefit. Personal notes and calls led to an all-time high of 1,192 contributors in 1943, 1,384 in 1944. *A Visionary Voyage on S.S. Friendship, Red, White and Blue Line*, an inspired wartime benefit, raised $8,000. The White Elephant Shop's silver anniversary celebration (1943) brought in $22,375—$8,000 more than in the previous year. A special tea at the Casino (admission a piece of silver) produced 1,200 pieces for sale. The Junior Auxiliary Board polished the silver to a high gloss for the opening day of the sale. In the middle of the silver that day was an etching of the White House, signed by President and Mrs. Franklin Delano Roosevelt. Someone on the silver anniversary committee had remembered that a gift from President Theodore Roosevelt had been a conversation piece at the opening sale of the Rummage shop at 27 East Ohio Street twenty-five years earlier. "Teddy" had sent a bullet with which he had shot a black elephant. It had sold for $200.

Gifts for special purposes also swelled the coffers in the forties. The National Foundation for Infantile Paralysis paid four dollars per day for the children it referred to the Hospital; the Community Fund underwrote the expenses of the nutrition clinic for several years. Dr. John Schweppe helped fund the new biochemistry laboratory; Mrs. Augustus Maxwell gave $5,000 to hire a special nurse for critically ill children, and the Preston Wells continued to support bronchoscopic work. The Walter Murray Foundation gave $5,000 for a special orthopedic nurse and another $5,000 to defray expenses for indigent orthopedic patients.

The rate of occupancy bore, of course, directly on operating expenses. As a result of remodelling and shifts in service, the number of beds had been reduced to 248 in 1943, but even that smaller number had an occupancy rate of only 48.2 percent. With beds to spare, the Directors looked once again at the top age limit for patients. Doctors frequently objected to dismissing patients arbitrarily when they reached their thirteenth birthday—many times the patients quietly remained. After a good deal of discussion the Board of Directors adopted a new policy: a few patients (not more than four or six at one time) could be kept up to their fifteenth birthday if a series of treatments needed to be completed, if death were expected shortly, or if a medical condition was of unusual scientific interest and hence of value in teaching.

A new Public Relations Department played no small part in the forties in increasing contributions by keeping the Hospital in the public eye. Director Gustavus Swift had become convinced that Children's needed a professional to coordinate its rather uncoordinated publicity. In 1940 he persuaded the Board to hire Mr. Harold E. Rainville for that purpose at $100 a month. The Public Relations Department developed slowly with some confusion as to its scope and purpose. In rapid succession two women followed Mr. Rainville as head. While Miss Marion Gridley held this post (from 1942-1947) she reported to the Auxiliary Board monthly the inches of newsprint and the number of pictures Children's had managed to get into the daily press. Under her successor, Miss Neola Northam (1948), the Department hit its stride as a vital force in the Hospital's affairs.

One story which caught the public's eye in November 1943 was the farewell tea for Dr. and Mrs. Aldrich. He left in January 1944 to head a research project in child development at the Mayo Clinic in Rochester.

Dr. Stanley Gibson was appointed the new Chief-of-Staff. His interest, like Dr. Aldrich's, centered on quality care for the "whole" child; his medical focus was rheumatic fever and congenital heart diseases. Since 1921, when Dr. Brennemann had brought him to Children's, he had worked in those fields. He was also deeply committed to quality education for the Hospital's medical students.

Through frequent visits to Auxiliary Board meetings and personal tours with the changing groups on its Visiting Committee, Dr. Gibson soon established an excellent rapport with the women. When his tours led, as they frequently did, to the cardiac wards, he explained the severe aftereffects of rheumatic fever and the great need for cardiac research, comparable to that in polio, stimulated by President Roosevelt's illness. The women reported that Dr. Gibson knew every patient by name, that smiles greeted him everywhere.

The side effects of the sulpha drugs and of penicillin, beginning to be studied in the mid-forties, was another subject about which he talked to the women. It was important to them—in 1945 Children's used 7,355 vials of penicillin at a cost of $6,608. During the war the

116

Hospital had been in the enviable position of having been designated as a penicillin distribution depot; after the war, it was buying supplies from pharmaceutical houses.

As the war drew to an end, doctors, in ever increasing numbers, began to return to Children's. Simultaneously, private patients almost doubled in number; by 1947 occupancy in those rooms was 91 percent—the highest in years. The Hospital was flooded with applications for residency; one year it refused 100. Returning doctors felt the need for refresher courses and the Hospital felt the need to strengthen departments weakened by staff shortages during the war. At Dr. Gibson's recommendation, Dr. Willis J. Potts, fresh from four years in the Pacific arena of war, was appointed chairman of the Department of Surgery, charged with making it equal to the Department of Medicine in services offered. Dr. Gibson also requested funds to improve the anesthesia unit, remodel the bronchoscopy operating room, provide more operating staff, and an assistant for himself.

If there was a feast of doctors, there was still a famine of nurses. They returned more slowly and they were restless. Those who had lived through the overworked war years at home and those returning from war service wanted higher salaries, a pension plan, good living conditions, a normal social life, and a definite place in the Hospital's program. The supply of nurses was further diminished by the withdrawal of Red Cross nurses' aides for assignment to veterans' hospitals. Children's raised salaries and devised a pension plan but still found it difficult to attract and hold a full staff. Even the head of the department changed often—there were five in the forties. The use and training of practical nurses began to be given serious consideration.

An examination of all salaries followed the rise in the nurses' salaries. Hughston McBain, President of Marshall Field & Co., had become a Director in 1945; he sent a man from the store's personnel department to help a Directors' committee review salaries both in the Hospital and in the community at large. Subsequently, the salaries were raised almost across the board. Inevitably, in 1947, the price of the Hospital's rooms rose too: fourteen dollars for private rooms and proportionate amounts for two-bed and four-bed rooms, and for ancillary services.

The last years of the forties were ones of "catching-up" and of planning for the future—with some degree of confidence. Children's had been held back for a long time. Dr. Gibson rejoiced in a full staff by the end of 1946, even a full roster of residents. Many of them, incidentally, were women—the war had given female medical students their opportunity. Income was higher, particularly from patients. Using some of the excess, the Hospital embarked on long postponed major repairs and alterations. Remodelling Martha Wilson, delayed in 1939 and again in 1941, was actually started in 1947 with the impetus of a gift from a social and philanthropic women's club.

The kindergarten opened again as the Sunbeam League turned their funds back from war bonds to a teacher's salary. And, after more than six years, a post graduate course in nursing with paid instructors was begun. Doctors began pushing for research in the cause and treatment of epilepsy, and in greater participation in public health programs, particularly in relation to tuberculosis.

As it planned for the future, a decision to affiliate with Northwestern University in 1946 had probably the most far-reaching effect of any of the Hospital's actions. It was a turning point in Children's history. The formal affiliation with the University of Chicago, dwindling in importance over the years, was terminated in the forties when that institution established its own Department of Pediatrics. But ties with Northwestern had been strengthening since 1931 when their first senior medical students had come to the Hospital for clinical experience and instruction.

Dr. Gibson was greatly delighted with the affiliation. "Under this arrangement," he announced, "the medical staff of the hospital will assist with the teaching of medical students from Northwestern." In time the mingling of hospital and medical school staff was complete: all of Children's full-time staff became members of Northwestern Medical School's faculty; the head of their Department of Pediatrics was Children's Chief-of-Staff; the University's department chairmen were heads of similar departments in medicine and surgery at the Hospital. It was, as Dr. Gibson predicted in 1946, an arrangement "beneficial to both institutions."

Disbanding the Junior Auxiliary Board was one change in the mid-forties which many regretted. During the war, plagued by dwindling attendance as young women moved to join their husbands in war work in Washington, New York, Boston, etc., the Junior Auxiliary had decided to hold meetings with the Social Service Committee. By 1945 the distinct lines of the Junior Auxiliary's activities had become blurred. The Social Service Department had absorbed some, the Hospital staff others. In November 1945 Mrs. Roy Flannery (Chairman from 1943) called the group together to discuss the Junior Auxiliary's role in the Hospital in post war times. Feeling that they were no longer useful as a separate entity, they voted to disband. Active members were added to other boards and committees; many remained as volunteers. The increasing need for the latter was a phenomenon of the forties as professional staff became scarce. The Annual Report for 1949 featured a "Salute to Volunteers."

War caused a spotlight to be turned on the emotional well-being of children. Absence of fathers, broken homes, mothers in the labor market, a national climate of suspense and fear—all had taken their toll. For years Children's had been aware of the relation of social problems to a child's illness whether they be fear of hospitalization, homesickness, or more deep-seated emotional disturbances. The Hospital had long brought a variety of disciplines to help diagnose and treat an illness: doctor, nurse, social worker, play therapist, dietician. After the war the "team approach" became something of a fad in hospitals; it had long been a way of life at Children's.

Children's concern for the emotional health of its patients was intensified in these years as the number of black children in the O.P. clinic increased sharply. Racial tension began to surface in Chicago and black families had to be handled sensitively. In 1947, the Welfare Council, reviewing Children's program and budget, asked why the Hospital had neither negro doctors nor residents on the staff. Miss Binner reported these questions to the Directors, adding "there is such a crying need in the community now for well-prepared people to care for members of their own race that I cannot see how we can disregard our community responsibility as a teaching hospital." In 1948 the first black physician, Dr. Oliver W. Crawford, joined the medical staff. It was 1950 before black nurses were accepted and housed in Nellie A. Black.

The American Pediatric Society in these years was also addressing the problem of the emotional well-being of children—particularly the newborn infant and the hospitalized child. A 1941 paper, "Lone-liness in Infants," helped revolutionize hospital care of babies. It held that isolation, not cross infection, was responsible for the high mortali-ty of the hospitalized baby. Rooming-in for mothers with newborn babies was tried and there was a growing trend to bring the pediatri-cian with his specialized knowledge into the picture before the babies left the hospital. A few years later everyone—parents, pediatri-cians, educators, et al.—were hotly debating "permissiveness": in diet, sleep habits, and general behavior. It was the age of Dr. Spock; he had written most of his book on infant care while he was in the navy.

Late in the forties a joint meeting of American and Canadian Pediatric Societies took as its theme "Humanizing Hospital Experiences." The symposium which followed, led by Dr. Milton Senn, discussed the psychotherapeutic role of the pediatrician. Dr. Aldrich was there from Mayo's to describe his program to foster adjustment in young, hospitalized children. Psychiatry was still a fairly new discipline of medicine; doctors in general felt its role in pediatrics still needed a great deal of research. Yet the concensus of the meeting was that "a large part of pediatric practice, whether in home, office, or hospital, is psychosomatic medicine. . . ."

In this climate, Children's lack of a Child Guidance Clinic was becoming something of an embarrassment. The peak of the Hospi-tal's achievement in the forties was in another area—the first "blue baby" operation of Dr. Willis Potts. In a three months' tour of surgical clinics before becoming head of Children's Department of Surgery, Dr. Potts had become interested in the Blalock operation used in correcting some forms of congenital heart disease. It consist-ed in joining one of the branches of the aorta to a pulmonary artery in order to carry more blood to the lungs. It was a successful surgical procedure but, unfortunately, it could not be used on young infants because their arteries were too small. Remembering the cyanotic babies brought to Children's, Dr. Potts decided to conduct a series of experiments to simplify and adapt the Blalock technique so that it could be used on infants. He called a former student, Dr. Sidney Smith (then a research fellow in pediatric surgery at Northwest-ern), asking him to join in the research, saying they might just be "chasing butterflies". Dr. Smith replied that he "loved chasing but-terflies" and the experiments began.

After dozens of trials and errors, they invented a clamp which would permit them to sew a baby's aorta and pulmonary artery together without obstructing the flow of blood during the operation. Using the clamp on laboratory animals was the next step. Caesar, the first dog to undergo the operation, became a hero around the Hospital as he recovered quickly and easily.

September 13, 1946, was a day of drama at Children's. Tension and excitement were high as Dr. Potts prepared to operate on a twenty-one-month-old baby girl—the first "blue baby" operation at the Hospital. When he reported success, the whole hospital "family" rejoiced—one young nurse is said to have danced, unrebuked, in the corridor. Local newspapers reported the triumph; the story spread across the country; and, as Dr. Bigler wrote, "Children's basked in reflected glory."

Dr. Potts served as Surgeon-in-Chief at Children's from 1946 to 1960. He was greatly beloved—his gentle manner and calm, reassuring approach to patients and their parents communicated his love of children. One small boy dubbed him "the tall man with the big hands"; every child reached out to him. He was the sort of man around whom legends grew: nurses told of his bursts of hymn singing during operations—"Christian walk carefully danger is nigh" at a critical point; "Oh how wonderful it is to walk in the path of the Savior," when an operation was successfully completed.

He had a way with words, was a witty speaker and writer, much in demand as both after his first successful operation. He was a superb fund raiser for the Hospital; it was said that at the end of one of his speeches there was "a tear in every eye, a check book in every hand." Probably his most quoted speech was *The Heart of a Child*. Its closing paragraph became famous:

The mystical heart of a child is a precious and beautiful thing. It is marred only by wounds of a thoughtless and not too intelligent world. In a physical sense the heart is a tough organ; a marvelous mechanism that, mostly with repairs, will give valiant pumping service up to a hundred years. In an emotional sense it is susceptible to wounds of indifference, thoughtlessness, and neglect and during episodes of illness is especially vulnerable. The heart of a child is mysteriously moulded by parents, teachers, playmates, and all those with whom it comes in contact. Physicians wish during those short but violent episodes of illness to avoid wounds that will leave irreparable scars. I am convinced that the heart of a child sunned by love, security, and understanding will be able to withstand the storms of illness and pain.

Dr. John Bigler was appointed Chief-of-Staff on Dr. Gibson's retirement late in 1946; Dr. Martin Hardy became Medical Director of the O. P. Department. Dr. Bigler had long ties with the Hospital; he had been a resident there and more recently had directed the O. P. Department under Dr. Aldrich and Dr. Gibson. His immediate goals, he told the Auxiliary Board, were to expand the laboratories and rearrange the surgical suite for greater efficiency. No small pressure had been put on the latter by the 240 "blue baby" operations performed at Children's in a little over two years. He hoped the space of the communicable disease unit, closed since 1941 when other community resources had developed, could be used for surgical research and staff offices and could also include an animal experimental operating room. A few months later, Public Relations was urging the Hospital to stay out of the animal vivisection controversy!

It was about this time that Dr. Potts wrote *Caesar Speaks,* describing wittily, through the dog's eyes, what really happened to some animals in research laboratories. By that time Caesar had been given a medal and a bronze plaque hung in the Hospital, inscribed:

To
CAESAR-DOG HERO
Who
Served in the Development
Of the Blue Baby Operations
CHILDREN'S MEMORIAL
HOSPITAL
For Distinguished Service to Humanity
NATIONAL SOCIETY
For MEDICAL RESEARCH

Not all of the Hospital's problems, however, were open to dramatic solutions. Two difficult ones faced the Social Service and Nursing departments when Dr. Bigler became Chief-of-Staff in 1949. Criteria for admission to the clinics was one. Established in the depression years of the thirties, they badly needed an objective review. Many doctors were challenging the definition of free care. Should the man who preferred to go on the recently inaugurated unemployment compensation rather than take a low paying job be entitled to free care at the expense of a doctor's livelihood? In a study of Chicago's free clinics a few years earlier, the Chicago Medical Society had suggested some guidelines for eligibility. They had set up an eligibility budget for food, clothing, and shelter— above the subsistence level but below the maintenance level of a self-supporting family. This budget, reviewed every six months by economic experts in the light of the cost of living, had become Children's yardstick for admission. But the Hospital had added a few qualifications of its own: the severity of medical need, whether the case would be long- or short-term, whether the patient was ambulatory, and whether treatment could be found closer to a patient's home. Patients were also rejected if their families were "over income," if they were under a private doctor's care, if they lived outside the Hospital's designated geographical area, or were under treatment at another hospital. Geographical lines were important to a Community Fund hospital. The Fund was committed to the medical care of the indigent and low-income family in Chicago only; Children's bore the expense of those from the suburbs or beyond.

Another problem was the acceptance of the licensed practical nurse. Chicago's Manley School offered basic training to young women in this field; and in the late forties the Board of Education certified the Hospital's six-week training course in pediatric nursing for Manley graduates. Children's trained forty of these women in 1948-1949 and cautiously accepted eight for work in the Hospital. Miss Audrey Short, new director of nursing in 1949, found they fitted well into her plans. She was actively reorganizing her department, trying to boost morale and bring the graduate nurse corps up to quota. Within the year the thirteen-week course in pediatric nursing was once more attracting large numbers of students—420 from fourteen affiliates (fifty more than in the previous year). The concept and philosophy of this course was, she wrote, an understanding of the whole child: his mental, social, and emotional needs as well as his physical ones. . . ." The course for the licensed practical nurse had the same emphasis. Both also stressed the team approach.

The general postwar forward movement at the Hospital made some minor irritations bearable. When an Illinois law prohibited coloring margarine yellow, small patients rebelled. They would not eat white margarine—lard, they called it. A flurry of writing-to-your-Congressmen merely vented the writers' irritation; the law was not repealed and the Hospital had to use butter, the "high-priced spread."

Children's had to accept, as well, a new transportation line which took noisy, clanging trolleys completely around the Hospital triangle. Board members appealed in vain to alter the route; Chicago had become too big and impersonal for such approaches.

CHAPTER X

Growth in
the Fifties

1950–1960

By 1950 the stresses of wartime were over and Children's was running fairly normally. But status quo had never been its hallmark; before the year was out, change was again the order of the day. Miss Binner and Mrs. Jennings resigned after twenty-six and twenty-one years of service respectively. Delbert Price was appointed Administrator; Mildred Jennings and Marie White became Directors of separate O.P. and Social Service departments—they had been administered as one unit for many years.

The make-up of the School of Nursing Committee under Mrs. William Mitchell's leadership changed as well in 1950. Like the Social Service Committee, this large committee had for many years acted like a separate board with almost complete autonomy—although it reported regularly to the Auxiliary Board. Its members had always been elected by the Board of Directors, not appointed by the Woman's Board as other committees were. Reflecting its wide interests, it added John J. Wilson, Jr., Dr. Bigler and representatives from the Chicago Board of Education and the Public Health nursing staff to the core of eight Auxiliary Board members. This broader membership enabled the committee to keep in touch with community problems and projects as well as with those at home. Children's own Dr. John Reichert, for example, was working with a Joint Committee on Health Services to the School Child to create a sound community health program—with emphasis on community. The Hospital's clinics had an important role in achieving such a program.

The immediate challenge for Marie White in social service was measuring Children's against the recommendations of the mid-century 1950 White House Conference. They were focussed, over-whelmingly, on assuring the emotional health of a child. Five professional organizations (social workers, including psychiatric, medical and group, and schools of social work) had joined to implement the recommendations in Chicago. It was obvious to all that Children's lacked an essential service—a child guidance clinic.

Dozens of voices had proclaimed that lack over the years. Dr. Brennemann, in spite of reservations, had listed it as an unmet need in 1941. Doctors Aldrich and Gibson as well as successive heads of social service, O. P., and nursing, had seldom failed to mention it in annual reports to the Boards. Space had actually been provided for it in Thomas D. Jones. And in 1949 the Welfare Council had pulled together a conference on the subject. With a psychiatric consultant from the office of the Regional Medical Director of U.S. Public Health Services and Albert Ropchan from the health division of the Council, Dr. Bigler and other Hospital personnel discussed steps to be taken in opening a guidance clinic. Out of that conference had come a statement of needs and facilities. The Hospital had sent that document to the National Institute of Mental Health, hoping to receive a grant.

There the matter rested in 1950 when Dr. Bigler wrote Mr. Wilson to express the medical staff's eagerness to plan the clinic. Mr. Wilson's reply advised caution—let Delbert Price settle in as Administrator and let all consider every side of the question. Money was a stumbling block; it was estimated that at least $30,000 would be needed to open the clinic and more in each subsequent year. The Board of Directors inched forward slightly in May 1950 when they voted approval in principle. But that approval was not accompanied by an item in the budget to start the clinic.

At the May meeting the Directors had approved several other potentially expensive projects: expanding the pathology laboratory and research facilities with Dr. Joseph Boggs as a full-time Director and permitting Dr. Mila Pierce to admit three leukemia patients for expensive treatment with a new drug, ACTH. It was estimated that the latter would cost from $2,000 to $10,000. The Board had also agreed to expand the Speech Clinic since, after a long search, a competent director, Dr. Harold Westlake, had been found to guide it.

Perhaps, in the face of these specific demands, the more nebulous requests of a child guidance clinic were more easily postponed. At any rate it was not included in expansion plans for 1951. A sharp rise in polio that year, coupled with a low bed occupancy, led to accepting a greater number of polio patients for after-care. Even though it meant instituting an inservice training program, the Hospital decided to use its own nurses for the services. After-care was expensive and operating costs rose, particularly when nurses' hours were, coincidentally, shortened to forty-four and later, to forty hours per week.

The Hospital also picked up the expense of the tuberculosis case-finding project (earlier funded by the Community Fund), opened a Tumor Clinic, and established a neurosurgical division.

Opening a Congenital Heart Center in 1952 broadened Children's cardiac services. The federal government encouraged this action with an initial grant of $30,000 to cover the costs for thirty children for one year. The Illinois Services for Crippled Children agreed to act as a referral center since patients from all over the state would be eligible for service. Approving the Center, the Directors noted, meant accepting federal and probably state aid. As always they were not eager to do this but the need was great and could not be met with Hospital funds.

The physical plant was improved by a passageway between the Agnes Wilson and Maurice Porter pavilions. Widespread redecoration brightened waiting rooms, wards, private rooms, offices, and corridors with new lights, fairy tale murals, and brilliant stretches of color.

Financing these projects and improvements strained resources. Contributions from individuals and organizations became increasingly important. The Marlene Appelbaum Auxiliary, for example, gave a special gift to buy ACTH and cortisone, used in increasing quantities. The Federation of Women's Organizations bought two ceiling projectors and ten films to entertain patients forced to remain flat on their backs. Members of the Auxiliary Board paid for most of the redecorating and for new clothes for ambulatory patients. Colored shorts and T-shirts for the boys and attractive dresses for the girls added a warm, gay note to the Hospital's appearance. Volunteers gave time and talent: one young artist decorated two patient rooms with storybook murals. Others worked in the laundry in a crisis, while three Board members substituted for Dr. Bigler's vacationing secretary. Memorial gifts for Mrs. James Hutchins (President of the Auxiliary Board 1941–1944), who died in 1952, were used to remodel the lobby of Martha Wilson. In the same year Mrs. Frederick Rawson furnished a new waiting room as a memorial to her mother, Mrs. Francis Kennett. And, in its thirty-fourth year, the White Elephant Shop found it had passed the $1 million mark in total contributions to Children's. Raising room rates to seventeen dollars for private and eleven dollars for semi-private rooms and varying amounts for operating rooms for cardiac and endoscopic patients added to income in the fifties as well. Somehow a way was always found for necessities and those extras that expressed tender, loving care for the children.

A child guidance clinic seemed really assured in 1952, Children's seventy-fifth year of caring for sick children. The Community Fund earmarked an extra grant of $7,625 for it; the Woods Charitable Fund pledged $5,000 for 1952 and $10,000 for 1953 and 1954, and the Junior League voted to make it their next special project. An annual budget for $40,000 was thus assured for three years.

Encouraged, Dr. Bigler invited Dr. Milton Senn, Director of the Child Study Center at Yale (he had led the symposium on the psychotherapeutic role of the pediatrician at the APS meeting in the forties) and Dr. William Lanford, Clinical Professor of Psychiatry at Columbia University and on the staff of New York's Babies Hospital, to meet with Board members, appropriate medical staff, and administration to chart the setting up of a guidance clinic. The discussion—informally, in small groups, at dinner, and at the symposium—ranged widely from identifying patients, the relation of pediatrician and psychiatrist, of parent and psychiatrist, the place of nurse, social worker, and volunteer in the clinic, to preventive psychiatry. The experts warned of unusual difficulties in adding this clinic to the Hospital's other services, but they also clarified two important points. The Director must be a qualified pediatrician as well as a psychiatrist, and teaching allied professions dealing with children must have equal priority with treating patients.

The search for a director began—it proved to be a long and far from easy task. While it continued there was a veritable explosion of activity in other fields at the Hospital. Research, underlying much of this activity, was a sign of the times. In abeyance during the long war years, it began to surface in the late forties and in the fifties with compelling force. With this research came specialization. Of the 105 medical staff members at the Hospital in 1954, a total of 48 were specialists; in the department of surgery alone there were 12 specialized fields.

It was, moreover, easy to find grants to support research in this period. The National Institutes of Health and the National Science Foundation stood ready to encourage research in broad medical fields. Smaller foundations, focussing on specific diseases such as heart, epilepsy, spastic paralysis, et al., had funds to support investigations into them.

Children's was quick to take advantage of the situation. With a grant from the Spastic Paralysis Foundation of Kiwanis International it began a research program in that field. Cardiac research was promoted by a heart catheterization unit (funded by the Seabury Foundation), and by a joint program with La Rabida in occupational therapy for heart patients. The former opened the way for more efficient diagnosis of heart malformations. Cardiac surgery was advanced by the establishment of an artery vessel bank to process and store arteries. The Chicago Heart Association made that facility possible with a gift of $1,000.

An electroencephalographic machine, bought by the Service Club of Chicago, advanced research in epilepsy. Adding a biochemist and an expert in viruses to the staff set off a series of inquiries into viral diseases.

The appointment of Dr. David Hsia as Director of Research in 1958 confirmed the beginning of a great surge of basic research at Children's—one that continues today. By 1959 the department numbered forty-seven: twenty-two doctors, two dentists, seven senior scientists, sixteen research technicians and assistants. Their research was supported by $210,000 in grants; one-third from private foundations. Two years later sixty-five men and women were engaged in research, and grants had more than doubled ($422,748).

"It is only through research that pediatric knowledge increases," Dr. Bigler wrote that year. The Hospital's activities bore witness to that observation. Every specialized service had a research component: bronchology, dentistry, gynecology, ophthalmology, otolaryngology, neurosurgery, orthopedics, plastic surgery, pediatric radiology, and others. Some were relatively new fields: pediatric anesthesia, for example, was in its infancy, struggling to develop a technique which would put a child to sleep so prepared psychologically that his ordeal would not be remembered as a nightmare in later life. Pediatric radiology was just gaining status as a specialty in the care of children. Plastic surgery was just beginning to learn how to correct burn defects. Even pediatric surgery had come to the fore fairly recently—only fifteen of the fifty-four pediatric hospitals in the United States had adequate surgical facilities. Dr. Potts recalled that just twenty years earlier, Children's had averaged forty operations a month; in 1960 the average was 174.

Children's was still thought of as primarily a clinical institution, but research was challenging that image.

When the Child Guidance Clinic finally opened in June 1954, Dr. Bigler noted with satisfaction that Children's now had all facilities—medical, surgical, psychiatric, as well as adequate laboratory and X-ray departments, to give "almost every diagnostic and treatment procedure that may be necessary." The Director, Dr. Henry H. Fineberg, was assisted by Dr. Irving Leiden, a clinic psychologist, two psychiatric social workers, a group social worker, a staff psychologist, and a secretary. The clinic announced three objectives: diagnostic and therapeutic service to patients; education of personnel attending patients; and research in psychiatry, psychology, and the psychological aspects of physical illness. To promote integration of the new service with other hospital services, the guidance staff went on rounds with Dr. Bigler each morning. It also offered consultation to in-patient and out-patient services, held an orientation class for each incoming nurses' group as well as for residents and social workers. It helped train, as well, a hand-picked group of Junior League volunteers to be used in the Clinic under the supervision of the group therapist.

The new clinic was a great success. Dr. Fineberg was much in demand as a speaker and writer on its goals and procedures. Group therapy was still a novelty in those days and many community organizations were eager to find out what light the clinic would shed on the behavioral problems of children enduring long hospitalization.

A 1940s remodeled lobby.

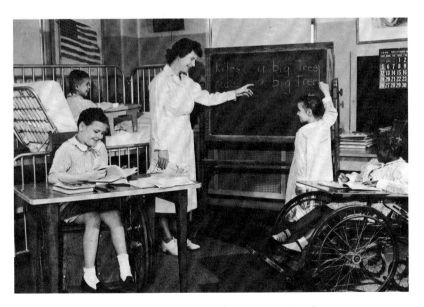

The children did not have to miss school.

Dr. Willis J. Potts, Caesar, and the first "blue baby."

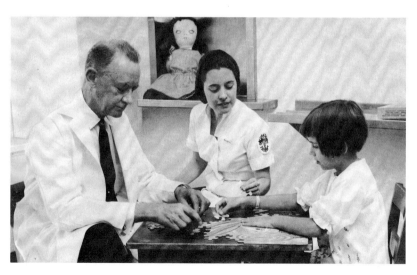

Dr. Potts found time to play.

Party time included some art therapy.

Outpatient clinics served growing numbers of community families.

Entertainment ranged from circus elephants to horse-drawn wagons.

Fun and games with volunteers have always been a part of caring.

A tribute to Dr. Bigler by famous cartoonist Carey Orr.

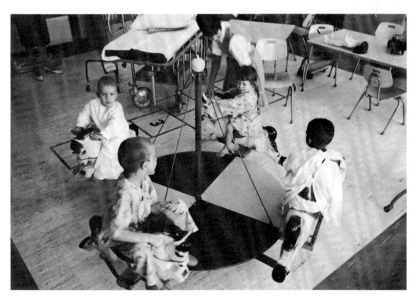

Playroom activities made the Hospital seem more like home.

Holidays always brought nice surprises.

To fulfill the educational goal of the clinic, the Hospital assigned each resident to one month's service there. The University of Chicago and Loyola (a new affiliate) sent psychiatric social workers for field work. And the psychology departments of both Northwestern and the University of Chicago sent students to study the emotional development and disorders of children.

The Child Guidance Clinic had become an integral part of Children's services when Dr. Fineberg resigned. Dr. Jerome Schulman was appointed his successor in July 1956.

The growth years of the early fifties saw a turnover in the Board of Directors. John Wilson was named Honorary Chairman in 1952 when John Jay Borland became President. He was succeeded by Dexter Cummings. The membership of the Board was enlarged from fifteen to eighteen on a three-year rotating basis.

During Mrs. William Mitchell's presidency, the Auxiliary Board in 1954 asked the Directors to change its name to the Woman's Board. The request was granted. The women also set three-year terms for their officers and committee heads. Mrs. Louis Watermulder succeeded Mrs. Mitchell in 1956.

An important staff change in 1954 was the appointment of Alice Saar as Director of the O.P. Department. She provided continuity in that key position throughout the turbulent years of the sixties.

Admission ages were raised in the late fifties to include sixteen-year-olds, and visiting hours were extended from 3 to 7 p.m. The longer hours permitted mothers to feed supper to their children and gave time for formal and informal conferences with doctors, nurses, and social workers. All personnel began to wear identification badges—the Hospital had outgrown its family atmosphere. And again the salaries of nurses and residents were raised.

Certainly in part as a result of this growth, Neola Northam asked that public relation policies be formulated. The thrust of the document, approved after ten months' consideration, was to establish one channel of information from the Hospital to the public —from doctors' articles to fund raising activities, all would flow through the Public Relations Department. "Dignity", not "sensationalism," was to be its hallmark. The statement reflected how big an operation Children's Memorial Hospital had become.

Within these guidelines the Public Relations Department told the Hospital's story with infinite variety. In 1953 the Woman's Board made Public Relations a standing committee. Mrs. Elliott Donnelley was its first Chairman. Under her spirited and imaginative leadership, the committee worked closely with Miss Northam to keep Children's in the public eye. Mrs. Howard Gillette continued the good work in 1955.

The use of the volunteer kept pace with the Hospital's growth. Dr. Bigler and the staff as a whole strongly supported their use—"they can do anything" was the usual comment. New fields opened as services expanded: the blood bank, the Spastic Paralysis Clinic, the polio after-care unit, play therapy in the Child Guidance Clinic. Puppetry was an exciting new volunteers' tool in the Audiology Department. Night volunteers were sought for those difficult hours when children were fed and prepared for bed.

Under the able and determined leadership of Mrs. Maxwell, Mrs. Watermulder, Mrs. Vilas, Miss Elsa Eisendrath, and Mrs. Uihlen (officers of the Volunteer Services Committee in the early fifties), the volunteer program was reorganized to meet the changing needs of the decade. Training classes were upgraded, placement made more effective. Always it was emphasized that volunteers *supplemented*, not *supplanted* professionals. The fame of Children's volunteer program caused the Chicago Council of Volunteer Directors to invite Mrs. Watermulder to join them. She was the only nonprofessional member, but they told her the Hospital had as professional a volunteer group as any in the city. Mrs. Maxwell was called the "patron saint" of the city-wide volunteer movement. Volunteers were given attractive green smocks to wear (jewellry was forbidden), and were honored with pins and certificates as they completed one hundred hours of service in prescribed periods. In 1956 the first professional Director of Volunteer Services, Mrs. Alfred Leiserson from Boston Children's Hospital, was hired. After a year, she was succeeded by Kloe Juers.

A non-medical field for volunteers after 1951 was the Hospital Shop, a brainchild of the Woman's Board. A generous gift of Mrs. Frederick Rawson, supplemented by contributions from other Board members, made possible redecorating and equipping an old dining room in NAB; the Hospital's own workmen built a counter for the shop end and a screen to separate it from the snack end. The

Shop in the beginning was run entirely by volunteers—in the first year sixty-four women worked 4,273 hours. Mrs. William O. Hunt was the first Shop Committee Chairman; other Board members selected attractive toys for the Shop, still others were responsible for planning menus and ordering food for the snack bar—with the advice of the head dietician. Mrs. Robert Carr, who handled the latter chore for several years, says she never knew there were so many ways to vary a basic cream cheese sandwich!

The Shop was begun as a service to visiting parents and the Hospital personnel; it was not expected to be a great money raiser. It did, however, turn over modest profits to the Hospital: from $1,500 to $5,000 in the first four years. The women were serving food to about one hundred persons daily by that time and felt they had earned a real place in the life of the Hospital.

The White Elephant Shop, on the other hand, continued to net large profits each year. Board members still supplemented the work of the manager and a few paid clerks. They still collected and priced goods and headed up special sales: book, spring dresses, dressmaker, Christmas, hats, and others. One year when hats were "in," they sold $2,000 worth of Bes-Ben creations in one day. Another year they created White Elephant perfume by combining the contents of twenty half-filled bottles of expensive perfume and bottling it in attractive small flasks. The Board still heard monthly reports, often telling of "great" donations: a pair of Chinese ceramic elephants, a Spanish toreador's cap embroidered in silver, three fur jackets, and a sable scarf.

The women were worried in 1953 when urban renewal forced them to leave 27 East Ohio and set up a new shop at 411 North La-Salle. Would their customers find the new shop? Sears Roebuck & Company helped arrange their new commodious interior; they held a grand opening with great newspaper coverage and ended the year with a gift of $43,000 to the Hospital—$1,000 more than in the previous year. In their larger quarters they introduced the 411 Shop, a specialty shop for brand name clothes and better furs—a money maker from the start. The Shop was still a focal point for the women; in the midst of a bewildering growth of medical services it remained peculiarly their own enterprise.

Pressed for money, the Woman's Board tried another benefit in

133

1957. With the help of the Directors they sold a large block of seats for the National Curling Championship matches. That effort raised $15,000. They also experimented, with the help of R.R. Donnelley, the Chicago-based printer, in a broadly based direct mail campaign. This venture was moderately successful but never replaced the personal touch in fund raising.

As Children's neared its seventy-fifth year of service (1957), it looked at its past and sought directions for its future. It questioned again, as it had on other big anniversaries, its role in Chicago's medical resources, its location, and its organization.

Dr. Bigler requested department heads to list their needs—and desires—and he appointed a committee to examine the Hospital's medical organizations. The direction for the future, inherent in the detailed recommendations of the department heads, was summed up in Dr. Bigler's report to the Board of Directors in 1957:

Several years ago doubt was expressed as to whether the specialized children's hospital would continue to be needed. It was advocated that all general hospitals develop pediatric departments, thereby decreasing the number of patients available to a hospital like ours. Actually, the reverse has been the trend. Competent and experienced pediatric resident staffs have never become available to the general hospital, specialized laboratory facilities became too expensive and each general hospital could not attract the large number of specially trained medical personnel to carry on an effective medical, surgical, and laboratory program.

In contrast, The Children's Memorial Hospital does have all of these facilities and it has developed a staff of specially trained medical personnel. We must be prepared to care for the infant a few hours old as well as the 15-year old child no matter what the emergency or how rare the medical problem. Your entire medical staff is convinced that The Children's Memorial Hospital will continue as an indispensable medical institution and that as we have been required to grow in the past, we will be required to grow in the future.

Our present hospital buildings permit us no further expansion. In fact, at the present we are unable to do many of the procedures that have become necessary. You are all familiar with the progress medicine has made. Unless we participate in this progress we will slowly regress.

The Board of Directors, in the meantime, had also appointed a planning committee to consider: (1) the physical plant; (2) desirable staff expansion; and (3) the need for expanded research facilities. On the recommendation of this, and the medical staff's organization committee, the Directors voted to retain the Chief-of-Staff type of organization. They also decided that Children's should stay at its present location, constructing there the buildings necessary to keep pace with the growing demands of a pediatric hospital.

Construction to satisfy a few of these demands had actually begun in 1955. A seventh floor had been added to NAB for additional nurses' rooms. And architects had been asked to submit drawings for a building to be erected on the site of the Maurice Porter Memorial, the oldest (1908) building on the Hospital campus.

Other considerations, however, shelved major construction plans for well over a year. Inevitably pressure for larger quarters continued to mount in that time. The O.P. Department was particularly hard hit. The expanded Dental and the new Child Guidance Clinics attracted hundreds of new patients. Many of them were the children of black migrant workers and of Puerto Ricans who arrived in Chicago in increasing numbers in the mid-fifties. Miss Saar reported that the clinics treated 12,458 children one year (5,317 new patients) and 13,600 the next.

The new divisions of clinical biochemistry, directed by Dr. David Hsia after 1958, requested space for a growing genetic clinic, and the time was ripe for a mental retardation clinic. In 1957 the U.S. Children's Bureau promised a grant of $133,500 (over three years) if Children's would open the latter.

An affiliation with the Martha Washington Home for Dependent Crippled Children in 1957 presupposed more space. The Home gave the Hospital $35,200 to offset the cost of an orthopedic operating room suite, together with a promise of $2,000 a year to care for indigent orthopedic patients. When more room would be available, the Home pledged to endow ten orthopedic beds in perpetuity ($100,000); they gave $20,000 for two beds at the outset. All of these facilities would have to be housed in a new building.

Most of the policy questions of the fifties were addressed by the Board of Directors, not the Woman's Board. For over fifty years the Hospital had not deviated from the policy adopted in 1903 of having separate men's and women's boards. But in the forties, and more frequently in the fifties, the Directors invited the President of the Woman's Board, the Chairmen of the Social Service, Nursing, and White Elephant Shop committees to their meetings. Often these

135

women knew facts essential to the Directors' decisions. In 1954 the Directors went a step further. They elected Mrs. Herbert Kennedy (President of the Woman's Board 1949–1952), Mrs. John B. Wilson, Jr., and Mrs. William Mitchell (President 1953–1955) full Directors with one, two, and three-year terms. In 1956 Mrs. Watermulder (President 1956–1957) and Mrs. Donnelley (President 1958–1959) took the places of Mrs. Kennedy and Mrs. Wilson. Women have continued to serve as Directors since that time—the President of the Woman's Board has been an ex-officio Director.

And it was a woman—Mrs. Donnelley—who in May 1957 reintroduced the question of a new building. She urged the Directors to dust off the building plans presented almost a year earlier and make some decisions. John Jay Borland was appointed Chairman of a new building committee; it was asked to report in June. It did, agreeing that something "must be done" but asking, must that something be so "expensive" and "expansive?" The architects' plans were passed to Dr. Bigler and the medical staff to set priorities. But the Directors still felt they needed an objective survey of community needs—in other words to establish whether a specialty hospital was really needed in Chicago (in spite of the doctors' reassurances) before they expanded.

Dr. Charles F. Willinsky, former President of the American Hospital Association and of the American Public Health Association agreed to do the job. His careful community evaluation and recommendations were in the hands of President Dexter Cummings in November 1957. His report expressed a solid conviction that a specialty hospital *was* sorely needed in Chicago even if pediatric units were developed in general hospitals. Pediatric research, for one thing, flourished best in a specialty setting. He recommended expanding Children's program on the grounds of a medical school if the present plant could be sold advantageously. If not, facilities should be enlarged on the present site. Beds should be added (to 225, possibly 240) and space found for expanded research—possibly in a new building. The cost would probably run as high as $5 million. He saw three roads to balancing, or at least containing, the budget: (1) increased endowment; (2) increase in third-party payments through insurance plans; and (3), greater government responsibility for the medically indigent. He advised strengthening ties with Northwestern Medical School and setting a retirement age for doctors (in December the Directors voted to give doctors emeritus standing at age sixty-five).

Many decisions faced the Boards as they finished their painstaking examination. They noted that in their seventy-fifth year of service, Children's had cared for 21,168 patients, performed 3,931 operations, given 16,921 X-ray examinations, made 104,816 laboratory examinations, filled 58,398 prescriptions, served 460,350 meals, and washed 1,214,860 pounds of laundry. Free care had cost $937,358—56 percent of the total cost of care. Its professional staff included 160 physicians and surgeons, 190 graduate and student nurses, and 465 other personnel.

What lay ahead in the sixties? Dr. Bigler's report as Chief-of-Staff in the seventy-fifth anniversary year noted the breadth of services which had developed over the years; it also commented on the Hospital's unchanging determination to meet the medical needs of children no matter what that stand had meant to generations of boards, physicians, and supporters:

The Children's Memorial Hospital today offers entire child care with all its complexities and ramifications. Because of compassion and love of children, the courage and foresight of the founders in meeting the medical needs of infants and children have been equalled through the years by the many men and women who have served on the boards and committees of the hospital, by the friends who have given financial support from their great or small means, and by the city's best known physicians. Let us hope that this philosophy will be our guide for the future.

PART FOUR   *1960–1981*

---

*"The hospital of the future will
have to be redefined legally,
medically, morally and
politically. . . . What a hospital
can do will have to be
determined by the community at
large, which is paying the bill."*

Overleaf: The White Hat volunteer program.

CHAPTER XI

The Sixties
Bring Changes

1958–1970

No ONE, perhaps, could have anticipated the
challenge to that philosophy in the turbulent years of social change
in the sixties. The Board of Directors seemed to have a clear mandate as it faced a building program under its new President, Hughston M. McBain, in 1958.

Two new committees were appointed: Planning with Charles
Folds as Chairman, and Ways and Means with Errett Van Nice and
John Borland as Co-chairmen. The first worked with the architectural firm of Schmidt, Garden, and Erikson to design a building—or
buildings—to house the great variety of Children's needs from
laboratories and clinic space to cafeteria, gift shops, and a meditation room. Many designs were submitted and modified before the
Committee recommended, and the Directors accepted, a plan to
erect two buildings—one for patient care and administrative offices,
the other for research. Since land was at a premium, it seemed best
to raze Maurice Porter and Agnes Wilson, two of the oldest and
least efficient Hospital buildings, and build on their sites. Entrances
to the buildings would be on Children's Plaza, a new street cutting
across the hospital triangle from Fullerton to Lincoln Avenue.

A grand kick-off dinner was held at the Hilton Hotel in October
1959; closed circuit television carried the message of expansion
from Dr. Bigler and Dr. Potts. An added excitement was the appearance of Dr. Potts' first "blue baby," now a young teenager.
Construction began. A year later, in November 1960, three small patients in hard hats took part in the symbolic ground breaking. The
Annual Report that year featured a four-year-old patient, Michael,

141

sporting a hard hat and carrying a shovel. The picture was titled "A Hole is to Dig . . . A Hospital is to Help."

At this point the Development Committee (also called variously Ways and Means, Finance, Campaign Fund) set a goal of $5.5 million to be raised by 1961. By December 31, 1960, they reached—and indeed surpassed—the goal with gifts and pledges amounting to $5,774,323. But the Development Committee had by this time enlarged *its* goals—the Medical Staff's pleas for more space seemed always to outstrip the amount planned. It would be necessary to redesign and modernize the interiors of the Thomas D. Jones and Martha Wilson buildings to accommodate various services. A new emergency unit and parking facilities had to be included as well in a complete program of expansion. An estimated cost of $7,465,254 was accepted by the Directors, and the Development Committee was authorized to let contracts.

Faced with a campaign of this magnitude the Directors hired their first Director of Development. President McBain had observed in 1959 that for the first time in its seventy-eight years of existence Children's was making an appeal to the public for capital funds. Now it was going back again for $2 million more—conceivably $3 million if all parts of the program were to be accomplished.

The Development Committee, under the leadership of Mr. Folds and later Mr. John Sturgis, worked with several professional fund raisers in the sixties. It was not an easy task, and the fund rose slowly. Children's told its story to businessmen, heads of foundations, and civic leaders over lunch at the Chicago Club. Directors invited key members of the community to tour the Hospital with Dr. Bigler or, after his resignation in 1961, with the new Chief-of-Staff, Dr. Robert Lawson. Films were developed to dramatize the Hospital's work. The committee divided the campaign into stages: (1) for new construction, (2) for altering Thomas D. Jones and Martha Wilson.

When the dinner honoring Dr. Potts on his retirement in 1960 raised $56,837, the Directors were strengthened in their belief that knowing what the Hospital did was the quickest way to a gift. They worked in teams and as individuals. They welcomed a substantial gift of $512,000 from the Martha Washington Home for Dependent Crippled Children—it would be used to establish the Martha Washington Orthopedic Center on the second floor of one of the new buildings. They instituted a more rapid depreciation of buildings to add to the fund, and estimated the amount of the Hospital's unrestricted funds and expected legacies which could be used to meet the goal. Mr. Sturgis in particular urged that new Board members be elected who would touch new geographical areas and hence new sources of money.

One avenue of money raising the Directors, as usual, approached reluctantly. In 1959, $300,000 in federal money had been earmarked to establish seventeen clinical research centers in the U.S. The Directors debated over several months whether they should apply to the National Institutes of Health for a share of these funds. The decision to do so was voted on at their annual meeting in October 1959—it was not unanimous: one director abstained, one voted "no." All were aware they were broaching a new, unknown source of support; most were apprehensive largely because they feared that government strings would be attached to the grant. It was five years before the Hospital received an initial grant of $217,000 and established a Clinical Research Center in the new research building. There doctors began to study organ transplants, rare metabolic disorders, kidney infections, and tumors.

The Hospital in the sixties saw the development of the research it had anticipated earlier, particularly in the fields of biochemistry, genetics, cardiology, hematology, and psychiatry. Dr. Hsia was investigating the carriers of hereditary diseases and the mechanism responsible for jaundice in the newborn. Dr. Robert Miller and Dr. Milton Paul in the new Division of Cardiology were studying cardiovascular defects and pulmonary hypertension. When Dr. Mila Pierce joined the Department of Hematology (directed by Dr. Irving Schulman), research was stepped up in hemalytic diseases with radioactive isotopes, leukemia, and the efficacy of new drugs. Dr. Jerome Schulman's research centered on the diagnosis and treatment of children with learning disabilities.

Dr. Bigler had been pondering the role of research at Children's for a number of years—particularly since Dr. Hsia's appointment. When he wrote his last annual report before retiring in 1961, he tried to put the whole matter into perspective. He recalled Dr. Brennemann's definition of Children's as "primarily a clinical institution" devoted to patient care and education. Research and the rapid

143

development of pediatric specialties had forced Dr. Bigler to evaluate that definition and to redefine the role of the Hospital in the sixties. The Hospital's Boards had shared in this task. The importance of research both as a tool for improved patient care and for teaching in the changing climate in pediatrics was unmistakable. Dr. Bigler had concluded that only by according research equal importance to patient care and teaching, could Children's become a leading pediatric hospital. That conclusion had been, Dr. Bigler felt, the underlying philosophy of his last years as Chief-of-Staff.

At Children's, accepting research as a third partner in its program meant planning for more space and finding more money. It explains the Directors' application for federal health research funds in 1959 and their search for foundation grants throughout the sixties. There were many of the latter. The Field Foundation supported an in-patient psychiatric unit to strengthen the Hospital's work (both treatment and teaching) with children who had an emotional component in their illness; and later underwrote a study on the effect of hospitalization on a child. The Kennedy Foundation supported research on mental retardation and on autistic children. When The Margaret Etter Crêche affiliated with the Hospital in 1967, its initial gift of $45,000 and subsequent generous annual contributions enabled Dr. Jerome Schulman to establish a learning center in his department through which he studied the diagnosis and treatment of children with learning disabilities.

The John A. Hartford grant of $309,000 advanced the study of urinary tract malformations. Viral and endocrinology research was heightened by a grant from the Brain Research Foundation; that of rheumatism and arthritis by money from the National Institutes of Health.

When the research building was dedicated in October 1963, Dr. Bigler was not there to help celebrate. He had died nine months earlier. But his portrait by William Draper, a memorial gift of friends and associates, hung in the Bigler Auditorium, where a symposium on the scientist and the child was held on dedication day.

Moving into the new building was a carefully planned and smoothly executed maneuver. Research scarcely missed a beat. In 1964–1965 Children's invested 40 percent more in research than in the preceding year; 1,404 percent more than ten years before. To meet the ever-increasing demand for services, Dr. Boggs' laboratories were divided that year into divisions, each headed by a pediatric specialist.

Dr. Boggs' own pioneer research in hepatitis and liver disease was funded through a contract with the U.S. Defense Department. Federal agencies also supported other research in the laboratories: the Research and Development Command of the U.S. Army; the Office of the Surgeon General of the Army; Health, Education, and Welfare; and the National Institutes of Health.

Research at Children's often provided good publicity for fund raising. In 1965–1966 the Public Relations Department (under a new Director, Blossom Porte) pulled together a list of fields in which the Hospital was active. It was impressive: organ transplants (Children's first was in 1964) and their concomitant, the preservation of whole organs; dialysis of patients with chronic renal disease; the development of drugs for respiratory therapy. Growth problems were under investigation from several points of view. Hepatitis serum studies advanced the hope of a vaccine. A study of the chromosome and genetic determinants of leukemia would, it was hoped, lead to earlier diagnosis of the disease and hence earlier treatment. Interuterine surgical research investigated the possibility of correcting deformities and abnormalities of fetuses. Epilepsy was a target of brain damage and amino-acid metabolic studies. One remarkable achievement was the discovery of the relation of PKU (phenylketonuria) to retardation. That research led to a state law that made it mandatory to test babies at birth.

This widespread research required sophisticated, and usually expensive, equipment. Unfortunately it often became obsolete in the rapid development of pediatric specialties. On the whole, equipment was bought and replaced with grant money. But as the amount spent on research mounted to over $1 million in 1966, and $2 million in 1967, a note of warning was occasionally sounded. If too much reliance were placed on government grants, research could be seriously impaired in a year of inadequate funding or of a changing political policy toward health care. And just that did happen in 1968 when, attempting to reduce federal spending in the area of medical research, the federal government curtailed grants and left many programs at the Hospital instituting rigid economies. A year later applications for research projects were often returned marked "approved but not funded." By 1970 some research programs could no longer absorb many of the collateral expenses—for example, the cost of transplant operations could no longer be covered by organ research grants. Dr. Henry Nadler, new Chief-of-Staff that year, reported to the Directors that the Hospital would have to bear that expense.

By the end of the sixties, however, no one questioned that research was an integral part of Children's purpose. Quality patient care was still regarded as its primary, and teaching as its secondary, responsibility. Research was a basic element to both. The Given Foundation in 1969 endowed the first professorships ever held at Children's. The chair of general pediatrics went to Dr. Robert Lawson; that of pediatric research to Dr. Henry Nadler. The latter had been on the Hospital staff since 1965, head of its Division of Genetics for two years before becoming Chief-of-Staff in 1970.

The new research building was just the first step in the physical expansion which the Directors hoped to advance in the sixties. While they spearheaded the development program, they were not alone either in planning or in raising money. The Woman's Board was a partner throughout. Women served on the Directors' planning and campaign committees; they also appointed a development committee of their own. As usual they planned special events: the kick-off dinner, the dinner for Dr. Potts, the ground-breaking ceremony, and dedication day. Mrs. Vilas even secured the artist who painted Dr. Bigler's portrait. Theirs was the primary responsibility for finding ways to honor donors. After Mr. and Mrs. Elliott Donnelley gave the Hospital a handsome leather Donor's Book in 1963, the Board appointed a committee whose duty it was to have the names of "generous friends" inscribed in the book in beautiful script. To the women, too, fell the job of designing and hanging plaques to honor donors. And they accepted without question the dictum: every Board member is a fund raiser. They solicited their own Board and hundreds of "outside" prospects. By 1963, 94 percent of the Board had given generously—51 percent active members, 43 percent associate.

By 1967 the Thomas D. Jones and Martha Wilson buildings were filled with workmen moving partitions, airconditioning, adapting rooms for new uses. An enlarged Development Committee—usually called the Long Range Planning Committee during this time—was engrossed in looking ahead from the vantage point of 1967 in order to set new short-term and long-term goals. A number of doctors, in addition to the Chief-of-Staff, had joined the committee. The Medical Staff had become increasingly dissatisfied with the slow progress of construction and planning; they wanted a hand in accelerating both.

This revitalized committee asked the Board of Directors three questions: what was Children's policy in regard to free care; what did it conceive its role in the community to be; and what place would it have in The McGaw Medical Center? The committee felt it needed answers to these questions in order to plan effectively.

The questions themselves point to situations which had indeed become stumbling blocks to the Hospital's planning in the sixties.

Free care was the founding philosophy of Mrs. Porter's hospital, and its basic tenet for over eighty years. But free care in the sixties had a different complexion from that of earlier days. Federal, state, county, and city governments had entered the field of providing medical care in ever-increasing volume for the medically indigent. The impact of these dollars had as well changed drastically from earlier times. Since the Hospital had reluctantly accepted tax dollars for operating expenses in the depression days of the thirties, it had become more and more dependent on them as a way to balance the budget—or at least reduce the deficit to manageable size. By the mid-forties Children's was receiving regular reimbursement for services to the indigent from the Illinois Department of Public Health, the Illinois Division of Services for Crippled Children, and the Chicago Welfare Administration. In 1945, for example, the Hospital received a little over $23,000 from these sources; in 1947 when the Illinois Department of Public Aid also began to reimburse the institution for the children it referred, the amount jumped to $57,557. These monies were a small percentage of the total operating costs, but they grew steadily. In 1953 they passed the $100,000 mark; in 1954 they totaled $177,841. The last amount was still a small fraction of the income necessary to run the Hospital that year ($1,638,069) but it was becoming an important source of income.

147

It grew in the sixties. In 1965 it was $250,000, but in 1968 when reimbursement from Medicaid had been received for a full year it reached $2,531,000.

It was as well a difficult source of income with which to deal. Government agencies at that time rarely, if ever, reimbursed the Hospital for the full cost of care; they were notoriously slow in payments; and they sometimes changed rules in midstream, leaving gaps in the Hospital's budgeted income. Those gaps had to be filled in by increasing the annual voluntary contributions, grants from the Community Fund, or from foundations with special interests: heart, polio, cystic fibrosis, rheumatism, etc. Many regarded the discrepancy between income from endowment, patient fees, and third party reimbursement, and the amount needed to run the Hospital, as the free care item in the budget. For years the Woman's Board ran its annual campaign for contributions on this basis.

Another problem of dependence on government money was the inflexibility of the reimbursement system. Having established a fee system, public agencies were slow to recognize changing factors in the institutions they reimbursed. Steadily rising salaries of nurses and house staff were a case in point in the sixties at Children's. Nurses' salaries, together with fringe benefits, had been consistently reviewed since World War II. To remain competitive in the sixties, a starting salary for a nurse had been raised from $375 a month in 1960 to $675 in 1970, with $100 more for the demanding service in intensive care. Nurses' hours had been shortened to forty per week in the fifties; in 1964 the Illinois Department of Education and Registration was pressing for a thirty-five hour week for student nurses. That change would mean hiring more nurses and consequently a large increase in the operating costs.

The Nursing Advisory Committee (Mrs. Paul Guenzel, Chairman) and the Board of Directors grappled with the problem. Mr. John Sturgis had become President in 1963–1964, following brief terms by Frank McNair ('61–'62) and Errett Van Nice ('62–'63). He raised the question of discontinuing the school entirely. An alternative might be reducing the pediatric nursing course from thirteen to eight weeks and perhaps charging tuition, since a thirty-five hour week would materially reduce the service the Hospital received from its students. Mr. Joseph Greer, the new Administrator in

1963, was opposed to closing; so was the Nursing Advisory Committee. It, however, recommended charging a tuition fee of $300 per year. Audrey Short, who had directed the School since 1950, strengthened in-service training, studied ways to make the pediatric nursing course conform to the broader scope of service expected of the pediatric nurse in the sixties, and supported community programs of nurse recruitment. Children's was not the only hospital with nurses in short supply. The situation improved for a while—at times Children's had a full quota of nurses—but never for long.

In 1969 the status of the School of Nursing was reviewed again. This time the Nursing Advisory Committee recommended closing the school but allowing students from affiliated schools, with their own instructors, to use the Hospital for clinic experience. The Directors accepted the recommendation. Cost of care went up as Miss Short was authorized to hire nine registered nurses and fourteen licensed practical nurses at a cost of $126,372. Situations like this which increased the cost of care were slow to be reflected in increased reimbursement.

House staff salaries also increased in the sixties, in part because, conforming to changing customs, residents were put on a straight cash basis in 1960. Before this change, pediatric residents were paid $1,500 plus room and board. By 1968, after two raises, residents received $6,000 to $8,000 (for one to four years of residency) and interns $5,500. The Personnel Committee of the Board of Directors in the sixties also set a schedule for medical staff salaries with built-in increments, and recommended health insurance and retirement plans for virtually all of its full-time employees. All of these improvements added materially to the Hospital's operating expenses.

There were several routes open to the Directors to recover these rising costs. They could raise room rates, or attempt to get more adequate reimbursement from third parties: public agencies and health insurance companies (Blue Shield, Blue Cross, or commercial companies). They did both. Room rates in the sixties rose from $28 to $75 for private rooms; $22 to $69 for multibed rooms; intensive care service from $26 to $119. Ancillary services—X-ray, laboratory work, anesthesia, operating rooms—rose in proportion. Per diem costs climbed from $40.53 in 1960 to $106.26 early in 1969. When they reached $121 later that year, Mr. Greer compared this price with those of other Chicago hospitals—the range he found was $50 to $123; Children's ranked second from the top.

Mounting deficits in the sixties disturbed both Boards and the Administrator. To show how free care contributed to the situation, Treasurers' annual reports began separating this item and estimating it as an expense arrived at after deducting "*unrecovered* clinic costs." In this decade that item never fell below $1 million; in 1967 when the Long Range Planning Committee asked its question, free care was estimated at $1,776,865.

Can we afford free care? The question came up again and again —and in many forms. Should patients be admitted on the basis of need or of value in teaching? How can the Hospital (as it went to the public for capital funds as well as annual contributions) reverse its "image" in the community as a rich hospital? How can it emphasize that it cannot continue free care in the old way without more voluntary contributions? Would the Hospital's "image" suffer if it limited free care, or should it be direct and cut its service to fit income? Can some clinic patients be treated in other places—is Children's regional boundary real or does it exist just on paper? Should priorities be set within financial limitations: teaching, research, and then the remaining funds for free care? There was more than one expression of concern that limiting free care would be letting down the long line of women and men who had served on Children's Boards since 1892. A few thought the volume of free care could be controlled only by the doctors, that they too needed to be shown that Children's was not a rich hospital. The discussion went on for years; there was not a clear answer to the question in 1967.

The magnitude of free care was, of course, closely tied to the committee's second question: what was Children's role in the community? The community in this case was not Chicago, from which the Hospital drew the bulk of its in-hospital patients, but the immediate Lincoln Park, near north area. Children's role there was hard to define in the social upheaval of the sixties. A Welfare Council Community Area Profile in 1965 described the neighborhood as one of the most deprived socio-economic areas in terms of low income, low education, and high juvenile delinquency. Its children were the Hospital's clinic patients; their composition, number, and actions delineated the community.

The growing number of black children in the clinic had been noticed in 1947, after World War II. In the fifties and throughout the sixties other minorities had joined them: Puerto Ricans, American Indians, and a minority group of another sort—Tennessee and Kentucky mountain people. In 1958 blacks formed 31 percent of the clinic patients, Puerto Ricans 12 percent. The latter presented new problems: language, suspicion of the Hospital's treatment (they still clung to their own remedies), and easily wounded feelings. Throughout the sixties, minority groups regularly accounted for 40 to 50 percent of the clinic patients. Since the parents had few employment skills, tax-supported agencies paid for their care—or at least part of it.

Coincidentally, the Hospital had, in 1958, abandoned its flat 50¢ clinic registration fee in favor of a graduated fee—50¢ to $3.00. An explanation of the fee scale was given to parents in Spanish and English, but social workers still had difficulty explaining the system to many parents who were barely literate. Need for Spanish was acute; when a Spanish speaking volunteer offered to give free lessons to clinic staff, a resident, several social workers, and two dietitians signed up immediately.

The O.P. Department was a troubled place in this decade. It considered various ways to meet the challenge of a changing society so clearly reflected in the clinics: hiring a full-time salaried doctor to direct the whole program, using case aides to relieve the hard-pressed social workers, and expanding the use of volunteers. The Woman's Board's Volunteer and Social Service Committee worked with the Director of volunteers, Shirley Bechtel, to improve the quality of the case-aide program. In 1964 the O.P. Department hired a case aide specializing in Spanish families; with the social workers she attempted to deal with the emotional problems of these volatile clinic families while the doctors coped with their physical ones.

Hard pressed to cover outpatient costs, the Hospital asked the clinics to make an all-out effort to increase income from patient fees. A new minimum fee of one dollar was set in 1964 and parents were notified—in Spanish and English. The new schedule seemed to be received without much grumbling, but the I.O.U. slips began to mount; they reached $1,000 per month before long. Then there was a marked change in the use of the clinics. Within six months of the fee change, there were 10 percent fewer free visits. The Hospital was concerned, but felt at least part of the decrease was attributed to an improvement in service. A new appointment system allowed residents and doctors to follow their patients through from admission to end of treatment. The greater individualization under this plan sometimes reduced the need for repeat visits. In addition, three more residents had been assigned to the clinics.

Clinic patients, however, continued to decrease—by the end of 1965 there was a drop of 90 percent in *new* free patients, 23 percent in all patients in the general medical clinics. On the other hand the number of patients coming to the specialty clinics (particularly cardiac, urology, neurology, and child guidance and development) increased as full-time salaried doctors extended specialized services to out patients. The Child Guidance Clinic began at this time, with the Planned Parenthood Association, to give birth control information to clinic mothers.

A primary referral source to the specialty clinics was the Near North Children's Center in the Olivet Community House on nearby Cleveland Avenue. It had been established with the U.S. Children's Bureau's funds through the efforts of the Chicago Board of Health. Medically indigent area children referred to it by that Board, the Board of Education, Infant Welfare, Headstart, and other public and private agencies received general primary care at the Center. For specialty services they were referred to Children's; the Center reimbursed the hospital $26.40 per visit. Children's also provided diagnostic work for the Center. The presence of this new neighborhood facility in the sixties accounted in part for clinic statistics at Children's.

The financial situation in the clinics continued to be precarious, however, as public agency cases skyrocketed to 44 percent of the total by the end of the sixties. Aid for Dependent Children mothers accounted for a sizable portion—that was a mixed blessing since reimbursement for that category was a relatively high $26.40 per clinic visit. An epidemic of rubella overwhelmed the Audiology Clinic with patients. Then the battered child began to be a factor to be reckoned with; at the request of the social workers, special files began to be kept on them.

Some improvement in reimbursement rates, however, followed an increase in public agency cases. The Board of Health promised to pay $12.98 per visit (actual cost) for referrals from its Infant Welfare Clinic. The Division of Services for Crippled Children, after designating the Hospital a Cystic Fibrosis Center, agreed on an equitable fee schedule for drugs and expensive ancillary services used in treating the disease. Public Aid raised its rates, and MANG (medical assistance no grant) picked up expenses for some families (largely Puerto Ricans) who could not meet residence requirements for other public aid.

The Hospital also found other sources to help ease the financial burden of the O.P. clinics. Private groups like New Eyes for the Needy, the Kappa Alpha Theta sorority, the Rice Foundation, the Elyse Rhond Fuchs Cancer Foundation, and others underwrote a good share of the expense of caring for indigent patients with special needs.

The overwhelming presence of the community in the clinics and its pressure for services had an added dimension at the end of the sixties. Medical care for those who could not pay had crossed that fine line from being a *privilege* to being a *right*. The community demanded, for example, that the O.P. clinics should be open twenty-four hours a day, seven days a week. They had complaints about other things too, shared at times by Hospital personnel. Alice Saar summed them up in her annual report to the Woman's Board in 1969:

> This has been a year of dissent; one calling for a good hard look at what we have and a harder look at what we have not. Complaints have been voiced within and without the hospital. Complaints about the physical appearance of the Clinic, the hard wooden benches, the sterile cold walls; complaints about the long waits, the impersonal atmosphere; complaints about the rudeness and unsympathetic attitude of some of the personnel; complaints of the fees charged clinic patients seen in the emergency room, and many others. And who are these people who have voiced these complaints—community action groups, it is true; but also our own Children's Memorial Hospital staff. And out of all of this has emerged a growing conviction that changes are due and must be made now if we are to maintain our reputation of providing the highest quality of medical services to the low income groups.

Complaints from staff (chiefly a few residents) were translated into what was called a "happening" in the sixties. During the night a group of residents and their wives, armed with paint brushes, brightened up the waiting rooms! The incident was discussed by the Directors, the Woman's Board, and Mr. Greer. The women, particularly, felt rebuffed; they were very much aware of the clinic's drab appearance but had held off redecorating because of the uncertainty of the clinics' location after the building program was completed. Part of the message of the "happening" was to point out the discrepancy in the appearance of clinic and private patient waiting rooms. In spite of a long-standing tradition that all patients were treated alike, the difference in decor, at least, was obvious. Dr. Swenson, Surgeon-in-Chief, feared there might be other incidents. A Director or two said the message was, "Get moving!" Chief-of-Staff Lawson felt a move had already been made to iron out discrepancies because he had earlier been authorized to hire a Director of Ambulatory Services (combined clinic and private).

The residents were rebuked for not "going through channels"; the Chief Resident was invited to the next meeting of the Decorating and Furnishing Committee; and Dr. Lawson intensified his search for a Director of Ambulatory Services.

By year's end the clinic waiting room had indoor-outdoor carpeting, brightly painted furniture, improved lighting and striped window shades. And Dr. Thomas Egan had become Medical Director of Ambulatory Services. Much of his time, and that of Dr. Robert Evans, new assistant to Mr. Greer (Mr. Greer's title changed to Executive Vice President, Dr. Evans was Assistant Vice President-Administration) was spent in improving the relationship of the Hospital and the community. The Directors appointed a Community Affairs Committee charged with developing a philosophy and policy to guide the Hospital through its encounters with its geographic community.

There was much to consider, for the Hospital was involved in a confrontation at the Near North Children's Center—at least it was an interested bystander. The Center's services to children had grown satisfactorily; now it wanted to expand to serving adults. But a group of local residents forced a work stoppage in the necessary remodelling for this purpose on the grounds that they wished to establish and control their own health center. Eight months and countless meetings later, the Center was allowed to go ahead with its plans, after it had added several experienced neighborhood health workers to its advisory board. Unfortunately, in January 1970, the original Children's Bureau grant ended and there was doubt that it would be renewed at the same level. Members of the Woman's Board visited the Center to lend moral support; the Board of Directors decided to continue accepting referrals (without reimbursement) and both Boards exerted what political pressure they could for a renewal of the grant. By June, money from the federal government was once more supporting the Center.

In July 1970 the Community Affairs Committee presented its report. After declaring the Hospital's primary role in helping sick children and preventing illness, it defined admission criteria, and stated that "although there are fees for services, no child has ever been refused emergency treatment because of an inability to pay." The report then addressed the important subject of Children's responsibility for social conditions which could affect a child's growth and development:

In pursuit of its traditional goal to improve the health of children, the Hospital Boards, medical staff and administration are concerned with the different aspects of the human condition that affect a child's growth and development. We recognize it is our responsibility to educate both our staff and the population served about the relationship of social deficits and health.

Such a course does not imply a choice between setting our goal on being an international referral hospital or on being a hospital interested in the general health needs of our community. While some might wish that we could concentrate on developing our capability towards the former goal, it would be irresponsible to state that as a specialty teaching hospital we should withdraw from concern for primary community care. We need to develop both facets of our program.

These concerns are evidenced by participation in fostering improvement, within the limits of our financial resources and areas of our competence.

The Department of Ambulatory Services improved after Dr. Egan's appointment. A public address system to call patients in turn was installed and the admitting area was modernized. Appointments were staggered further to reduce long waits. Two teams (supervising doctor, house staff, nurse's aides, and unit clerks) improved and individualized the care of patients. A full-time Head Resident served a six months' tour of duty in the clinics, and then

155

exchanged position with the Chief Resident in-hospital. A recreational therapist was sought to plan constructive play for the children while they waited their turns.

Children's place in The McGaw Medical Center, the third area about which the Long Range Planning Committee sought clarification, was first discussed in 1963. At that time Northwestern proposed establishing a medical center on its downtown campus with Children's, Evanston, Passavant, and Wesley hospitals as members. Each hospital would be completely autonomous but all would join in raising medical educational standards, fostering research, and improving patient care. At the outset, Children's approved the plan in principle, but insisted on the importance of each hospital maintaining its identity. When the Center (expanded to include V.A. Lakeside Hospital and Glenbrook) was established in 1966, it sought ways to benefit its members by suggesting a salary scale for house staff (Children's adopted that in 1967), and initiating studies of the feasibility of a centralized laboratory and a centralized computer system—both at McGaw.

Obviously, centralizing some functions at McGaw had space implications for Children's, but a more crucial question facing the Directors in 1967 was should the whole Hospital be moved to McGaw Center's downtown campus. That suggestion had been made by Northwestern University. The Directors asked Mr. Earl Frederick of Cresap, McCormick, and Paget, a management consultant firm, to study the idea from every angle: space, financing, the impact of the move on free care, the relation of federal aid to medical care, and trends and changes in pediatrics in Chicago. His report recommended that Children's move to the Center but first asked if McGaw were willing to help with land and financing. While the Directors, the Woman's Board, and the Medical Staff debated the pros and cons of moving, Mr. Frederick continued to study whether the change were feasible and practical, as well as desirable.

The matter was still being discussed in 1969. Land was available for leasing, but there would be no financial aid. Roscoe Miller, President of Northwestern, assured Children's that it would remain the medical school's pediatric arm even if it remained on Fullerton Avenue; there was no plan to build another pediatric hospital at the Center.

While the discussion continued, Mr. Frederick was asked to develop interim plans—particularly for relocating the Psychiatric Department, centralizing the clinical laboratories, and providing parking.

In March 1970 the Board of Directors voited to remain at the old location. It was a majority vote, not unanimous; so too was the consensus of the Woman's Board and the medical staff. Children's responsibility to its community and fear of losing autonomy swung the decision to "stay."

With location settled, the Hospital had a clear direction for physical planning. Land was sought on Lincoln Avenue for a parking garage; it was thought additional land would not be needed to accommodate proliferating programs. Closing the School of Nursing had freed, for example, several floors in NAB into which the Psychiatric Department could be fitted. That move in turn would free space in Thomas D. Jones for centralized laboratories. Reshuffling was a familiar exercise; Children's was ready to go ahead.

CHAPTER XII

Changing Roles of the Board of Directors and the Woman's Board

1960–1970

THE HOSPITAL entered the seventies a large complex institution reshaped in part by outside social forces in the sixties. The responsibilities of its Board of Directors and the Woman's Board had changed as well in that decade. The Directors' role had grown enormously as financial obligations expanded, location had to be decided upon, and policy set as to Children's place in the community. Five Presidents had led the Board through the turbulent decade: Hughston McBain, Frank McNair, Everett Van Nice, John Sturgis, and Bowen Stair. Fourteen new Directors (men) had joined the Board in the sixties, as compared to six in the fifties, five in the forties. They provided a broader base for interpreting the Hospital's work to Chicago and for raising money. One of them could also interpret social pressures to the Board; he was the first black director. To keep the interest of Directors who wished to resign from active membership, they had instituted an Associate Member category.

The role of the Woman's Board had also shifted gradually during this decade. Their presidents were able, talented women: Mrs. Chauncey Hutchins, Mrs. A. Loring Rowe, Mrs. John P. Wilson III, and Mrs. Homer Hargrave, Jr. And the channels of communication with the Directors and administration were clear. Women served on the Board of Directors and its committees; they received monthly reports from Mr. Green on hospital statistics (number of patients, cost per diem, rise in salaries, etc.). But the agendas of their monthly meetings in the sixties reflect little policy making. They were clearly intended as a vehicle for receiving information;

decisions were made—and recommended at times to the Board for a vote—in the Executive Committee or in standing committees which grew in number (thirteen by 1969) and strength during the decade. The important Nursing Advisory Committee was still not a Woman's Board standing committee, although it too reported to the women every month. Its recommendations to close the School of Nursing, however, were made to the Board of Directors.

As expressed in their Bylaws, the responsibilities of the Woman's Board had not changed since 1904—full charge of the internal management of the Hospital. As frequently happens, however, the Bylaws had not kept pace with reality. As the Hospital grew, there had been a good deal of erosion in the women's "full charge." In the rapid growth of the sixties there were further shifts in emphasis, and the women were well aware of them. They were attempting to find their unique place in the "different" Hospital. Mrs. Rowe commented on the situation in her 1965 annual report:

The 83rd year of Children's Memorial Hospital has seen our continued advancement in the fields of pediatric medicine, research and teaching. When a hospital such as ours grows into a large and complex institution there are by necessity many changes, some accompanied by regrets for the passing of old days and old ways. Looking back to the time of the 'Lady Managers' the Woman's Board would have to agree with Robert Browning that 'Progress is the law of life.'

During the past year the Woman's Board has worked in close cooperation with the Nursing, Outpatient, Social Service, Volunteer, Public Relations, Occupational Therapy and Housekeeping departments. Our members have volunteered in many capacities both in and outside the hospital, raised considerable sums of monies and last but not least have interpreted the purpose, philosophy and spirit of Children's Memorial to the community at large. In this era of specialized medicine, complicated and sophisticated techniques, it becomes increasingly easy for doctors and hospitals to think of their patients in terms of an IBM card rather than a person. To me one of the most important functions of the Woman's Board is to help our hospital and staff maintain the personal touch, and show by the warmth of our interest that we care. This we do by volunteering in the hospital and working to keep it the attractive, friendly place it is. Thus we will continue to play a most important role in the destiny of Children's Memorial.

Their next President, Mrs. John P. Wilson, Jr. (1966–68), embodied many of those qualities necessary to keep the "personal touch." A plaque hung in the Woman's Board office honors her for her "complete dedication to the Children's Memorial Hospital, to the children who must be here, to the staff and employees who work here, to the reasons the Hospital was created. She was committed to caring for children and she personally shared herself with them and with every person connected with the Hospital."

The women's function as money raisers neither changed nor diminished in this decade. Since early days they had been imaginative in that area—several of their enterprises had become ongoing important sources of income. The White Elephant Shop was forty-one years old in 1960; it celebrated its birthday in a new shop (the old Aetna State Bank Building) in the apex of the Hospital triangle. A pair of handsome ceramic elephants (the gift of the mother of a young Board member) stood at the entrance on opening day. Old clientele followed the Shop, it picked up new, and that year it made more money than ever—$52,000.

The 411 Shop struck a gold mine with Pauline Trigere clothes in 1962. Thirty-five Board members modelled their own Trigere dresses and then gave them to the Shop for resale. Trigere herself, with her son, gave the commentary at the Ambassador West's fashion show and luncheon, the special rummage collecting "event" that year. A new fall Trigere dress was the door prize—that, and colorful invitations designed by a Board member, lured 437 women to the luncheon, all with attractive rummage to restock the Shop.

The Hospital Shop had also become a steady, if smaller, source of income. After its move to the basement of the main building in the mid-sixties its trade grew rapidly. Volunteers, by that time, worked under a paid manager and four assistants. Board members' chief concern in 1966 was keeping the shelves stocked with gift items. As for food—six loaves per day were enough for sandwiches in 1965; in 1966, sixteen were needed. Advancing opening hour from 9:30 to 9:00 a.m. brought in forty dollars more per day. In the sixties, the Shop gave $89,000 to the Hospital.

A new benefit in 1961—with a promise of continuity—was a Professional-Amateur Golf tournament. It was a success from the start, contributing $60,000 to income that year, $283,500 in the first four years. Dozens of Board members worked year-round on invitations, sponsors, locations, prizes, press parties—with their usual flair they made the parties surrounding the event as well as the tournament itself great social occasions. Although Pro-Am was run by the women, Director John Ames was for years its patron saint. It joined the White Elephant Shop and the Hospital Shop as an annual money raising project.

Occasionally the Board accepted a one-time benefit. Racing for Charities brought in $5,000 one year, selling a block of tickets to a Beatle concert $4,000–$5,000 another.

But the Board was more interested in ventures with continuity. Organizing a number of guilds throughout metropolitan Chicago and the suburbs in 1958 was one of these. They were formed chiefly to carry Children's story to new areas in the hope of opening up new sources of contributions. At first the guilds had a central organization (Mrs. Norman Gerlach was its first President, Mrs. Thomas Boodell her successor). In addition to active members—more than 100 in a short time—it had affiliates: the Service Club, the Marlene Appelbaum Memorial Foundation, the Junior Women's Club of Lake Bluff, Lincoln Park Senior Center, Homewood Junior Women's Club, and many others. It was a large and rather amorphous group. Smaller (largely regional) units within the membership met to roll bandages, sew or make toys or organize parties for the children, or to plan dances, bridge parties, bake sales, etc., to raise money. Once a month the whole group met at the Hospital. They also came together in a number of services there; the most important were wrapping Christmas presents and running a holiday bazaar. Their unique service, however, was making a nurse puppet to give each child who was hospitalized. That was an enormously successful project; it continued through the sixties even though they needed 5,000 puppet heads the year their price soared to 45¢ each (1968). In 1970 they distributed 4,200 puppets and still gave the Hospital $23,292.30.

The disparate nature of the guilds was recognized in 1964 by a change in organization and name. Called the Executive Council of Service Guilds and Affiliates with two coordinators (Mrs. Victor Lewis and Mrs. John Bigler), it included autonomous groups, some service-oriented, some fund raising, some interested in special projects. The Margaret Etter Crêche was an affiliate in 1968. Raising money for the Hospital was the goal of all groups.

The womanpower needed to manage all these enterprises was enormous, but for years the Board had been large. Averaging forty-

The Woman's Board created a charming garden court for outdoor play.

The Ronald McDonald House a few blocks from the Hospital.

*A famous patient, television star Gary Coleman,
helped Mr. and Mrs. Kroc lay a cornerstone.*

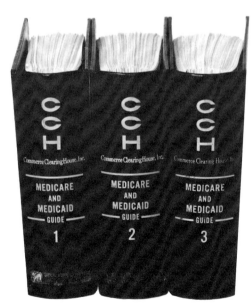

Social programs had far-reaching impact on the Hospital.

The Hospital builds for its second century of caring.

*After sixty years, The White Elephant Shop found a
permanent home at 2380 N. Lincoln Avenue.*

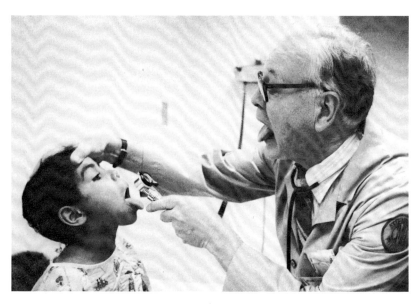

Sophisticated technology improves patient care,
but is always accompanied by the human touch.

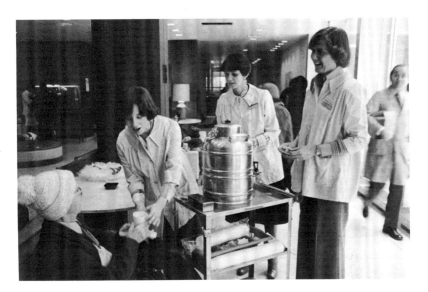

*Dedication of supporting Guilds and Affiliates
includes volunteer service in the Hospital.*

*The Woman's Board Hospital Shop
is a major fundraiser.*

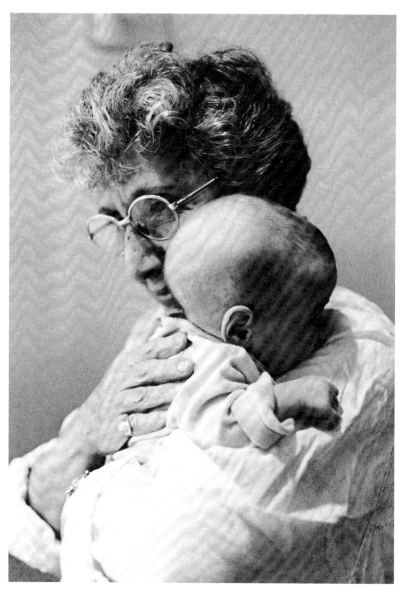

An *"element of love."*

eight active members and twenty-two associates through the early fifties, it had increased to seventy-two active members in 1958 when the women decided to invite all the members of the very large Clinic and Social Service Committee to join them. After this move, and throughout the sixties, the Woman's Board combined active and associate members averaged ninety-five.

And they needed every one, for their financial responsibility did not end with managing fund-raising events. Year in and year out they carried on a personal solicitation. Each one had a list of names (revised every year) to whom she went for annual contributions. That task became more difficult when it coincided—as it did all through the sixties—with the drive for capital funds. But they persisted.

Spurring their enthusiasm was their work on the standing committees—fifteen by 1970: executive, advisory, budget, clinic, decorating and furnishing, development, finance, garden court, guilds and affiliates, Hospital Shop, membership, community relations, social service, volunteer, and the White Elephant Shop. Work on these committees brought them an understanding of the goals and problems of the Hospital's many departments. The make-up of committees changed frequently to broaden a member's knowledge—it was difficult to comprehend the whole complex institution. Reports at Board meetings helped—presidents struggled against the superficiality of this device. The high point of the monthly meeting was not reports but the talks by the doctors explaining vividly the work they were doing in the clinics, the operating room, the research laboratory.

Board members were urged to volunteer—the field for individual service was wide and deeply rewarding. Accelerated use of the volunteer begun in the fifties, continued in the sixties—particularly after Lucille Crawford became Director in 1966. She revitalized volunteer services, extending them in innovative ways. Evening volunteers increased in numbers; so did summer ones (particularly teenagers). Mrs. Crawford reorganized the admissions and placing of volunteers, strengthened their orientations, and worked hard to have them accepted as partners of the staff—nurse, resident, social worker, or therapist. As volunteers were accepted in delicate areas (the Department of Psychiatry, for example), Mrs. Crawford realized that orientation should be in the hands of the medical personnel as well as nurses and social workers. And she succeeded in securing appropriate staff for this purpose. The service of volunteers was enormously heightened by these innovations; so was their personal satisfaction.

Mrs. Crawford was quick to see possibilities for service: manning the Hospital Shop, reading a bedtime story (the evening story ladies included two men one year), helping in occupational or recreational therapy, playing with children waiting in the clinic. To alleviate the fears of small patients entering the hospital, a puppet program similar to the one used in preparing children for operations was worked out. The Mother Bank project grew to three volunteers giving six hours a day each to cuddling babies in need of love.

Dr. Schulman suggested that volunteers from the Woman's Board serve coffee to parents who, for one reason or another, spent so many hours in the hospital's waiting rooms. The coffee and bun cart became a popular service for Board volunteers; contact with parents gave them a deepened sense of the Hospital.

From small beginnings projects grew. From a navy captain's visit to a sick child who loved ships, Project White Hat developed. A navy bus brought a group of sailors (often thirty or forty) to Children's every Saturday. The director of recreational therapy provided orientation and background information; in a short time the staff welcomed the sailors enthusiastically. When they began staying to lunch one therapist reported happily that the scene was a "hilarious military mess!" The sailors filled a void for many a child from a fatherless home; themselves from many backgrounds and nationalities, they understood the broad spectrum of emotional problems found in the children.

The thousands of hours which volunteers gave to the Hospital were reported monthly to the Woman's Board. In 1969 Mrs. Crawford looked at these hours in a new way—the total, she estimated, could be equated to the time of twenty-two full-time staff. That year volunteers were drawn from twenty-eight communities beyond the city limits, with twenty-six high schools and colleges sending students. Particular honor was paid to Mrs. Querin Dorschel in 1969—she was presented with a special gold Bambino charm to honor her long years of volunteer service.

As individuals the women gave many hours to volunteer work in the Hospital; as a hard working Board they masterminded a dozen other activities during the sixties. They continued to give beautiful annual teas to honor the doctors, sometimes in the Hospital, more often in these years in their own homes. They had been doing this since 1934. They inaugurated annual parties for the house staff and their families with a picnic (with train rides!) at the Elliott Donnelleys' in 1964; and an employees' award lunch at the Hospital in 1969.

They celebrated the ninetieth birthday of Mrs. Frederic Upham in 1965. Her lifetime spanned the life of the Hospital, for she was born seven years before it had been founded. She had joined the Auxiliary Board in 1910, served as its President from 1924–1928, and was still working for Children's fifty-five years later. Her devotion to the White Elephant Shop was indicated by tiny elephants on the birthday cake and on her corsage. With gifts from Board members and friends in honor of her birthday, Mrs. Upham chose to sponsor two amateur golfers in the Pro-Am tournament. A few years later the Board honored her further by naming two school rooms for her.

The Decorating and Furnishing Committee had its hands full in the sixties coping with paint, furniture, draperies, and pictures for the new and remodelled buildings. For the first time they hired a professional decorator to facilitate their access to the Merchandise Mart and to help coordinate the huge task. When she was reduced to an "on call" basis, they worked with Donald Scalzo who joined the administrative staff in 1962.

By the mid-sixties Garden Court had been added to the Board's standing committees. In the building and remodelling of the early sixties, the Garden Court had been born. It was designed by Gertrude Kuh in honor of her sister Elsa Eisendrath, whose death in 1962 ended almost twenty years of service to Children's. Income from memorial gifts for Miss Eisendrath and other members maintained the Court for years.

It was an outdoor retreat for children recovering from illness and surgery, a place where mothers could play with their children or just sit in the sun waiting for news. It became a focus of creative activity for the women. At Christmas it housed a tall lighted tree, decorated at times by ornaments made by the children themselves. At Easter one year, a larger-than-life papier-maché Easter bunny dominated the scene; at Thanksgiving bright orange pumpkins and shocks of corn marked the season. With the help of Mr. Scalzo they built a gazebo and a bird cage over the fountain as a background for spring flowers and live birds. They planted daffodils and tulips, impatiens and petunias. With bright red geraniums they won first prize in the Mid-north Association of Gardens and Patios in 1965. The Garden Court was the campus of earlier years.

While patients enjoyed looking at the changing scenes in the Court, they used it as well. An ambitious recreational therapist had them baking cookies there one warm day; on another, they built sand castles. Ingenious raised sand boxes allowed wheel chair patients to participate.

Like the Board of Lady Managers in 1892, the Woman's Board in the late fifties had become concerned with the absence of a religious program in their Hospital. In earlier days they had experimented with Sunday School for the children. In this period, after a conference with the Dean of McCormick Theological Seminary, they decided upon a nonsectarian chaplaincy program. Four seminary students spent ten hours a week each visiting the children and counseling the parents. Rabbis, priests, and ministers continued to be encouraged to visit, as they had for years.

When the building program began, the Woman's Board suggested that it include a Chapel, a quiet place for meditation and prayer—and an occasional service. The Chapel was given in honor of Mrs. Robert Wood (Mrs. William Mitchell's and Mrs. A. Watson Armour's mother) by her family. Statues of two children stood against russet curtains at the entrance; a simple altar within was backed by a gold curtain. Later, friends stitched twenty needlepoint kneeling cushions with the theme, God's World. The Reverend Robert Hall of St. Chrysostom's dedicated the kneelers. Thanksgiving, Christmas, and Easter services were held in the Chapel fairly regularly over the next few years.

In 1970, the program changed slightly. Children's began a religious program with Grant Hospital. A full-time chaplain was employed, who divided his time equally between the two hospitals. The new chaplain, the Reverend Palmer Temple, told the Woman's

Board he thought a chaplain's job was to listen, to be with, and to be available. Five students from various denominations shared his duties; Sunday services were conducted each week.

Changes in the roles of the Boards as well as in the Hospital itself in the sixties were not peculiar to Children's—they were signs of the times. Ray Brown, Executive Vice President of the McGaw Medical Center, predicted that the future would hold more:

> The hospital of the future will have to be redefined legally, medically, morally and politically. We will see more and more influence about the financing come from the national level, not only because the reimbursement policies of Medicare and Medicaid will continue to have substantial impact, but also because money from the private sector will become more national in scope.
>
> What a hospital can do will have to be determined by the community at large, which is paying the bill. The future demands that trustees have a different perspective. They are going to have to admit that the complexity of the internal operation is such they will have to stay out . . . they are going to serve in the same way as industrial boards of directors—to determine major direction, and to constantly evaluate their progress.

CHAPTER XIII

The Ferment
of the Seventies

1970–1980

Social Forces in the sixties had brought changes in the operation of Children's and new emphases to its services, but it had not altered its mission. The Hospital's commitments were still clear; quality care, excellent education, and research—now equal partners. It was responsible as well for providing a physical plant adequate to meet the needs of each component of its mission. In deciding to remain at its eighty-eight-year-old site, the Hospital had also committed itself to continue serving the Lincoln Park community. That was a demanding role—and likely to become more so.

The Directors and the Woman's Board knew that meeting its commitments would not be easy, but the challenge was exciting and Children's had a long history of facing obstacles and achieving the impossible.

Getting the next phase of the expansion program out of planning committees and off architects' drawing boards to the reality of steel, bricks, and mortar had first priority. An earlier building plan was reviewed. To it were added specific requests: a new office building; space for modern operating rooms with intensive care units close by; better ambulatory facilities; an adolescent medical unit; centralized laboratories; burn and trauma units; and new and expanded radiology facilities—including nuclear medicine. The list also included an old but greatly needed item—an adequate parking garage. Could the Hospital afford this program, or at least pieces of it? Once again the question of money loomed large.

Generous gifts from Mr. and Mrs. Ray Kroc in 1972, spurred

plans for a capital drive. The Directors began shaping up a Centennial Fund campaign. Recast several times, its goal was finally set at $50 million: $32 million for construction and renovation; $18 million for additional endowment. Mr. Harold Byron Smith, a Director since 1961, accepted the chairmanship of the Fund.

This forward momentum was slowed, however, by a renewed invitation from Northwestern to move Children's to the grounds of the McGaw Medical Center. The Directors turned to Cresap, McCormick and Paget to update their 1968 study on the advisability of such a move. Earl Frederick came back to look at Children's in 1973. The tremendous growth of the Hospital in five years focussed the new study on how best to accommodate this great development in services both in 1973 and in the years ahead. In either location a large expenditure of capital would be needed to keep the Hospital viable, able to meet its commitments. With Mr. Frederick's report in hand, the Directors weighed the question of space at both locations, the effect of "place" on long-term and short-term goals, the Hospital's responsibility to the Lincoln Park community. The earlier question of how best to preserve autonomy was discussed, so too were the benefits of twenty-seven years of close affiliation with Northwestern Medical School—the close ties of staff and a shared medical education program. Would physical proximity on the Chicago campus strengthen these ties? The Directors felt the two-way benefits of the affiliation were too great to be affected by location. When a vote was finally taken, nineteen Directors voted "stay," five "go"; eventually the decision to stay was unanimous. Mrs. Howell Hardy, President of the Woman's Board (1972–1975), reported that their Executive Committee's vote had also been divided—in fact, split down the middle. It was not an easy decision, but the die was cast.

There was an unexpected dividend to this reexamination of location. When Mr. Greer resigned as Administrator in 1973, Earl Frederick was asked to lead the Hospital in the important years ahead. He became Executive Vice-President for Administration in July 1974; his title changed to President within the year. Mr. Frederick needed no orientation. Within months he was deep in reorganizing the financial management of Children's, considering ways to attract new revenue, and urging a reexamination and strengthening of the institution's relation to the community. Under his sure, firm direction Children's was about to turn an important corner in its long history.

Mr. William Swartchild became a strong partner in achieving these objectives when he succeeded Mr. Meers as President of the Board of Directors in 1975. Under his leadership the Board joined Mr. Frederick in facing squarely the problems of these pivotal years. The Woman's Board, led by Mrs. Frank Kelley, was ready to do its part; so too was the medical staff under a relatively new Chief-of-Staff (1971), Dr. Henry Nadler.

The impact of a changing and inflationary economy was felt both in expansion plans and in the day-to-day operation of the Hospital. In 1976 a plethora of financial problems came into sharp focus; Mr. Swartchild and Mr. Frederick came to the Woman's Board to discuss them. Mr. Swartchild listed some of the surface reasons for Children's financial difficulties:

"... inflation affecting costs of everything we buy and use; increased premiums for the health insurance we provide employees, amounting to about $130,000 a year in additional costs to the Hospital; rising costs of sophisticated hospital equipment which because of rapid technology becomes obsolete comparatively quickly (the Hospital is considering purchasing an EMI Scanner at the cost of about $600,000 for example); and the tremendous increase in our malpractice insurance."

But these reasons were, he felt, but the "tip of the iceberg;" underneath was a basic philosophical question which must be addressed by the Hospital:

"We are living in a society which has claimed that everyone is entitled to the most sophisticated medical care available, whether they can pay for it or not. While this is a worthy idea, there are not enough dollars to pay for it, and the financial squeeze is on the health care institutions, medical schools and insurers. The country is going to have to face the issue of whether we can continue this policy.

There are two alternatives: raise taxes to pay for health care costs, or establish priorities as to who will receive health care that can be paid for. It is obvious that it is not politically expedient to raise taxes. Establishing priorities, as has been done in some foreign countries with socialized medicine, raises profound moral questions, such as do we provide care to the young or old; how long do we prolong life?"

In this context, Mr. Swartchild reported, the Directors had made several important decisions for the immediate future:

"We have concluded that the Hospital will impose a moratorium of one year on new programs and services until operating costs of the Hospital can be brought in line with revenue. Each year's budget will be based on the fact that our operating loss will not exceed revenues we can anticipate from investment income and contributions. We will engage in a strong campaign to increase our annual giving from about $575,000 a year to $1 million. And the expansion program of the Hospital will go forward, but will proceed in steps of established priorities. Our goal will be raising a dollar for endowment support for every dollar raised for bricks and mortar, recognizing that the Hospital must be able to finance the operations of whatever new facilities it builds."

Far from being pessimistic about the future of the Hospital, Mr. Swartchild was determined that it should be positioned to adapt to future changes in the health care system. That there would be changes no one doubted.

Nor was Mr. Frederick discouraged—he preferred to regard Children's perplexing problems as "challenges," a word he used often in these years. He pointed out that health care funds had been poured out generously by social and political leaders since World War II; but now the public was greatly concerned about the proportion of the tax dollar devoted to health. This concern was forcing hospitals—and other segments of the health care system—to take stock of their operations to "be sure," he said, "that what we are doing is necessary and right for the long term," and that we "maintain our professional and financial viability."

Although Children's had ended fiscal year 1975/1976 with a deficit of $1.7 million, Mr. Frederick still felt the Hospital was in a strong financial position. It was determined, however, that it must commit itself to find new income and to cut operating expenses 10 percent (about $3 million) in the coming year.

To reach these goals, many groups were already at work. A cost containment committee of administrative staff and physicians was charged with suggesting how each medical department could achieve one or both objectives. A medical committee was reviewing medical programs to recommend priorities for the future. Administration was working on a variety of problems; among them an Illinois Medicaid freeze, and that perennial, below cost reimbursement for Public Aid patients.

The women had much to think about when Mr. Frederick suggested that the time had come for the Hospital to move away from the old free care concept in the light of the government's concern with health care for the medically indigent, and to think in terms of raising money for a program need—such as oncology or one of the new clinic programs. Moving away from the old concept was already reflected in new policies of in-patient admissions: each applicant was questioned to discover what public agency or insurance coverage he had; and at the time of admission a system for collection payments was worked out. Personnel were there to help parents register for financial help with an appropriate source if they did not know what was available.

Mr. Frederick regarded Children's development program as a "sound launching pad for the future." He believed the goals of $50 million for the Centennial Fund and $1 million in annual giving achievable. He affirmed the Directors' decision that new construction and renovation should be undertaken only if there were funds in hand to support the new facilities thus generated. Priority had to be given in 1976 to a Diagnostic and Treatment Center and to a parking garage.

The tone of the future was unmistakeable. But there was too little uninterrupted time in the Hospital setting to take a long objective look at the years ahead. The Hospital's leadership felt the need to rethink its philosophy and the mission statement, assess the financial future in broad terms, look at new directions in medical programming, and ways to improve communication—and thus cooperation—within the Hospital and with the community around it. Directors, physicians, and administrative staff met, therefore, in a weekend retreat in June 1976 to address these questions.

Out of this meeting came significant action on many fronts. It was agreed, for example, in order to preserve and foster referral sources, that Children's should strengthen its liason with other north side hospitals serving children (in 1972 it had joined the newly organized Lincoln Park-Lake View Health Planning Association). In the important area of financing—particularly cutting costs—it was agreed that administration should continue to refine its cost effectiveness studies so that medical programs thus identified could be assessed by the medical board for value either in patient care or in education. The physicians were strongly in favor of going to the public for support, saying frankly that Children's services were outstanding and an asset to the whole Middle West, but that the institution could not be self-supporting; it must be subsidized.

The retreat ended on a positive note as all groups which made up the Hospital family voiced determination to pull Children's through this difficult period. This spirit of cooperation was to be a hallmark of Mr. Swartchild's leadership through the remaining years of the seventies and into the eighties.

The Board of Directors' mandate to Mr. Frederick to balance the budget in 1977 was but another indication of the direction of the future. That he succeeded was a tribute both to him and to Mr. Swartchild. In the firm belief that an institution must be financially sound if it were to fulfill its mission, they led the Hospital through some difficult financial years.

Setting monetary goals and determining priorities in building were just the beginning of the strong expansion in the seventies. As there were outside economic forces which influenced the Hospital's financial planning, so too there were government agencies and interested voluntary groups which looked over Children's shoulder at its building plans. Every phase of a five-year plan upon which the institution wished to embark had—if it required spending more than $100,000—to be approved by the Illinois Comprehensive Health Agency and the Health Facilities Planning Board. They were the watchdogs to avoid duplication of services and contain medical costs through control of beds. In Chicago, the Department of Urban Renewal had to approve land acquisition, but before they could do that, the Lincoln Park Community Conservation Association had to indicate its approval. There were still other steps—the City Planning Commission and the Chicago Commission on Building and Zoning had to approve the buildings themselves which were to be erected on that land. And there were smaller community groups alert to preserve the residential character of their neighborhood. In particular in 1976 they fought the construction of a parking garage. But a green light was finally received for it and the Kroc Diagnostic and Treatment Center. The garage was completed in September

1977 and a gala groundbreaking ceremony was held a month later for the Kroc building.

Then Phase II—a four-story addition to the bed tower—began winding its way through the approval process!

It is understandable that improving communication within the Hospital and with the Lincoln Park community was high on Mr. Frederick's list of priorities. Knowing the problems facing the Hospital was the first step toward solving them. In earlier days, when Children's was smaller and fewer outside forces shaped its life, communication within the institution was easy—it scarcely needed to be planned. Word travelled fast and everyone knew everything. But in the mid-seventies, it was a different story. While every part of the Hospital: physicians, Boards, administration, nurses, employees, parents and patients were necessarily involved in solutions of day-to-day and long-range problems, too often one group did not know what the others were doing nor how it fit into the whole. Better communication was imperative.

The Public Relations Department under Suzanne Edwards (its Director in 1973) became Mr. Frederick's strong right hand in this endeavor. *The Children's Voice,* a bimonthly magazine started under Blossom Porte but later discontinued, was revived. It was sent to 20,000 persons: donors, Board members, parents, friends of the Hospital, and staff. *Newsbreak* kept 1,500 employees abreast of the Hospital's and their own activities. *Administrative Highlights,* a monthly news sheet designed to inform the medical and dental staffs of major hospital events, policies, procedures, etc., was also sent to Directors, Woman's Board members and the administrative heads of departments. The May 1981 issue, for example, set forth the impact on Children's of proposed cuts in government spending for health care in the year ahead.

News of the Hospital has reached the Lincoln Park-Lakeview community in the last two years through releases to the semi-annual *F.Y.I.* (For Your Information), a publication of Augustana, Children's Memorial, Grant, Illinois Masonic, St. Joseph's, and Columbus hospitals. Recently a member of the Public Relations staff has been assigned as liaison between the Hospital and neighborhood residents, businesses, and community organizations.

From time to time, Children's, appropriately enough, has

entertained area children: with a huge Children's Festival—complete with clowns, balloons, and a parade; and a party for 350 children and their parents in the new parking garage just before it opened. Perhaps the latter helped soften the neighbor's attitude toward the garage—that, plus one of Chicago's snowiest winters, when everyone was happy to see 550 cars off the street! The Lincoln Park School children added a note of gaiety to the scene at one stage by painting a bright butterfly mural on the fence surrounding the construction site.

Communication with parents took a giant step forward when Nancy Wachs was appointed Children's ombudsman in 1975. She is the middleman, the liaison between patients and their parents and the Hospital. She is a child advocate, but perhaps more often now her job is interpreting the institution—the system—to the parent. She listens to all sides without judging and attempts to bring understanding to difficult situations. As the Hospital has grown as a referral center, Miss Wachs is a force against its becoming impersonal. Her work, and that of the many volunteers she supervises, benefits the Hospital as well, for often that work is a catalyst which effects changes that ease life for Hospital personnel as well as for patients and their parents.

In these days of rising hospital costs she often finds herself discussing the question "How am I going to pay this bill? What does this item mean?"

Facts, figures, and the crucial decisions necessary to assuring a financially sound institution dominate Children's story in these years leading to its 100th year of service. But the story unfolds against a background of children; the reasons for its existence are always present. Suzanne Edwards expressed it well in the 1975/1976 Annual Report:

Concerned as we must be with finances, budgets, planning, data-gathering and managing, we never lose sight of why this organization of people and facilities exists.

It's for the children.

For the children who come here with serious medical problems, the children throughout the world who will be cared for by the physicians and others we train here; for the future generations we may be able to give more hope through our research efforts.

As we go about our business we are always surrounded by children—

some sitting quietly with tense, still faces; others happily playing a rowdy game in the lobby; or on patient floors riding round and round in a little red wagon; some on the way to a playroom, pulling IV poles behind them.

Woman's Board "business" still took the women into the Hospital—the entrance lobby, the admitting rooms, the intensive care units, the wards, and the playroom—a physical proximity unfortunately seldom asked of the Board of Directors. Back in 1965 Mrs. Rowe had written that the women's most important function was "to help our hospital and staff maintain the personal touch, and show by the warmth of our interest that we care." Increasingly in the seventies as running the Hospital became "big business," the Board recognized its responsibility to promote the human touch—the "element of love" which had distinguished Children's since 1882.

There were for the women many natural ways to do this. As the Decorating and Furnishing Committee (in 1977 called the Design Committee, in 1979 the Department of Design with Donald Scalzo head) selected bright color schemes for the ambulatory department, bought indestructible furniture for the psychiatric unit, or tested the comfort of sofa beds and reclining lounge chairs for parents who needed to stay with their children overnight, the committee's focus was human needs. Through this committee the women could even look at expansion from a point of view other than that of money raising. Each stage of furnishing and decorating the new and remodelled buildings was reported to the Board; often tours were arranged to show off a finished area.

Redecorating the Chapel was part of this committee's responsibility in 1974. The women slipped down before and after meetings to inspect William Moulis's murals. They had as their themes the twenty-third psalm and the tree of life. Parents and patients too came often to stand before the paintings.

Maintaining the Garden Court was another expression of the women's concern. Whether this committee was creating Mr. McGregor's garden for Easter, planting 500 tulip bulbs—a gift from a north shore nursery—or helping Public Relations plan mini-golf tournaments for the children, the activity was patient-oriented. It was part of the Board's desire to create a warm and attractive environment to nourish a sick child, make him a little less fearful of being in a hospital.

Even their "odd" jobs kept the women close to the institution. They bought new books to replace the dog-eared ones in the children's library; they searched for a child's drawing appropriate for the Hospital's annual Christmas card appeal. They transferred $5,000 from a special fund into a revolving fund for loans to student nurses for housing. For several years they sponsored two black high school students in a summer program at Children's, designed to show under-privileged youth some career possibilities in the health field.

Some of the Woman's Board's standing committees, however, did not necessitate active participation. In the sixties, committees like social service, recreational therapy, volunteer, and nursing had become primarily channels of information from professional staff to the Board. That trend continued in the seventies.

Child Life was a new standing committee in 1976, a new name for the old recreational therapy committee. It had not just changed its name, however; a new role for it had been evolving over several years. The new name indicated the broader scope of its work and identified it with similar programs nationwide. Child Life's function was to maintain the normal patterns of a child's growth and development during hospitalization. "Play" was the tool it used to do this. Through play, the department helped hospitalized children to "explore and master their environment, learn about the world, and express their feelings." It was an interdisciplinary effort: everyone who was a part of the child's hospital life—doctor, nurse, social worker, volunteer—as well as members of his family—was enlisted to make a patient's stay a positive experience. Mrs. John B. Hutchins was Chairman of the first Child Life Committee.

Under the enthusiastic direction of its Director (Myrtha Perez), the work of Child Life passed from a tolerant acceptance on the part of the doctors to a what-would-we-do-without-you attitude. The nurses appreciated its value from the outset—the Vice-President of Nursing, Ann Henningsen, keenly aware of the psychosocial as well as the physical needs of the patient, worked closely with Child Life as its program expanded. Parent groups were formed, sometimes just to bring together parents of hospitalized children; at other times to develop contact between parents of children suffering from the same serious illness—spina bifida, cancer, cystic fibrosis. Staff, with the help of volunteers, supervised activities for all the children from the infant to the adolescent. A popular spot for the latter was The Hangout, a club room where teenagers could get together to play games, cook a snack, listen to music, or just talk. The Child Life Committee reported to the Board one month that The Hangout needed a small refrigerator to add to its kitchen facilities; earlier it had requested—and received—a piano, a stereo, and a ping-pong table. Those requests must have had a familiar ring to some of the long time Board members!

Today Child Life finds new challenges in its work. Phenomenal medical advances have prolonged the lives of children suffering from serious—and often multiple—illnesses. Often these children must endure long, and sometimes painful, treatments. To help maintain the best possible quality of life for these patients and to support their parents through weeks, months, and even years of treatment demands all the knowledge and skill Child Life has.

The Volunteer Committee, like Child Life, had changing patterns to report to the Woman's Board in this decade. Volunteers still clock an astonishing number of hours: 52,499 in 1971; 54,592 in 1980. While still continuing traditional jobs of reading bedtime stories and cuddling babies, they offered their help in the new medical services which have opened in the seventies or in the ombudsman program inaugurated in 1978. Project White Hat is still going strong. In 1977 alone, when the Woman's Board helped celebrate the project's tenth anniversary, 320 men had given 3,083 hours of service.

But there are changes. Joan Rehm, Director of the department, sent a questionnaire to all volunteers in 1979. The answers pointed up interesting trends in volunteerism in the seventies. Of 420 new volunteers in 1979, 181 were employed, only 44 were retired. Students numbered 189, including 27 college students. Volunteers had limited time and a great variety of priorities and commitments in their own lives.

Elizabeth Schwartz, succeeding Miss Rehm as Director in 1980, finds these trends continue. She commented on the kind of person who is volunteering in 1981: more bankers, lawyers, businessmen, teachers, and a few from the FBI—she calls them the "corporate" volunteers. There are fewer housewives, women with time on their hands because their children are in college or married. Of the 421 volunteers in 1980, 280 were between ages 18-29; only 15 in the 50-64 age bracket, and only 18 over 65. White collar workers and students accounted for 185 and 176 persons respectively.

The Woman's Board has continued to man the coffee cart once a week. Their volunteer hours aside from this project are given on the whole to the Hospital Shop and the White Elephant Shop—if one does not count the hundreds of hours spent in committee work and fund raising.

The Social Service Committee has remained the Board's window to the clinics and in many ways to the community. Glenn Sheldon Key has been Director of Social Service throughout the seventies. A major reorganization and an enlarged staff strengthened the department's work in 1976. Today's staff of nineteen social workers, several interpreters, and fifteen volunteers is, like its clients, varied in racial, ethnic, and religious background. Many are bilingual—Spanish is still a second language in the clinics.

The social work required at Children's today, Mr. Key says, has changed. As a referral center for critically ill children, Children's now sees, as well, parents with more difficult problems. The impact on a family of caring for a chronically ill child, faced with long-term treatment, is tremendous. "Friendly visiting" is no longer sufficient; parents need great support to meet their problems—often an underlying one now is the financial burden of expensive hospitalization.

The department continues to be an important field work resource for social service students from the University of Chicago and Loyola. It plays a part as well in some courses for medical students. A home visit with a social worker and attendance at an interdisciplinary conference on child abuse were required for a few years in an elective course in ambulatory pediatrics.

There is a good bit of informal interchange between the Social Service and Pastoral Care departments. The latter has grown since the first five seminarians began training in hospital pastoral care under the Reverend Palmer Temple in 1969. Two hundred students (seminarians and ordained ministers and priests) have been trained at Children's. The Reverend Lyonel Gilmer, Director of Pastoral Care since 1977, compares his program to that of the medical resident. Like the resident who learns the reality of medical life in the clinics and the wards, the seminarian also learns there the reality of one phase of a minister's life. Alleviating a child's feeling of separation, the most prevalent emotion of a hospitalized child, if the focus of the student in pastoral care. His work encompasses work with parents and staff as well.

Child abuse, just beginning to be identified as a distinct problem in the late sixties, became a primary concern of the Social Service Department in the seventies. Physicians had become adept at recognizing abuse victims among their patients, but the legal aspects of reporting cases and seeing them through the courts were time consuming and difficult. In 1974, Mrs. Querin Dorschel, a member of the Woman's Board, interested her husband's law firm in the problem. The method it worked out with Children's became a model for expediting child abuse cases through the courts.

The following year the Hospital was one of a sizable group of public and private agencies given a grant of $1 million by HEW to fund a three-year demonstration project on the problems of the abused and neglected child. This Metropolitan Protective Services Project showed successfully the value of a network of private and public agencies working on a social problem. It included such disparate agencies as the Juvenile Court, the Illinois Department of Child and Family Services, the Youth Division of the Chicago Police Department, Illinois Children's Home and Aid, and Chicago Child Care. Children's was the only hospital in the group.

When the project ended, additional grants became available to extend the positive effects of its findings. Children's received one of $53,000 to develop social work programs for children who have been sexually abused, children of seriously disturbed parents, and teenage parents of children with serious medical problems. The grant was renewed for further studies in 1981.

Supportive services for the families of chronically ill children have become increasingly important at Children's. One group of parents, led by Charles Marino, solved their problems in this situation themselves with the help of Dr. Edward Baum from the Department of Oncology. Their children had leukemia and needed continuing treatment. When the family lived at a distance—often out-of-state, the hardship and expense of travel and overnight lodging sometimes made continued treatment virtually impossible. With a gift of $150,000—raised by Chicago's McDonald's restaurant managers—the parents bought a house on nearby Deming Place, installed a young couple to run it, and offered accommodations to out-of-town parents. The Chicago Bears supported the program and within a year Ronald McDonald House was an ongoing facility. It continues today, a shining example of parents' creativity in the face of need.

The Nursing Advisory Committee was an interesting assignment for members of the Woman's Board in the seventies for it saw a turn around in the philosophy of nursing. Shortages of nurses continued to be a problem in the early years of the decade in spite of another round of salary raises in 1971 to meet competition. To this difficulty was added a growing dissatisfaction with the status of the Director of Nursing on the administrative staff. Should she not be given a title to indicate her place in the Hospital's planning?

When Dorothea Fee became Director of Nursing (following Audrey Short's retirement in 1973) the matter was resolved by naming her Assistant Vice-President of Nursing, equal with the heads of ambulatory, professional, and general services. Ann Henningsen, her successor in 1975, was made a full Vice-President.

Nursing shortage reached a critical point that year. For several years studies were made to determine underlying causes: one looked closely at the function of the clinic nurses (ambulatory services were growing steadily); another, the use of the operating nurse; a third, the strain of nursing infants. The last was a particularly sensitive area after Children's newborn unit opened in 1972. The high mortality rate among these critically ill infants was difficult for many nurses to accept; the required constant nursing was demanding.

The basic problem, however, was felt to be density—the Hospital's occupancy rate remained unrelentingly high. As Children's reputation grew, referrals of seriously ill children grew as well. Usually they required longer and highly specialized care. A corollary to the shortage of nurses and density was arbitrarily moving a nurse from one patient or service to another in times of crisis. That practice met with resentment and did much to increase a nurse's tension.

Operating room nurses felt the pressure of a dramatic rise in the number of operations performed at Children's in the seventies, particularly after Dr. Lowell King became Surgeon-in-Chief in 1973 (succeeding Dr. Swenson). Between 1971 and 1975 there were between 5,300-5,700 operations a year; by 1980 there were approximately 7,000. Since many of the operations crossed medical and surgical specialty lines, after-care frequently involved difficult long-term stays in intensive care—another source of tension.

Out of this background in 1977 came the adoption of a new philosophy of nursing care at Children's—primary nursing. Focusing on the child and his family, this method provided the best of individualized care. Each child was assigned to one nurse who planned for his total care from admission to discharge. She was responsible for that care on a twenty-four hour basis; she left specific written instructions for the associate nurses (LPN and NA) who carried on in her absence. Such nursing embraced a patient's—and hence his family's—psychological needs as well as his physical ones. It relieved a parent's bewilderment by giving him a single person to whom to turn for information and advice.

The nurses were enthusiastic about primary nursing, feeling it contributed to their personal, as well as professional, growth. Its philosophy both attracted and held nurses.

From the surgeon's point of view, Dr. King reported enthusiastically on the results of appointing nurses and clinicians to work with a specific service as their primary endeavour. An increasing use of nurse clinicians and nurse clinical specialists was a phenomenon of the seventies. Their training in specific medical specialties made them a valuable asset to the doctors. The clinicians had, in part, a teaching function—explaining to a diabetic or asthmatic child, for example, the details of diet and treatment. The clinical specialists worked most efficiently with doctors in specialty divisions at Children's. Dr. King paid tribute to the system in a report in 1977: "This has improved morale, and the surgeons, in general, feel that working with the same scrub and circulating team tends to shorten surgery and makes the procedure more efficient. It certainly improves the morale of all members of the staff, resulting in more effective team care." That someone on the team visited a child before his operation to explain what would happen meant that the patient was more secure and might even see a familiar face as he was wheeled into the operating room. One little boy's comment must have been

183

typical: "I'm not scared any more, 'cause I have surgery lots of times; and I'm not scared any more, 'cause I know what it is now."

The nursing staff grew from 377 in 1970 to 613 in 1980. Under Vice-President of Nursing Ann Henningsen and acting Vice-President Barbara Jones (1979-1980), after the adoption of primary nursing, the department stabilized.

The Woman's Board had long accepted fund raising as a major responsibility, although their By-laws still carried only that 1904 mandate "full charge of the internal management of the Hospital." But in 1973 when a newly elected Director, carefully reading Children's Constitution and By-laws, asked in amazement if this statement were true, it was revised to read "The Woman's Board shall assist the Board of Directors . . . and the committees of the Board of Directors in the management of the Hospital's operations." Certainly a large part of that assistance was raising money—a "necessary evil," one Board member called it. Given Mr. Swartchild's emphasis on the cooperation of all segments of the Hospital toward meeting the goal of a financially sound institution, plus the presence of women on the Board of Directors (four to six in the seventies), and on its planning, budget, and campaign fund committees, the women knew the realities of the financial situation.

No small part of the challenge and burden of the Presidents of the seventies (Mrs. Howell Hardy, Mrs. Frank Kelley, and Mrs. Newton Burdick) was sustaining the fund raising efforts of the Board. These included, as usual, the White Elephant Shop, The Hospital Shop, Pro-Am, and those fifty or more personal appeals. In 1978 the White Elephant Shop "packed its trunk" and moved "home" to permanent quarters across the street at the corner of Lincoln and Fullerton Avenues. It opened with a new boutique, a men's shop to complement the 411 shop for women. The Hospital Shop a few years earlier had become a gift shop only. Rising food prices in a time of inflation had forced the women to turn over the food part of their operation to the dietary department of the Hospital. The gift shop continued to show a steady profit. Pro-Am was still a major money raiser.

In 1978 the Woman's Board added ArtisTrees to its ongoing money raising events. Christmas trees trimmed by well known

Chicagoans—civic leaders, politicians, TV personalities, actors, decorators, et al.—had a public and private viewing in a prominent location on Michigan Avenue; the John Hancock building was a favorite. At the party hosting the private viewing, the trees were sold at a silent auction. The first year ArtisTrees cleared $13,000; the second, $25,000.

For many years the money raised by the Guilds and Affiliates was included in the total yearly contribution of the Woman's Board. That amount was significant in the seventies, reaching a high of $131,240 in 1976. Recognizing, however, its lack of involvement with those money raising efforts, the Board decided in 1978 that the Guilds' and Affiliates' contributions should more properly go directly to the Hospital. At the same time Coordination of Guilds and Affiliates was dropped from the Board's standing committees.

One way or another, through increasing effort, the Woman's Board met their steadily mounting goals with steadily mounting contributions: $454,192 in 1970; $600,000 by 1975. They never dropped below the latter figure after that year. They were ready, therefore, to consider two requests which were made in 1978 during Mrs. Burdick's first year as President. They were asked to guarantee $600,000 in annual giving; and, as their part in the Centennial Funds drive for capital funds, to assume a major commitment to support a specific part of the Hospital's medical program. Granting the latter request would shift the women's fund raising motivation from the traditional free care stance to focus on a service.

Believing deeply in the future of the Hospital as a great center of care, education, and research, Mrs. Burdick led her Board through consideration of the changes that accepting these requests would bring. She appointed an Ad Hoc Committee (Mrs. Robert Ingersoll, Chairman) to suggest possible projects and a dollar goal for Board discussion. By the end of the year the Board was ready to act: it accepted a goal of $2.2 million to be reached by Children's 100th anniversary in 1982; and it selected the new pediatric cardiology unit as its project. The project was named The Heart Center Fund.

By the time Mrs. Burdick wrote her annual report for 1979-1980, the Fund stood at the half-way mark—$1,064,722. On July 1, 1981, it reached $1,800,000—just $400,000 was left to be raised by the centennial year.

The annual-giving target of $600,000 has been reached each year as well—anything raised over that amount has been added to The Heart Center Fund. For 1980-1981, Mrs. Henry Wheeler's first year as President, that goal was raised to $625,000.

In Children's seventy-fifth year, Dr. Bigler had written with quiet satisfaction: "The Children's Memorial Hospital today offers entire child care with all of its complexities and ramifications." Twenty-five years later, that statement would include an astonishing number of new services or old ones developed almost beyond recognition. It would count equipment undreamed of and techniques unheard of then. Each decade of the Hospital's long history has witnessed the growth and development of pediatrics. Problems of infant feeding, of measles, typhoid fever, and mumps, of polio and crippling orthopedic diseases, of mental retardation and emotional disorders—these, and a host of others, were in turn the focus of earlier periods. When cures or alleviating treatments were found, the Hospital's medical staff had been quick to make them part of Children's quality care of sick children.

Being ready to offer entire child care in the seventies meant, indeed, many things unheard of in 1957. Dr. Henry Nadler, Chief-of-Staff, wrote of these changes as well as of the still unmet needs of children in his annual 1975/1976 report:

The continued rapid accumulation of new and sophisticated knowledge in areas of child health has taken place at an amazing rate. This has resulted in significant changes in patterns of illness and, therefore, the types of services that the hospitals are now required to supply. The problems of infectious disease and malnutrition have given way to those of prematurity, congenital malformations, malignant disease and other chronic conditions which are now the major reasons for hospital utilization. The demands on the hospital in providing services for these patients involve not only a significant increase in personnel and specialized equipment but an increase in the use of ambulatory facilities. In addition, the problems of mental and emotional health, the unique problems of adolescence, and the problems of learning disabilities are some examples of what are considered to be largely unmet needs of children. There are more children needing these services than ever before and the role of the hospital in the provision of this care clearly must be evaluated.

To meet some of these demands had meant establishing new specialties: gastroenterology, immunology, nephrology, a neonatology, nuclear medicine, intensive care, and respiratory care. It had meant adding staff to the enlarged and reorganized departments of anesthesiology, medicine, pathology, radiology, and surgery. The overall full-time staff had grown from 47 to 115 in 11 years, with corresponding increases in nursing and ancillary personnel. In ambulatory services it had meant adding a primary care clinic and a health screening and maintenance clinic for well children to the already established thirty-three specialty clinics. It had meant extending the operating day to 6 p.m. in order to meet the demands of orthopedic and cardiovascular-thoracic surgery. It had meant neurosurgeons offering a new procedure for the closure of myelomeningocele (a spinal defect), and plastic surgeons offering a new technique in skin grafting. It had meant expanding intensive care patient days until they accounted for 18 percent of total patient days.

In another area of care it had meant adding five new services to the department of psychiatry: an in-patient unit; a day-care program; a 7- to 11-year-old group with learning disabilities; a few preschoolers with multiple handicaps; and a small group of adolescents with marked emotional disorders.

Looking back over his eleven years as Chief-of-Staff, Dr. Nadler talked to the Woman's Board in June 1981 about the significance of that period. As preventive medicine—immunizations—had been a major thrust of pediatrics in the twenties, he said, and the use of antibiotics that of the forties, the seventies could be called the period of technology. The single most important advance in that time was hyperalimentation (feeding fluids containing essential nutrients directly into tiny veins through a catheter). Next in importance were improved anesthesia techniques and more skilled intensive care.

Seriously ill children live longer now than they did in the sixties. A leukemia patient can, perhaps, look forward to a normal life span. Children suffering from cystic fibrosis may live now to twenty instead of eleven or twelve years—with repeated treatments. Extension of life is particularly dramatic among premature babies, even those weighing only 800 to 1,000 grams at birth. Hyperalimentation, lung ventilators, and expert intensive care pulls many of them through the critical first days of life. But neonatology has still much to learn, since many of these babies return to the Hospital later with other problems—often respiratory.

Today's pattern of illness at Children's includes a high percentage of chronic, disabling diseases. Readmission is high—40 percent now; it will probably be 60 percent, Dr. Nadler feels by 1985. Chronic diseases, such as asthma, arthritis, and lupus, account for many readmissions—asthma is the most common one today.

Dr. Nadler ended his talk with a strong plea that the Woman's Board continue its traditional role of preserving the human side of the Hospital. Medical care for children, he affirmed, must always be connected with loving and caring.

Educating undergraduate medical students, postgraduate residents, and staff physicians to practice pediatrics in the complex medical world of the seventies was a vital part of life at Children's. Education had long been an important segment of its mission.

Dr. James E. Eckenhoff, Dean of Northwestern Medical School and new ex-officio member of the Board of Directors (1977), took a look at the place and quality of education at Children's in an interview for *The Children's Voice.* "It is generally accepted," he said, "that any institution, especially a hospital, that is not actively involved in the education of young people will stagnate. Young people with their incisive questions, probing minds and unwillingness to accept dogma keep an institution on its toes. Over a period of years, if an institution is not involved in education its standards will deteriorate."

Since Children's is its pediatric arm, Northwestern Medical School is of course responsible for its educational programs. Always good, they were strengthened measurably by the creation of The McGaw Medical Center in 1966. One of the Center's principal functions was to upgrade educational standards. A few years later (1969), it introduced a graduate medical education program with the first private, interhospital agreement in the country. All functions of education in the member hospitals—such as seeking the approval of certifying boards, recruiting trainees, and evaluating programs—were centralized and placed under the jurisdiction of Northwestern. This plan greatly improved graduate education at Children's.

In 1971 Dr. Nadler invited Dr. Wayne Borges to administer the daily conduct of medical education at the Hospital. He became the Given Professor of Pediatrics and was soon, with Dr. Nadler, deep in reevaluating the scope of the institution's medical programs. Together they redesigned the concept of the medical resident's education, that most formative period of a doctor's life. Children's insisted on a three-year residency (the American Board of Pediatrics required only two at that time). By the third year, following a recast in the curriculum of the second and third years, residents were ready to act as supervisors of all major hospital services under the guidance of senior physicians.

The residency program for surgeons is one of the most extensive in the area. Under Dr. Lowell King and Dr. Casimir Firlet (Acting Surgeon-in-Chief, 1981), each surgical division maintains a formal teaching program and provides practical experience for residents, as well as daily contact with the distinguished surgeons at Children's.

A minor rebellion of the residents broke out in 1977—similar to those happening all over the country. Residents began to question some of the long accepted patterns in their education; they were restive under the demanding, tightly structured training. They found it at times unreasonable, frustrating, and unrewarding; at all times it provided a "quality of life" unacceptable to young persons in the late seventies. There was another factor in the situation at Children's not, perhaps, perceived clearly at the time. Residents were constantly exposed to critically ill patients, they saw children die, and were confronted with the difficult ethical questions of prolonging the life of a badly afflicted child. It was a far cry from the concept of the pediatrician dealing with essentially healthy children—immunizing, curing common ailments.

Dr. Nadler and the staff took another look at the life and problems of the resident. Adjustments were made to alleviate tension and improve education. Applications for residency, which had begun to fall off noticeably, improved dramatically. Today there are approximately 100 residents at the Hospital.

Research in the seventies has revolved around the patient and his care, as it has from the beginning. Rooted in a physician's need to know the "whys" and "hows" of diagnosis, treatment, and care of his patients, it has embraced a wide spectrum of programs. It ranges from the basic physiologic sciences, which permit early prenatal diagnosis of genetic diseases to the causes of the anomalies of birth, to the techniques effecting changes in social behavior, to understanding the motivation of child abuse. It includes efforts to discover the underlying causes of rheumatoid arthritis, sickle cell anemia, hematologic and cardiac problems, cystic fibrosis, and degenerative diseases. In the department of surgery there has been active research in the important fields of neurosurgery and urology. With another focus, studies have begun to investigate the neurological, psychological, social, and educational development of children suffering from such severe diseases as spina bifida and malignancies.

While many of these programs have generated their own funds, there must be a never-ending search for money to support this component of Children's mission.

Just as social and economic forces of the seventies shaped the administration of the Hospital, so did they affect the practice of medicine. Dr. Nadler addressed the impact of these forces which had led to a review of Children's programs as the medical staff looked to the future:

One of the major social forces is the general acceptance of society's obligation to provide high quality, comprehensive health care to all children. The development of more complicated and time consuming components for both preventive and curative medicine places tremendous demands on the resources of our community and society in general. A comprehensive health care program for children will shortly be in effect. The specifics of such a program are yet to be defined; however, it is very difficult to believe that such a program will not be undertaken. This may well impact upon the type of patient served, the scope of our program, and the methods of financial and medical review.

Another recent change has been the increasing involvement of consumers in determining the acceptability of medical care and medical decision making. The evolution of programs of patients' bills of rights and better methods of informed consent have been recently implemented. It is obvious that the problem of medical malpractice is a complex one and involves review of medical performance because of dissatisfaction of patients, lawyers, juries, and other individuals. Medical costs have continued to increase at a frightening pace significantly above that of the general rate of inflation. A major problem faced by all hospitals is the ability to offer care to patients at prices which can be afforded. The higher costs of hospitalization as well as rates for ambulatory services are at a level which may well make medical care inaccessible to many of our potential consumers.

The recent publicity regarding the inability of the medical profession and specifically hospitals to fulfill their traditional role in supplying free care to the poor has added to much resentment towards hospitals and physicians. It has become impossible for many families of lower and middle incomes to pay for the care of their children. Many who are willing find it difficult to obtain adequate insurance programs and relatively few of these cover the costs of well child supervision. . . .

Many of the problems in the health care system and their ultimate solutions are not within our direct control. We will, in any case, be forced to find more efficient and effective methods of providing care to children, both in our inpatient and outpatient settings. The Medical Staff plays a critical role in attempting to recognize its responsibilities in each of these areas and to react in a responsible way to enable us to meet our goal of providing optimal health care for children with the resources available to us.

As a basis for evaluating programs, medical audits were made under Dr. Margaret O'Flynn's direction. They served several purposes—they supplied information needed by the Joint Commission for Accreditation of Hospitals, an important standard setting body, and they informed the Board of Directors of the quality of patient care. The latter became increasingly important as this Board became directly responsible for that part of the institution's operation.

Positioning the Hospital to meet the challenges of the eighties was, in effect, the rallying cry of its leadership at the end of the seventies.

The second phase of the building program—four additional floors to the bed tower—was underway, it would be completed by 1982, the Centennial year. Children's was in a sound financial position as it entered the eighties. Mr. James Cipriano, Vice President for Development and Public Relations in 1978, was assessing the public's image of the Hospital in order to develop new and more effective ways to broaden understanding and support of its work. Operating income had increased; annual contributions were reaching the enlarged goals set each year; the Centennial Fund's construction committee had raised $29.7 million by June 30, 1981. The Endowment Fund was rising more slowly—it stood at $1,226,249 on that date.

The Board of Directors with an enlarged membership (thirty-four active and eight ex-officio as opposed to twenty-six active and three ex-officio ten years earlier) had accepted a vastly greater role than that of earlier days. Their current By-laws define that role as having "charge, control and management of the property, affairs and funds of the Corporation." It recognizes that the Board, as a policy-making body, is ultimately accountable not only to the people it serves, but also to the community and to the government. These are no small tasks in the climate of today's rules and regulations imposing financial constraints and the public's great concern over the increased cost of health care.

Per diem cost at the Hospital is about $700. Private rooms were discontinued in March 1981; semi-private rooms cost $325. Special care units are higher: $500—$725 for intensive care, $645 for the neonatology unit.

The Board of Directors has reviewed and tightened its structure to meet its greater responsibilities. It has reworded the Hospital's mission statement:

> To provide infants and children the maximum quantity and quality of comprehensive health care within the available resources of the hospital.
>
> To teach students and health professionals through educational programs in dentistry, medicine, surgery, nursing and the allied health professions.
>
> To advance medical knowledge through research on the cause, treatment and prevention of childhood disease.
>
> To be a leader in the implementation of coordinated pediatric health services for its immediate community and for the wisespread regions served by the hospital.

This statement, adopted in 1980, does not minimize the traditional commitments of Children's; however, it does, by adding the phrase "within the available resources of the hospital," bring Children's into the reality of the eighties.

The Woman's Board as well has analyzed its purpose and structure in the light of the changes of the seventies. It has divided its committees into two categories: fund raising and hospital-centered services. The first includes finance (the annual appeal), The Heart Center Fund, The Hospital Shop, Pro-Am, ArtisTress, and the White Elephant Shop. An overall committee in this category—Fund Raising and Communications—is charged with reviewing, coordinating, and helping to implement fund raising and public relations.

The Hospital-centered committees coordinate many of the former standing committees into four comprehensive ones: ambulatory, Garden Court, nursing, and hospital services. Without exception, the charges to these committees stress active participation, not just collecting information. The entire committee structure in this category is aimed at involving Board members in work for—and in—the Hospital.

The Woman's Board's purpose as restated, is concise and clear: "to support the hospital in fund raising, communications, and volunteer activities." The Long Range Goal reaffirms the women's commitment to preserving the "element of love" at Children's: "The Woman's Board shall provide the human element for this growing professional hospital."

The challenges of the eighties to the Hospital will be no easy ones. But the Board of Directors, the Woman's Board, the medical staff, and administration are ready to meet them. For one hundred years Children's Memorial Hospital has been caring for sick children; it will continue to do so as it enters its second century.

Appendix

Below are lists of the men and women who have served The Children's Memorial Hospital from 1882-1981 as members of the Boards, Chiefs-of-Staff, Administrators, and heads of the departments of nursing and social service. The names are listed exactly as they appear in the hospital's records: minutes in the earliest days, annual reports later. They are listed alphabetically under the year of joining; no effort has been made to note the length of service.

1882

Porter, Julia Foster
(Mrs. Edward C. Porter)

1892

Adams, Mrs. George E.
Bowen, Mrs. J. T.
Field, Mrs. Henry
Mead, Mrs. E. R.
McClurg, Mrs. A. C.
North, Mrs. Robert
Ogden, Mrs. Mahlon
Smith, Mrs. Orson
Taylor, Mrs. S. G.

1894

Adams, Mrs. George E.
Adams, George E.
Fay, Charles Norman
Fay, Mrs. Charles Norman

Lathrop, Mr. & Mrs. Bryan
McCagg, Mrs. E. B.
McClurg, Alexander C.
Porter, James W.
Smith, Orson

1895

Cobb, Mrs. Ives
Goodwin, Mrs. Daniel
Kohlsaat, Mrs. Herman H.
McConnell, Mrs. Luther
Smith, Mrs. Dunlap

1896

Hadduck, Mrs. Frank
McCormick, Mrs. Alexander
Nelson, Mrs. Murry, Jr.

1897

Cramer, Mrs. Eliphalet W.
Dyar, Mrs. Hugh

Meeker, Mrs. Arthur
Tyson, Mrs. Russel
Waller, Mrs. Robert

1898

Harlan, Mrs. James
Truesdale, Mrs. Wm. H.

1899

Howe, Mrs. Richard
McCormick, Mrs. Harold F.

1900

Deane, Mrs. Ruthven
Hunt, Mrs. Platt

1901

DeLaur, Mrs. F. A.
Porter, Mr. James F.

1902

Black, Mrs. John
Martyn, Mrs. E. J.
Pike, Mrs. Charles
Porter, Mrs. James F.
Smith, Miss Mary Roget
Wilson, Miss Martha

1904

Armour, Mrs. J. Ogden
Babcock, Mrs. Orville
Baker, Miss Ethel
Bartlett, Mrs. Frederic C.
Bass, Mrs. John F.
Booth, Mrs. W. V.
Borland, Mrs. Chauncey
Burnes, Miss
Carpenter, Mrs. A. A.
Carpenter, Mrs. Hubbard F.
Carpenter, Mrs. John A.
Caruthers, Miss Fanny
Chalmers, Mrs. W. J.
Chapman, Mrs. Clarence
Clark, Mrs. Edwin
Clark, Mrs. George

Clark, Mrs. Mancel
Clow, Mrs. James C.
Coleman, Mrs. Joseph G.
Cox, Miss Jane
Cramer, Mr. Eliphalet W.
Crane, Mrs. Richard., Jr.
Dempster, Mrs. Charles W.
Deck, Miss Mabel
Dunham, Miss Belle
Dunham, Mrs. Wirth
Dunn, Morrill
Eldridge, Mrs. Harold
Elting, Mrs. Howard
Euston, Mrs. Edwin
Fair, Miss Helen
Ferguson, Mrs. George M.
Field, Mrs. Marshall, Jr.
Field, Mrs. Stanley
Follansbee, Miss Eunice
Galt, Mrs. Hubert
Gaylord, Miss Louise
Gillette, Mrs. Edwin
Goodrich, Miss Juliet
Hamilton, Miss Adelaide
Hamlin, Mrs. Harry L.
Heyworth, Mrs. James O.
Higinbotham, Mrs. Harry
Honore, Mrs. Lockwood
Hoyt, Miss
Hoyt, Miss Edith M.
Hoyt, Mrs. Phelps
Hulburd, Miss Ethel
Hull, Morton D.
Johnston, Mrs. Morris
Jones, Thomas D.
Kales, Mrs. Albert M.
Keith, Mrs. Edson, Jr.
Keith, Mrs. W. W.
King, Mrs. Charles Garfield
King, Miss Marjorie
Kohlsaat, Miss Pauline
Lawrence, Mrs. Dwight
Linn, Miss Mabel
Lord, Miss Helen
Lord, Miss Mary

Marshall, Miss Gertrude
Marston, Mrs. Thomas B.
Mott, Miss Genevieve
Musgrave, Mrs. Harrison
McClurg, Mrs. Ogden T.
McCord, Mrs. Alvin C.
McCormick, J. Medill
McCormick, Mrs. J. Medill
McCullough, Miss Florence
McFadon, Miss Margaret
McIlvaine, Wm. B.
McMurray, Miss Elizabeth
McMurray, Miss Kathleen
Newell, Mrs. Ashbel
Odell, Mrs. Wm. R.
Olmstead, Mrs. Oliver
Otis, Miss Louise
Packard, George
Palmer, Mrs. Honoré
Patterson, Mrs. Joseph M.
Patterson, Mrs. Stewart
Peck, Miss Haroldine
Peck, Miss Josephine
Pelouze, Mrs. Wm. N.
Pike, Charles B.
Pope, Mrs. Charles
Porter, Mrs. H. H., Jr.
Potter, Miss Gertrude
Ridlon, Miss Hester
Runnells, Miss
Russell, Miss Mary
Rutter, Mrs. Dudley
Ryerson, Mrs. Edwin W.
Ryerson, Miss Mary
Shumway, Miss Mary
Smith, Miss Harriet
Smith, Mrs. Kenney
Sprague, Mrs. A. A. II
Stevens, Mrs. Redmond
Stevenson, Mrs. Robert
Stone, Miss Louise H.
Stone, Mrs. Robert
Street, Miss Agnes
Taylor, Mrs. Francis W.
Thompson, Mrs. Gale (Leaverett)

Thorne, Mrs. James W.
Tyler, Mrs. Theodore
Tyson, Russell
Wakem, Mrs. Wallace
Walker, Mrs. Bertrand
Waller, Mrs. Francis
Walsh, Mrs. Richard
Warner, Mrs. Ezra, Jr.
Washburn, Mrs. J. Murray
Williams, Miss Cornelia
Wilson, Mr. John P.
Wilson Mrs. John P., Jr.
Winterbotham, Mrs. John H.
Winterbotham, Miss Katherine
Winterbotham, Miss Margaret A.

1906

Allen, Miss Dora
Blair, Watson F.
Blair, Mrs. Watson F.
Borland, Mrs. John Jay
Bross, Mrs. Mason
Canby, Miss Mary
Corbin, Mrs. Dora
Cowles, Alfred
Deering, James
Gray, Miss Florence
Higginson, George, Jr.
Janeway, Mrs. John H.
Lynde, Miss Isabelle
McCormick, Mrs. Robert Hall
Mitchell, Mrs. Leeds
Nelson, Murray, Jr.
Norcross, Mrs. Frederick
Rosenthal, Lessing
Ryerson, Edward L.
Smith, Mrs. Walter Byron
Strobel, Charles L.
Walker, James R.
Walker, Mrs. James R.
Walker, Dr. Samuel J.
Walker, Mrs. Samuel J.
Walsh, Mrs. Vincent
Willing, Mrs. Mark S. K.
Wilson, John P., Jr.

1907

Beebe, Mrs. Wm. H.
Brewster, Mrs. Walter S.
Burke, Mrs. Edmund
Forstall, Miss Celestine
Isham, George S., M.D.
Keep, Mrs. Albert II
Spoor, Mrs. John A.
Woolley, Mrs. Clarence M.

1908

Brentano, Mrs. Theodore
Brown, Miss Margaretta
Carr, Mrs. Clyde M.
Chase, Mrs. Samuel
Dickinson, Mrs. Wm. R.
Eckhart, Mrs. Bernard
Fairbanks, Mrs. Warren C.
Fitch, Mrs. Lawrence
French, Mrs. George B.
Fuller, Mrs. LeRoy
Gary, Mrs. John
Gillett, Mrs. Charles
Grannis, Mrs. Uri B.
Harahan, Mrs. James T.
Harvey, Mrs. Byron S.
Henry, Mrs. W. G.
Hubbard, Mrs. Charles W.
Hubbard, Mrs. Henry
Huck, Mrs. L. C.
Ingalls, Mrs. George H.
Johnston, Mrs. Hugh McB
Keith, Miss Bessie
Long, Mrs. Joseph B.
McLennan, Mrs. D. R.
Moore, Mrs. Philip W.
Morris, Mrs. Edward
Neff, Miss Florence
Ortmann, Mrs. Rudolph
Paxton, Mrs. Charles F.
Peabody, Mrs. Augustus
Pietsch, Mrs. Frank H.
Pitcher, Mrs. John C.

Pollack, Mrs. Edward L.
Rehm, Mrs. Wm. H.
Rosenthal, Mrs. Lessing
Rosenwald, Mrs. Julius
Schuttler, Miss Lillian
Schwarz, Mrs. Herbert E.
Simpson, Mrs. James
Stephens, Mrs. Redmond D.
Taylor, Mrs. George H.
Williams, Mrs. Harry F.
Winchell, Mrs. Benjamin L.
Winter, Mrs. Wallace
Wrenn, Miss

1909

Adams, Mrs. Cyrus
Booth, Miss Agnes
Burrows, Miss Louise
Carpenter, Mrs. A. A., Jr.
Chandler, Miss Isabel
Coleman, Mrs. S. Cobb
Conger, Miss Cornelia
Counselman, Mrs. Charles
Crane, Mrs. Harold
Cummings, Mrs. D. Mark
Dewey, Mrs. Charles
Enders, Miss Margaret
Insull, Mrs. Samuel
Meeker, Mrs. Arthur
Upham, Mrs. Frederick W.

1910

Martin, Mrs. Wm. P.
McAuley, Mrs. Henry S.
McCormick, Mrs. R. H., Jr.
Pike, Mrs. Eugene
Spoor, John A.
Wilson, Miss Irene

1911

Morris, Edward
Patten, James A.
Peterson, Mr. P. C.
Welton, Mrs. Emil

1912

Adams, Mrs. Hugh
Armour, Mrs. A. Watson
Ballard, Miss Margaret
Billings, Miss Margaret
Blair, Miss Mildred
Bond, Miss Rachel
Borland, Mrs. Bruce
Bowen, Mrs. deKoven
Browne, Mrs. Aldis
Bull, Miss Hilda
Bull, Miss Margaret
Carton, Mrs. Alfred T.
Chandler, Miss Ruby
Chandler, Miss Virginia
Conover, Miss Margaret
Cooke, Mrs. Henry E., Jr.
Countiss, Mrs. Frederick D.
Craig, Mrs. Alexander
Crane, Miss Dorothy
Cudahy, Miss Helen
Cudahy, Mrs. Joseph
Cummins, Miss Julie
Dickinson, Mrs. Francis
Ely, Mrs. Jay Morse
Farwell, Miss Katherine
Farwell, Miss Olive
Farwell, Miss Sarah
Felton, Miss Beulah
Fisk, Miss Beulah
Fitzgerald, Miss Gertrude
Forgan, Miss Ethel
Forgan, Miss Marian
Freeman, Mrs. Charles J.
Given, Miss Erma
Greenlee, Mrs. Wm. B.
Gregory, Miss Ruth
Haines, Mrs. J. Allen
Hall, Mrs. Robert
Hambleton, Mrs. C. J.
Hamill, Mrs. Alfred E.
Hamline, Miss Josephine
Hawes, Miss Fanny
Healy, Mrs. Paul

Henry, Mrs. Huntington
Herrick, Miss Margaret
Holdredge, Mrs. C. J.
Keep, Miss Margaret
Kimball, Mrs. Charles
Langmore, Mrs. W. B.
Lyon, Miss Harriett
Meller, Mrs. Ford
McCluney, Mrs. James
McClure, Miss Harriet
McCormick, Miss Mildred
McFatrich, Miss Florence
North, Miss Dorothy
Osborne, Mrs. Glidden
Owsley, Miss Edna
Peabody, Miss May
Peak, Miss Martha
Poole, Mrs. Ralph
Prindiville, Miss Cora
Ranney, Mrs. George
Raymond, Miss Lucy
Reilly, Miss Margaret
Robbins, Miss Dorothy
Robbins, Miss Marjorie
Ryerson, Miss Suzette
Sprague, Mr. A. A. II
Stuart, Mrs. John
Swift, Mrs. Alden
Swift, Mrs. Gustavus, Jr.
Swift, Miss Ida May
Throop, Mrs. George
Turner, Mrs. Tracy
Viles, Miss Helen
Viles, Mrs. Lawrence
Walker, Miss Sarah
Walker, Mrs. Wm. Ernest
Waller, Miss Mary
Walsh, Miss Dorothy
Walton, Miss Harriet
Watson, Mrs. Hathaway
Wilson, Mrs. Milton

1913

Baldwin, Mrs. Rosecrans
Buckingham, Miss Alice

Clark, Mrs. A. Sheldon
Forgan, Mrs. Donald
Goodman, Mrs. Kenneth S.
Helmer, Miss Myra
Hill, Mrs. Frederick
Hutchins, Mrs. James C., Jr.
Johnson, Mrs. Francis J.
Jones, Miss Catherine
Key, Miss Marian
Leatherbee, Mrs. Robert
Mabbatt, Miss Judith
Mitchell, Miss Gwendolyn
Morris, Nelson S.
Morton, Miss Helen
Peck, Miss Martha
Robbins, Isabel
Ryerson, Mrs. Donald
Spoor, Miss Caryl
Wilson, Miss Marjorie
Withers, Mrs. A. L.

1914

Baum, Mrs. J. E., Jr.
Bennett, Mrs. E. H.
Delano, Miss Louise
Dox, Miss Dorothy
Gardiner, Mrs. Paul
Hibbard, Mrs. Frank
Shaw, Miss Doris
Stillwell, Mrs. Addison
Stuart, Mrs. Douglas
Walcott, Mrs. Chester
Wells, Miss Dorothy
Woodruff, Miss Emily

1915

Armour, Mrs. Laurence
Atherton, Mrs. Ray
Blair, Miss Anita
Daughaday, Mrs. Hamilton
Hambleton, Miss Eleanor
Hambleton, Miss Gladys
High, Miss Gladys
Maxwell, Mrs. Augustus
Meeker, Miss Grace

Simpson, James
Stevenson, Mrs. John
Walker, Miss Jeanette
Wallace, Miss Florian

1916

Ames, Mrs. James C.
Armour, Miss Lolita
Baur, Mrs. Jacob
Bond, Mrs. Ralph
Boyle, Miss Elizabeth
Brackett, Mrs. Wm.
Braun, Mrs. George
Broome, Mrs. Thornhill
Brown, Mrs. A. Wilder
Carry, Mrs. Edward F.
Carry, Miss Emma
Cramer, Mrs. Ambrose
Douglas, Mrs. James H.
Ellis, Mrs. Ralph
Freeman, Mrs. Halsted
Gardner, Mrs. Robert
Geraghty, Mrs. Frank
Gowen, Mrs. Albert
Gurley, Miss Helen
Howard, Mrs. Harold
Johnson, Mrs. Oscar W.
Leonard, Mrs. Clifford
Lytton, Mrs. Walter
Meller, Miss Janet
Niblack, Mrs. Austin
Nicholas, Mrs. George R.
Rend, Mrs. Frank
Shaw, Mrs. Henry
Shearson, Mrs. Harry H.
Whiting, Mrs. Bradford
Wilson, Mrs. Eloise S.
Winston, Mrs. Hampden
Young, Mrs. Hobart

1917

Blair, Mrs. Parker
Crane, R. T., Jr.
Forgan, Mrs. Robert
Freund, Mrs. Ernst

Lingle, Mrs. Bowman
Reynolds, Mrs. Earle
Rickcords, Mrs. Stanley

1918

Comstock, Mrs. Robert
Dixon, Mrs. Alan
Eaton, Mrs. Barrien
Jerrems, Mrs. Donald
Keith, Mrs. Harold
Keith, Mrs. Stanley
Montgomery, Miss Frances
Nicholson, Mrs. Wm.
Nielson, Mrs. Francis

1919

Litsinger, Mrs. E. R.
Pirie, John T.
Wilhelm, Mrs. Frank

1920

Dewes, Mrs. E. P.
Gilbert, Miss Clara
McCormick, Mrs. L. Hamilton
Rawson, Mrs. Frederick
Salisbury, Mrs. Warren
Seaverns, Mrs. G. A., Jr.
Theurer, Mrs. Peter
Tilt, Mrs. Joseph E.

1921

Evans, Mrs. Floyd
Gould, Mrs. Gordon
Graves, Miss Virginia
Green, Miss Lucretia
Holden, Miss Eleanor
Lake, Miss Clara
Lord, Miss Lucy
Marston, Miss Dorothy
McKinlock, Mrs. George A.
McLaughlin, Miss Harriet
Offield, Mrs. James
Owen, Miss Mary Dale
Perkins, Mrs. Charles
Pierce, Miss Adelaide

Rinaker, Mrs. Samuel
Rockwell, Mr. H. H.
Smith, Mrs. Harold
Voight, Miss Alice
Ware, Miss Elizabeth
Wheeler, Mrs. Robert

1922

Bowes, Miss Katherine
Boyden, Mrs. Preston
Boyden, Mrs. W. C., Jr.
Brown, Mrs. Charles E., Jr.
Chapin, Mrs. Henry K.
Chase, Miss Elizabeth
Clow, Miss Marion
Cowles, Mrs. Thomas
Cummings, Miss Edith
Cunningham, Mrs. Secor
Dick, Mrs. Albert B., Jr.
Dixon, Mrs. Homer
Edwards, Miss Marjorie
Field, Stanley
Jones, Mrs. Owen B.
Packard, Mrs. Frank
Pierce, Miss Adelaide
Smith, Miss Helen
Smith, Miss Mari
Storm, Mrs. Frank

1923

Blair, Mrs. Wm.
Clow, Mrs. Kent
Foster, Mrs. Chas. K.
Kohlsatt, Miss Edith V.
Letts, Miss Hollis
Lowden, Mrs. Frank
Marquis, Miss Anna
McCord, Miss Marjorie
Orr, Mrs. Robert C.
Russell, Miss Maroussa
Wacker, Mrs. Fred G.
Winston, Mrs. Farwell

1924

Rawson, Frederick H.

1925

Addington, Miss Florence
Bartholomay, Miss Elsa
Beidler, Miss Elizabeth
Brunker, Mrs. Albert
Carpenter, Miss Alice
Carpenter, Mrs. Kenneth
Chandler, Mrs. Fremont
Childs, Miss Madeline
Dennehy, Mrs. Thomas
Dixon, Mrs. Arthur
Drake, Mrs. John B., Jr.
Emerson, Mrs. E. Waldo
Hambleton, Miss Margaret
Harding, Miss Mary
Hettler, Mrs. Sangston
Holden, Mrs. Hale, Jr.
Hubbard, Mrs. Wm. C.
LeForgee, Mrs. Charles Granville
Lowden, Miss Harriett
Mitchell, Mrs. Clarence B.
Naugle, Miss Jane
Norcross, Miss Catherine
Noyes, Miss Florence
Ritchie, Miss Jeanette
Rodman, Mrs. Clifford
Scott, Miss Emily
Smith, Mrs. Potter L.
Thompson, Miss Laura
Tyler, Miss Louise
Woodruff, Miss Lyla

1926

Allen, Mrs. Harry A.
Bartholomay, Mrs. Henry C.
Blossom, Mrs. Frances
Clay, Mrs. John, Jr.
Collins, Miss Virginia
Coonley, Mrs. John S., Jr.
Covington, Mrs. Wm.
Drake, Miss Elizabeth
Greenlee, Mrs. Robert
Kennedy, Mrs. Herbert

King, Mrs. Joseph H.
Laflin, Mrs. Lloyd
Madlener, Mrs. Albert F., Jr.
McLaughlin, Mrs. George D.
Peabody, Mrs. Howard
Stuart, Miss Joan
Valentine, Mrs. Patrick A.
Van Hagen, Mrs. George, Jr.
Withers, Mrs. Pickett

1927

Drake, Mrs. Wm. McClellan
Hord, Mrs. Stephen Y.
Keernan, Mrs. Francis K.
Kennedy, Mrs. Herbert, Jr.
Morse, Mrs. Milton
Neilson, Mrs. Francis
Osborne, Mrs. Nathan G.
Pike, Eugene R.
Salisbury, Mrs. Kimball
Sinclair, Miss Margaret
Stuart, Miss Ellen
Thompson, Mrs. John
Wetten, Albert H.

1928

Booth, Mr. Frederick S.
Borland, Bruce
Brewer, Miss Louise
Dennehy, Miss Eleanor
Drake, Miss Katherine
Dunbaugh, Mrs. George, Jr.
Hammond, Mrs. Gardner
Harvey, Miss Roberta
Higgins, Miss Jeanette
Hopkins, Mrs. James, Jr.
Laflin, Mrs. Claire Childs
McArthur, Mrs. Billings
Newcomet, Miss Edith Louise
Osborne, Mrs. Catherine B.
Otis, Miss Sorane
Phillips, Mrs. McCord
Richardson, Miss Frances
Scott, Frederick H.

Watkins, Mrs. W. A. P.
Wehmann, Mrs. Charles
Wetmore, Mrs. Horace
Whitecomb, Miss Georgiana

1929

Agar, Mrs. Woodbury S., Jr.
Benello, Mrs. Lytton
Borland, Miss Beatrice
Clow, Mrs. Brach J.
Osborne, Mrs. Bartholomay
Scudder, Mrs. Barrett

1930

Cosalis, Mrs. Maurice
Foster, Miss Marguerite
Gray, Mrs. William
MacCaughey, Miss Mary
McBride, Mrs. W. Paul
Poole, Mrs. George A., Jr.
Sidley, Miss Rosemary
Swift, Miss Narcissa

1931

Agar, Mrs. W. Stearns, Jr.
Cable, Arthur G.
Crawford, Mrs. Walter Webb
Insull, Samuel, Jr.
King, Joseph H.
Leonard, Miss Harriet
Vaughn, Mrs. James

1932

Castle, Mrs. Latham
Cox, Mrs. A. C.
Holden, Mrs. Royal
Parker, Mrs. Woodruff J.
Peterkin, Miss Jeannette
Ripley, Miss Jane
Stevens, Mrs. C. Gardner, Jr.
Swift, Miss Geraldine
Theurer, Miss Jane
Vilas, Mrs. Royal C., Jr.
Walsh, Miss Ann Elizabeth
Watson, Miss Chloe

1933

Dudley, Miss Lillian
Flannery, Mrs. Roy
Kelly, Mrs. T. Lloyd
Taber, Mrs. David

1934

Alexander, Miss Elizabeth
Bastien, Miss Barbara
Bouscaren, Mrs. Pierre
Davis, Miss Isabel
Davis, Mrs. Johnson
Freeman, Mrs. Charles Y., Jr.
Gardner, Miss Marie Louise
Hunt, Mrs. William
Hurley, Mrs. John R.
Isham, Mrs. Ralph N.
Lawlor, Mrs. William J., Jr.
Morse, Mrs. John B.
Newcomet, Miss Marian
Sullivan, Mrs. Denis E., Jr.
Taylor, Mrs. A. Thomas

1935

Armour, Lester
Armstrong, Mrs. Frank
Drum, Mrs. John
Foley, Mrs. Charles S.
Goodwillie, Mrs. W. S.
Hays, Miss Mary Lou
McNair, Frank
Offutt, Mrs. Seymour
Schuyler, Mrs. William M.
Wetten, Miss Elinor

1936

Blodgett, Mrs. Delos A. II
Brydon, Miss Louise
Ferguson, Mrs. Alan
Jeffery, Miss Frances
King, Mrs. John L.
Schuyler, Mrs. Daniel M.
Sterling, Miss Virginia

1937

Burton, Miss Babbs
Critchell, Mrs. Robert S.
Elliott, Mrs. F. Osbourne
Goodwillie, Mrs. Johns
Haverkompf, Mrs. John III
Noble, Mrs. Newton S., Jr.
Offutt, Mrs. Battelle
Search, Miss Madalon
Sherman, Miss Eleanor
Swift, Miss Marie

1938

Coffin, Mrs. Charles H., Jr.
Gleim, Mrs. Frederic, Jr.
Harwood, Miss Yvonne
Irving, Mrs. John L.
Symonds, N. M.

1939

Bouscaren, Mrs. Henri
Hutchins, Miss Margaret
King, Mrs. Joseph H.
Lill, Mrs. George II
Peabody, Mrs. Stuyvesant, Jr.
Pierce, Mrs. Frank, Jr.
Porter, Mrs. Lefens
Tredenick, Mrs. J. Beacham
Vanderworker, Mrs. Richard
Vilas, Mrs. Jack, Jr.
Wastcoat, Mrs. John W.
Woolf, Mrs. Edward B.
Zimmerman, Miss Jane

1940

Barnes, Mrs. Nelson L., Jr.
Beatty, Mrs. John T.
Gillette, Mrs. Howard F., Jr.
Howe, Mrs. Edward C.
Mather, Mrs. Joseph
Minor, Mrs. J. Ramsey
Pennington, Mrs. James S., Jr.
Ryerson, Mrs. Anthony M.
Sims, Mrs. Edwin W., Jr.

Upham, Mrs. Robert B., Jr.

1941

Adams, Miss Mary S.
Cherry, Mrs. Walter L.
Cummings, Dexter
DeClerque, Miss Natalie
Gardner, Mrs. T. Sewall
Gillespie, Miss Elizabeth
Osborne, Mrs. Frank G.
Rodormer, Mrs. E. Winston
Spiel, Mrs. Robert E.
Thompson, Miss Lois

1942

Brown, Mrs. Donald A. K.
Cain, Mrs. George R.
Coffin, Mrs. John
Kramer, Mrs. LeRoy
Roberts, Mrs. William E.
Schueler, Miss Martha

1943

Elmer, Mrs. Charles T.
Holinger, Mrs. Paul
McBain, Hughston M.

1944

Babcock, Mrs. Alexander
Young, Mrs. George Berkeley

1945

Adams, Cyrus H. III
Borland, John Jay

1946

Watermulder, Louis F.
Welles, Edward K.

1947

Armour, Mrs. Philip D., Jr.
Bachman, Mrs. Harold A.
Clay, Mrs. John
Cummings, Mrs. Dexter
Douglas, Mrs. Donald B.

Eisendrath, Miss Elsa
Hosler, Mrs. Wyndham
Holabird, Mrs. John A.
McKenna, Mrs. James J.
Rogers, Mrs. Hopewell L.
Rowley, Mrs. Henry N.
Simpson, Mrs. Constance B.
Straus, Mrs. Henry Horner
Swift, Mrs. T. Philip
Whiting, Mrs. Harris A.

1948

Donnelley, Mrs. Elliott
Fetridge, Mrs. William
Watermulder, Mrs. Louis

1950

Addington, Mrs. James R.
Ames, Mrs. John D.
Carr, Mrs. Robert Adams
Farrar, Mrs. John T. P.
Hutchins, Mrs. Chauncey Keep
Sizer, Lawrence B.
Wilson, Mrs. John P.
Winston, Mrs. James H.

1951

Burdick, Mrs. W. Newton, Jr.
Clay, Mrs. Eastman
Meers, Henry W.
Starosselsky, Mrs. Nicholas

1952

Mitchell, Mrs. Wm. H.
Swift, Mrs. Edward F. III

1953

Guenzel, Mrs. Paul W.
Kennedy, Mrs. Herbert H.
King, Garfield
Mitchell, Mrs. William H.
Taylor, Mrs. Wm. C.
Van Nice, Errett
Wilson, Mrs. John P., Jr.

1954

Dickinson, William R., Jr.

1955

Addington, Mrs. Wood
Nichols, Mrs. Frank B.
Wheeler, Mrs. Henry P.

1956

Armour, Mrs. T. Stanton
Armour, Mrs. Vernon
Bowers, Mrs. Lloyd W.
Buhse, Mrs. Howard
Cathcart, Mrs. Silas S.
Chandler, Mrs. G. M.
Clausen, Mrs. Henry W.
Cudahy, Mrs. Wm. B.
Cummings, Mrs. D. Gregg
Dickinson, Mrs. Wm. R., Jr.
Dorschel, Mrs. Querin P.
Douglas, Mrs. Donald
Gorham, Mrs. Sidney S., Jr.
Graham, Mrs. John A.
Ingersoll, Mrs. Robert S.
Lewis, Mrs. Victor L.
Matter, Miss Mary
McCormick, Mrs. Brooks
McIlvaine, Mrs. Wm. B., Jr.
Meers, Mrs. Henry W.
Mullett, Mrs. Aidan I.
Ottman, Mrs. John B.
Runnells, Mrs. John S.
Seaman, Mrs. Irving, Jr.
Straus, Mrs. Henry Horner
Sturgis, John C.
Williamson, Mrs. Jack A.
Willing, Mrs. Mark S., Jr.

1957

Bartholomay, Mrs. Wm. C.
Folds, Charles W.

1958

Doering, Mrs. Edmund J. II

Henry, Mrs. C. Wolcott, Jr.
Kelley, Mrs. Frank J. III
Knoy, Mrs. Maurice G.
McBain, Mrs. Hughston M.
Merlin, Mrs. Peter H.
Monroe, Mrs. J. Hampton
Rowe, Mrs. A. Loring
Searle, Mrs. Wm. L.
Stinson, William A.
Wilson, Mrs. Christopher W.

1959

Rockwell, Mrs. Matthew L.
Swartchild, William G., Jr.

1960

Addington, Mrs. Whitney W.
Birmingham, Mrs. Rutledge, Jr.
Dick, Mrs. C. Mathews, Jr.
Hardy, Mrs. Howell B.
Hargrove, Mrs. Homer P., Jr.
Miller, Dr. J. Roscoe
McLaughlin, Mrs. Claude R.
Nichols, Frederick A.
Peabody, Mrs. Preston
Stair, H. Bowen

1961

Bennett, Mrs. Sturgis
Donnelley, Mrs. Thomas E. II
Sivage, Mrs. Gerald A.
Sturgis, Mrs. John C.

1962

Ames, John D.
Baxter, Mrs. James P.
Coulter, Mrs. James R.
Grabower, Mrs. Franklin L.
Madden, Mrs. John, Jr.

1963

Searle, William L.

1964

Addington, Mrs. Keene II

Billingsley, Robert P.
Block, Mrs. Andrew K.
Dixon, Mrs. Stewart S.
Gardner, Robert A., Jr.
Guenzel, Paul W.
Piggott, Mrs. Aubrey D.
Pope, Mrs. Henry, Jr.
Smith, Harold Byron
Wilson, Christopher W.
Wilson, Mrs. John P.

1965

Birmingham, Mrs. G. M.
Crown, Lester
Frankenthal, Mrs. Lester E. III
Greer, Mr. Joseph P.
Loomis, Mrs. Daniel P.
Loucks, Mrs. Vernon R., Jr.
Reid, Mrs. Bryan S.
Scribner, Mrs. Gilbert H., Jr.
Swift, Mrs. Phelps H.
Uihlein, Mrs. Edgar J., Jr.
Williams, Emory

1966

Armour, Mrs. A. Watson III
Bowman, Mrs. Marquis, Jr.
Cohen, Mrs. Stephen Z.
Dole, Mrs. Arthur III
Ireland, Mrs. Melville H.
McCulloch, Mrs. Paul L., Jr.
Monroe, Mrs. Boswell
Roberts, Mrs. John H.
Slaughter, Thomas B.
White, Mrs. Walter H.
Wilkins, Julian B.

1967

Blank, Mrs. Allan S.
Ish, Mrs. Stanley, Jr.
Palmer, Mrs. Potter
Studebaker, Mrs. Clement A.
Willner, Mrs. Benton J.

1968

Cohen, Mrs. Milton H.
Donahoe, Mrs. Daniel J. III
Donnelley, James R.
Gray, Mrs. Walter F., Jr.
Henry, C. Wolcott, Jr.
Hutchins, Mrs. John B.
Knight, Robert P.
Swift, Mrs. McKelvy

1969

Alter, Mrs. James M.
Dugas, Lester J.
Fairbank, Mrs. Livingston
Gorter, Mrs. James P.
Hunt, Mrs. Robert P.
Milliken, John F.
Sullivan, Mrs. John W.
Williams, Mrs. Albert D., Jr.

1970

Bogan, Ralph, A. L., Jr.
Davison, Mrs. Charles H.
Edwards, Mrs. Stephen W.
Koldyke, Mrs. Martin J., Jr.
Marquardt, Mrs. Gilbert H., Jr.
Siragusa, Mrs. John R.
Strubel, Mrs. Richard P.
Warner, Mrs. Douglas A., Jr.

1971

Davidson, Mrs. Donald B.
Dixon, Stewart S.
Dunne, Mrs. Arthur L.
Folds, Mrs. Charles W.
Knight, Mrs. Charles F.
Nadler, Dr. Henry

1972

Abboud, A. Robert
Bacon, Mrs. William T., Jr.
Block, Philip D. III
Briggs, Mrs. Stephen F. III
Cain, Mrs. Tyler R.

Christopherson, Weston R.
Gramm, Mrs. W. Patrick
Henry, Mrs. Hoyt
Misthos, Mrs. George E.
Potter, Mrs. Charles S.
Schoenhofen, Mrs. Leo H.
Siragusa, Mrs. Richard D.
Van der Eb, Henry G.
Wright, Mrs. Kenneth T.

1973

Gatlin, Mrs. Allwyn H.
Gilmore, Mrs. John C.
Goldblatt, Mrs. Stanford
Graham, Mrs. William B.
Meyer, Charles A.
Monge, Mrs. Jay Parry
Ryerson, Mrs. M. Hutchins
Stiffel, Mrs. Jules N.
Strubel, Mrs. L. F.
Tucker, Mrs. Alice A.
Van Cleave, Mrs. Peter
Walker, Mrs. Robert G., Jr.
Wells, Mrs. Thomas E. IV

1974

Anderson, Mrs. Paul F.
Benninghoven, Mrs. Daniel
Clarke, Mrs. Charles F., Jr.
Frederick, Earl J.
Frey, Donald N.
Hargrave, Mrs. Pirie
Hughes, Mrs. Howard
King, Dr. Lowell R.
Strotz, Mr. Robert H.
Traisman, Dr. Howard S.
White, Dr. Harvey
Williams, Mrs. Donald C.

1975

Briggs, Mrs. L. S.
Douglas, Mrs. William C.
Dubinsky, Mrs. William G.
Klutznick, Mrs. Thomas J.

Lewis, Mrs. Victor L., Jr.
Moorhead, Mrs. Thomas J.
Quinn, Mrs. Edward V.
Wheelan, Mrs. John G.

1976

Davis, Mrs. Carl B. III
Frank, Mrs. Clinton E.
Hand, Mrs. Elbert O. III
Ireland, Mrs. J. Taylor
Martin, Mrs. James F.
McNally, Mrs. Andrew IV
Notz, Mrs. John K., Jr.
Redondo, Dr. Diego

1977

Bliss, Charles M.
Burr, Mrs. John S.
Eckenhoff, Dr. James E.
Goldstein, Dr. Richard I.
Gorter, James P.
Haffner, Mrs. Charles C. III
Johnson, Elmer W.
McCardell, Archie R.
Walsh, Ms. Linda E.

1978

Adams, Leland C.
Buchanan, Mrs. DeWitt, Jr.
Crane, Mrs. William A.
Donnelley, Mrs. C. C.
Egan, Mrs. Donald
Hoge, James
Langdon, Mrs. James P.
Mecklenburg, William G.
Merritt, Mrs. Thomas W., Jr.
Mills, Mrs. John W.
Rodhouse, Mrs. Thomas

1979

Davies, Mrs. Paul E., Jr.
Ewing, Mrs. Robert
Given, Dr. Gilbert Z.
Griffin, Roger S.
Kennedy, George D.

Patterson, Mrs. O. Macrae
Ross, Norman
Smith, Mrs. Louis A.
White, H. Blair

1981

Firlet, Dr. Casimir F.
Lawlor, Mrs. William III
Newman, Mrs. James W., Jr.
Sennott, Mrs. William J.

Chiefs of Staff

Miller, Dr. Truman Washington, 1882
President
Harris, Dr. M. L., 1900
Henrotin, Dr., 1902
President
Walker, Dr. Samuel, 1909
President
Houston, Dr. J. P., 1905
President
Churchill, Dr. Frank S., 1917
President
Helmholtz, Dr. Henry, 1918
President
Brennemann, Dr. Joseph, 1930
Officially Chief of Staff in 1930, but carried responsibility from 1921.
Aldrich, Dr. C. Anderson, 1941
Gibson, Dr. Stanley, 1943
Bigler, Dr. John A., 1949
Lawson, Dr. Robert B., 1962
Nadler, Dr. Henry L., 1971

Administrators

Gilmore, Genevieve, 1886
Superintendent
Cutler, Miss Eva C., 1891
Superintendent
Hewitt, Miss Catherine, 1895
Superintendent
Watson, Miss Grace, 1899
Superintendent
Waugh, Dr. J. F., 1908
Superintendent

Henderson, Miss Bena, R.N., 1909
Superintendent
Stewart, Mary C., R.N., R.R.C.,
  1924
Superintendent
Binner, Mabel W., R.N., 1930
Superintendent
Price, Delbert L., 1951
Administrator
Sellers, Richard Wayne, 1960
Acting Administrator
Greer, Joseph P., 1961
Administrator
Frederick, Earl J., 1974
Executive Vice-President
President, 1974

Nursing

Gregory, Miss Muriel, R.N., 1910
Superintendent of Training School
Burks, Elsie L., R.N., 1911
Principal of Training School
Henderson, Bena M., 1914
Superintendent
Miller, Henrietta, R.N., 1923
Principal, Department of Nursing
Allan, Jane, R.N., 1924
Principal, School of Nursing
Asseltine, Elizabeth Ann, R.N.,
  1926
Director of Nurses
Potgieter, Sophia, 1928
Director
Howe, Minnie E., 1929
Director of School of Nursing
Ingersoll, Margaret M., 1940
Acting Director
Morse, Alice M., R.N., B.S., 1941
Principal, Department of Nursing
Brink, Frances V., R.N., 1945
Director of School of Nursing
Travis, Hettie Belle, 1948
Director of Nursing
Upp, Margaret W., 1949
Director of Nursing

Short, Audrey, 1950
Director of Nursing
Sandbloom, Hildur, R.N., 1972
Acting Director, Nursing
Fee, Dorothea L., 1973
Assistant Vice President of
Nursing
Henningsen, Anna Wainio, 1975
Vice President
Jones, Barbara, R.N., 1979
Acting Vice President, Nursing
Hicks, Judith, 1981
Vice President

Social Service

Walsh, Miss Adelaide Mary, R.N.,
  1910
Director of Social Service
Binner, Mabel W., 1925
Director of Dispensary and Social
Service
Jennings, Babette S., 1929
Director, Social Service
Waite, Marie, 1951
Social Service
Jennings, Mildred L., 1951
Social Service
Mixon, Rosalie W., 1952
Social Service
Lynch, Miss Helen, 1953
Director of Social Service
Out Patient
Saar, Alice, 1953
Director, Out Patient and
Social Service
Regner, Marian, 1956
Director, Social Service
Levinson, Sema, 1957
Director, Social Service
Clark, Mary Jean, 1960
Director, Social Service
Yoshimura, Kiyo, 1966
Acting Director, Social Work
Key, Glenn Shelton, 1967
Director, Social Work

Index

Abt, Isaac Dr., 96, 106
Adams, Adele (Mrs. George E.
  Adams), 17, 21, 23, 24, 28, 39,
  42, 56
Adams, George E., State Senator,
  12; 26, 27, 42, 47, 55
Addams, Jane, 22, 71
Adler, Herman, Dr., 82
Administrative Highlights, 175
Aetna State Bank Building (White
  Elephant Shop, 1960), 161
Agnes Wilson Memorial Pavilion,
  68-9, 77, 78, 83, 114, 127, 141
Aid for Dependent Children, 152
Aid to Dependent Children Act,
  112
Aldrich, Charles Andrew, Dr., 96,
  102, Chief-of-Staff III; 113, 116,
  120, 126
Aldrich, Charles Andrew, Mrs.,
  116
Ambulatory Services, 154, 155,
  182
American Academy of Pediatrics,
  96
American Association of Hospital
  Social Workers, 98
American Hospital Association,
  136
American Indians, 151
American Journal of Nursing, 72
American Medical Association
  (A.M.A.), 18, 31, 72

American Pediatric Society, 17,
  18, 19, 30, 44, 65, 66, 67, 72, 82,
  96, 99, 102, 119, 120
American Psychiatric Society,
  100, 128.
American Public Health
  Association, 136
Ames, John, 162
Anesthesia unit, 117
Annual Reports, 1891, 17; 1894,
  26, 31; 1898, 37, 38; 1904, 57;
  1909, 64; 1975/1976, 176
Antisepsis (Listerism), 20, 29
Anti-smoke ordinance, 6
Archives of Pediatrics, 18
Armour, A. Watson, Mrs., 166
Armour & Co., 91
Armour, Lester, 90, 112
Armour, Ogden, 68
Arthur Young & Co.
  (accountants), 89
Art Institute of Chicago, 11, 22
ArtisTrees, 184, 192
Assembly Balls, 7
Associated Jewish Charities, 63
Associate Memberships
  (Children's Memorial), 38
Austin, Richard, Dr., 65
Auxiliary Board, The (of
  Children's Memorial), renamed
  55; 57-61, 64, 67, 70-72, 76, 78,
  79, 81, 82, 84, 85, 87, 90-92,

Index

Chicago Public Library, 103
Chicago (and adjacent) Social
Agencies, Henry Booth House;
Chicago Commons; Gad's Hill
Center; Northwestern
University Center; Jewish Aid
Dispensary; United Charities;
Cook County Welfare Agent;
Mother's Pension; The Home for
Disabled Children; Bethel Home
for Convalescents; St. Vincents'
Orphanage; The Foundling
Home; Municipal T.B.
Sanitarium, 70
Chicago Streets and Wards,
Belden Ave. 11, 12, 14;
Children's Plaza 141; Clark St.
N. 11, 13; Deming Pl. 182;
Cleveland Ave. 152; Fullerton
Ave. 7, 14, 15, 32, 57, 62, 77, 79,
141, 156, 184; Grand Blvd. 7;
Halsted St. 14; Harrison St. 23;
Lakeview Ave. 97; LaSalle St.
N. 133, 161; Lincoln Ave. 57,
107, 141, 157, 184; Madison St.
6; Michigan Ave. 78, 185; North
Ave. 20; Ohio St. E. 78, 115,
133; Orchard St. 15, 23, 57, 77,
79, 89, 106; Prairie Ave. 7; 20th
St. 6; Washington Blvd. 7;
Fourteenth Ward 7
Chicago Theological Seminary, 68
Chicago Tribune, The, 25
Chicago Welfare Administration,
147
Chicago YMCA, 26
Chief Short Wing, 91
Child abuse, 181, 189
Child Guidance Clinic, 120,
126–128, 130–132, 152
Child Life Committee, 178, 179
Children, patients (1891),
Nationalities, 16, institutional
origin 16, diseases 16, 17
Children's Aid Society, 16, 29, 30
Children's Diseases, anemia 16;
arthritis 188; asthma 188; birth
anomaly 189; chicken pox
(varicella) 23, 93; chorea 16;
chronic disabling 188; cleft
palate, hare lip 82; congenital
heart 116; cystic fibrosis 148,
178, 187, 190; debility 16;
degenerative 190; diarrhea 5;
diphtheria 5, 6, 47, 97, 99;
emotional disorder 186; epilepsy
118, 129, 145; fetal abnormality
145; genetic 189; growth
problems 145; heart 97, 116;
hematologic 190; hepatitis 145;
idiocy 16; learning disability
143; leukemia 126, 145, 181,
187; lupus 188; malnutrition 93;
measles (rubella) 5, 47, 186;
mental retardation 186;
meningitis 64, 65; mitral
regurgitation 16; mumps 186;
paralysis (spastic) 129;
phenylketonuria (PKU) 145;
pneumonia, lobar 16, 93, 99;
poliomyelitis 65, 114, 116, 127,
132, 148, 186; renal 145;
respiratory 145; rheumatism 17,
148; rheumatic fever 116;
rheumatoid arthritis 189;
scarlatina (scarlet fever) 5, 16,
47, 99; sickle cell anemia 189,
190; smallpox 5, 16, 97;
spina bifida 178, 190;
thrombosis 17; tonsillitis 17;
tubercular pneumonia 93;
tuberculosis 19, 65, 66, 93, 118,
127; typhoid fever 5, 7, 16, 30,
31, 35, 47, 186; venereal 65–67,
97, 99; whooping cough 5, 29,
30, 47
Children's Diseases, Operations,
listed for 1890, 17; blue baby
122; organ transplants 145; rise
in volume 182, 183
Children's Festival, 176
Children's Hospital Association,
101
Children's Hospital, Boston, 13
Children's Hospital, Cincinnati, 26
Children's Hospital Society
(1903), 51, 64
Children's Library, 104

DESIGNED BY
MOBIUM CORPORATION FOR DESIGN AND COMMUNICATION,
CHICAGO, ILLINOIS
PRINTED AND BOUND AT
R.R. DONNELLEY & SONS COMPANY,
CRAWFORDSVILLE, INDIANA